From Your Friends at The MAILBOX®

The BIG BOOK of MONTHLY IDEAS

GRADES 1–3

Project Manager:
Karen A. Brudnak

Editors:
Cayce Guiliano
Leanne Stratton

Art Coordinator:
Teresa R. Davidson

Cover Artists:
Nick Greenwood
Clevell Harris
Kimberly Richard

www.themailbox.com

©2001 by THE EDUCATION CENTER, INC.
All rights reserved.
ISBN #1-56234-433-1

Except as provided for herein, no part of this publication may be reproduced or transmitted in any form or by any means, electronic or mechanical, including photocopying, recording, or storing in any information storage and retrieval system or electronic online bulletin board, without prior written permission from The Education Center, Inc. Permission is given to the original purchaser to reproduce patterns and reproducibles for individual classroom use only and not for resale or distribution. Reproduction for an entire school or school system is prohibited. Please direct written inquiries to The Education Center, Inc., P.O. Box 9753, Greensboro, NC 27429-0753. The Education Center®, The Mailbox®, and the mailbox/post/grass logo are registered trademarks of The Education Center, Inc. All other brand or product names are trademarks or registered trademarks of their respective companies.

Manufactured in the United States
10 9 8 7 6 5 4 3 2 1

ABOUT THIS BOOK

Get a year's worth of seasonal and holiday ideas in this handy resource! We've compiled outstanding curriculum-related activities, ready-to-go reproducibles, and timely themes from our best-selling Monthly Idea Books for grades 1–3. You'll find

- Super starters for the first days of school
- High-flying activities for Thanksgiving
- Dozens of December holiday delights
- Outstanding ideas for commemorating Black History Month
- Legendary activities for St. Patrick's Day
- Earth-loving ideas for observing Earth Day
- Memorable suggestions for wrapping up the school year
- And much more!

TABLE OF CONTENTS

August
A Watermelon Welcome 6
Cooking Up New Friendships 14
Count on Me! 20

September
Totally Awesome Autumn 28
An Open House to Remember 35
Grandparents Are the Grandest People! 45

October
Fighting Fire With Facts 50
Columbus Day Celebrations 58
Happy Halloween! 66

November
National Children's Book Week 74
A Feast Full of Thanksgiving Ideas 82

December
Hanukkah Lights 88
A Christmas World Tour 94
Kwanzaa 109

January
A Parade of Penguins 116
Remembering Martin Luther King, Jr. 121

February
Black History Month 134
Valentine's Day Delights 146
By George, It's Honest Abe! 151

March
Look Out for Leprechauns! 162
Up, Up, and Away! 175

April
Raindrops Are Just Ducky! 186
It's an Easter "Eggs-travaganza"! 193
The Endangered Earth 200

May
Festive Fun for the Fifth of May 208
A Cowpoke Roundup 214
It's Been a Great Year! 226

Index 235

A Watermelon Welcome

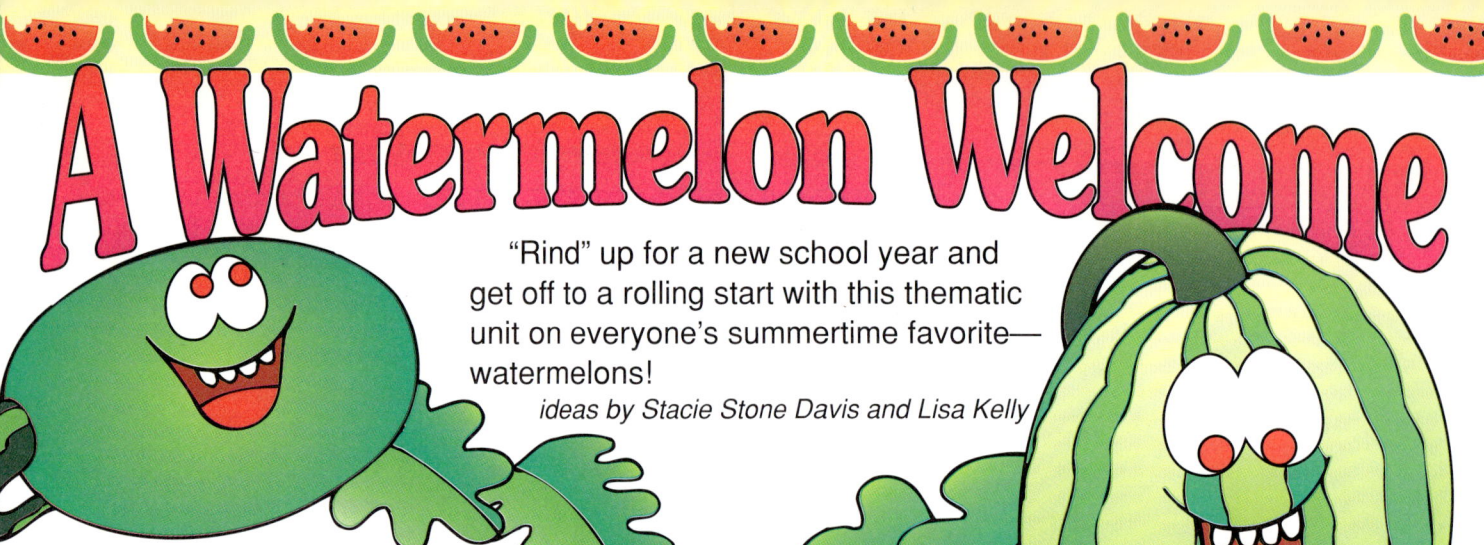

"Rind" up for a new school year and get off to a rolling start with this thematic unit on everyone's summertime favorite—watermelons!

ideas by Stacie Stone Davis and Lisa Kelly

What A Melon!

Here's a nifty way to start the school year! Prior to the start of school, collect the names and addresses of your future students. Copy the letter shown onto the watermelon pattern on page 12; then make student copies. Personalize the letters and mail them to your students. When the first day of school arrives, place a large watermelon atop a table in a prominent classroom location. Invite students to each use a permanent marker to write adjectives describing this juicy melon on the watermelon. Then slice the watermelon, provide each student with a sample, and discuss with students their reactions to the food. My, what a tasty first day of school it was!

Dear _____,
I am looking forward to meeting you on the first day of school. I have some special activities planned for us! All of the activities will have to do with a juicy summer food. The food is green on the outside and pink on the inside. It has lots of seeds inside, too. It's very juicy! Can you rearrange the letters below to spell the name of the mystery food? See you soon!

From,

It's a _ _ _ _ _ _ _ _ _ _ !
(MNOEATWRLE)

Watermelon Nametags

This neat nametag project doubles as a getting-to-know-you activity. To make a nametag, a child glues a pink or red construction-paper semicircle atop a slightly larger green construction-paper semicircle as shown. He uses a black crayon to personalize his watermelon half and then glues a desired number of clean watermelon seeds (or construction-paper seeds) to the nametag. Next he punches two holes at the top of his nametag. Finally he threads a length of yarn through the holes, ties the yarn ends, and wears the nametag around his neck.

After completing the projects, gather students in a large circle on the floor. Encourage each child to introduce himself; then, for each seed that is glued to his nametag, ask the child to share a fact about himself. No doubt students will enjoy this appetizing activity!

"Who Me?"

Melon Patch Fun

This enjoyable game is perfect for helping students learn each other's names at the beginning of the school year. As children become increasingly confident with the rhyme, challenge them to add a clap and a snap movement while they are chanting.

Who Took The Melon From The Melon Patch?
(chanted to the rhythm of "Who Stole The Cookies From The Cookie Jar?")

All: Who took the melon from the melon patch?
Leader: [Student's name] took the melon from the melon patch.
Student named: Who me?
All: Yes, you!
Student named: Couldn't be!
All: Then who?

Student named: [Another student's name] took the melon from the melon patch.
Second student named: Who me?
All: Yes, you!
Second student named: Couldn't be!
All: Then who?

Repeat the rhyme in this same manner until each student has had a chance to be named. The last person called is "in the melon patch" and starts the game as the leader the next time it is played.

Juicy Jobs

Looking for a great way to grow a crop of responsible students? Try this deliciously easy idea! From bulletin-board paper, cut a large watermelon shape and mount it on a bulletin board. Also cut several seed shapes from black construction paper and attach those to the watermelon. Print the name of a classroom job—such as line leader, messenger, caboose—above each seed cutout. Next have each student draw a likeness of herself on a piece of white construction paper (smaller than the seed cutout). Or, if desired, take a photograph of each child. Laminate the drawings or photographs; then store them in a resealable plastic bag pinned to the bulletin board. When you're ready to assign jobs, simply pin a student's drawn picture or photo atop the black seed cutout bearing the name of the job that the student will perform.

A Patch Of Graphing Practice

Sweeten your students' graphing skills with this daily activity. Reduce a copy of the watermelon pattern (page 12) to 50 percent. Then duplicate student copies on white construction paper. Have each student color, personalize, and cut out her watermelon pattern. Laminate the watermelon cutouts for durability and store them in a container near the chalkboard. Then, each morning, write a watermelon-related fact on the board (see the provided list) and the words "true" and "false" below it in two columns. When each student arrives, have her read the fact, decide whether she thinks the statement is true or false, and then tape her watermelon cutout in the appropriate column. Before the end of the day, analyze the data collected before revealing the answer.

True Watermelon Facts

- Egyptians grew watermelons more than 5,000 years ago; wall paintings were decorated with them.
- Watermelons are about 93 percent water.
- Most watermelons weigh from 5 to 40 pounds.
- Some watermelons weigh up to 100 pounds.
- Watermelons grow on vines.
- As many as 15 watermelons may grow on one vine.
- In some places watermelons are fed to farm animals.
- Watermelons are considered as vegetables by horticulturists.
- A ripe watermelon makes a hollow thud when thumped.
- Every part of the watermelon may be eaten.

The Scoop On Watermelons

Most people think that watermelon is a fruit. Actually, because it grows on a vine and must be replanted annually, horticulturists consider it to be a vegetable. It belongs to the gourd family, which includes squash, pumpkins, and cucumbers. Just like many other plants, a watermelon's roots grow underground and its vine acts as a stem. After sharing this information with your students, invite them to join you in the following chant.

The Watermelon Chant
(chanted to the rhythm of "Peanut, Peanut Butter")

Chorus:
Water, watermelon—(whisper) tastes great.
Water, watermelon—(whisper) tastes great.

Verses:
First you plant a seed and it grows. It grows.
It really, really grows.
Pretend to plant a seed.

Then you pick the melon. You pick it. You pick it.
You really, really pick it.
Pretend to pick a watermelon.

Now it's time to slice it, to slice it.
You really, really slice it.
Pretend to slice a melon.

Then it's time to eat it, to eat it.
You really, really eat it.
Pretend to eat watermelon.

Once upon a time, a little _____ went into a watermelon patch. He couldn't believe his eyes! Before him was a large _____ watermelon that weighed at least _____ pounds. The tiny critter _____ to the watermelon and tried to lift it, but it wouldn't budge. So the little critter decided to eat the watermelon. He ate it in _____ bite(s)!

1
2
3
4
5

Wacky Tales From The Watermelon Patch

Here's a wacky way to spur on some watermelon-related tales! To begin, have each student number a sheet of lined paper from 1 to 5. Then read aloud the descriptions below. For each description, the student writes a word or a numeral on his paper.

1. the name of a small animal
2. a color
3. a large number
4. a past tense action verb
5. a number less than ten

Afterward give each child a copy of a story frame like the one shown. Instruct each child to copy the words from his lined paper onto the corresponding story blanks. Then encourage each student to draw a corresponding illustration for his story. Invite students to share these wacky tales with their classmates. If desired, have students rewrite their stories on special watermelon writing paper (see "Sweet Stationery").

Sweet Stationery

The idea of writing on this pretty paper will have your pupils penning poem after poem, story after story. To make the stationery, students will need sheets of white construction paper, pink or red tempera paint, sponges that have been cut into semicircles, and green and black felt-tip pens. First have each student dip a sponge shape into the paint, then gently press the sponge onto the construction paper to create a watermelon border. After the paint has dried, ask each student to use a green felt-tip pen to add watermelon rinds. To complete the project, have him use a black pen to draw watermelon seeds. Encourage students to use the paper to publish watermelon-related tales, poems, or letters.

A Perfect Patch

Any way you slice it, this display is sure to whet your students' appetites for reading. Give each child a white construction-paper copy of the watermelon pattern on page 12. Each student personalizes the rind and then colors it green. Next he sponge-paints the remainder of the watermelon pink. After the projects dry, mount them on a bulletin board titled "A Perfect Patch Of Readers." Then, each time a child completes a book, have him glue a black construction-paper seed atop his watermelon cutout. When a child earns ten seeds, reward him with a small prize or privilege.

Problem Patch

Melon-Seed Manipulatives

Younger students often need manipulatives to help them solve operational problems. While studying watermelon, use its seeds to help your students' math skills grow. To prepare for practicing math problems, provide each student with a construction-paper copy of the watermelon pattern (page 12) to serve as a workmat and a supply of watermelon seeds. (Beans and construction-paper seeds could also be used.) Provide oral and written story problems similar to the ones shown and challenge students to use their seeds to solve the problems. What a way to ripen students' math skills!

Mike Mouse ate four seeds. Then he ate six more. How many seeds did he eat in all?

Charlie Chipmunk followed a pattern. On Monday he ate two seeds, on Tuesday four seeds, and on Wednesday six seeds. How many did he eat on Thursday? On Friday?

Sarah Squirrel ate five seeds. Her friend Sam ate four seeds. How many more seeds did Sarah eat than Sam?

Melon Math

How do your students measure up when it comes to math skills? Find out when you put them to work at these hands-on watermelon tasks. Use the guide below to set up five stations in different areas of your classroom. Also place a supply of pencils at each station. (For management purposes you may wish to enlist the help of parent volunteers to supervise the stations.) Provide each student with a copy of the "Melon Math" reproducible on page 13. Divide the students into five groups and send each group to a different station. Allow time for each student to complete the activity. Then, on a predetermined signal, have students rotate clockwise to the next classroom station. Continue in this manner until each student has completed each activity. Have the students return to their desks; then lead students in a discussion of what they learned. And if you're looking for a tasty way to use up all that watermelon, see the recipe on page 11!

Materials Needed:
Station 1: a watermelon, a large tub of water, paper towels (for cleanup)
Station 2: a watermelon, a yardstick, yarn, scissors
Station 3: a watermelon, a yardstick, yarn, scissors
Station 4: a watermelon
Station 5: slices of watermelon (one per student), paper plates, napkins

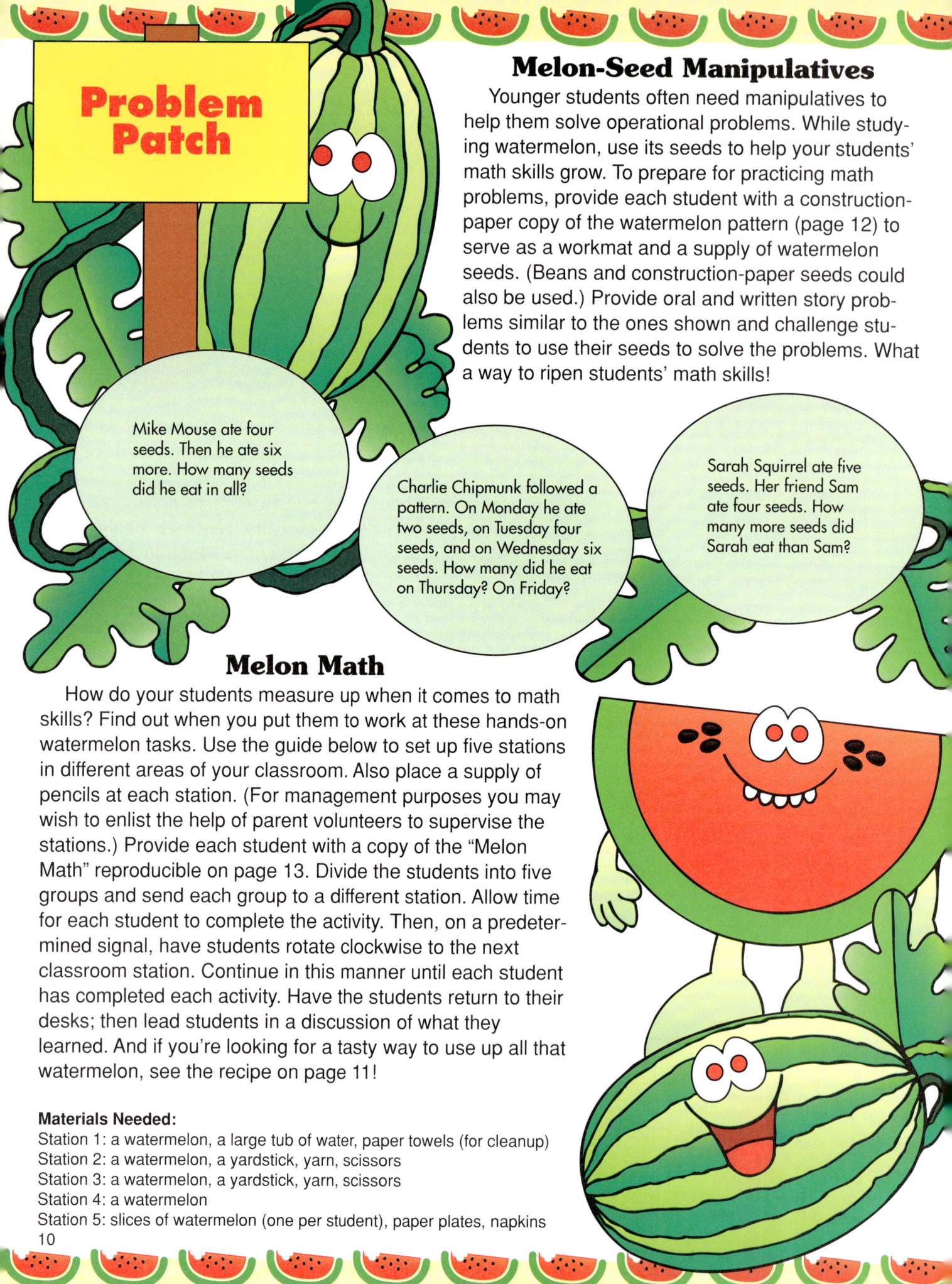

Pick-Of-The-Patch Literature

Eating The Alphabet: Fruits And Vegetables From A To Z
written and illustrated by Lois Ehlert
(Harcourt Brace Jovanovich, Publishers; 1996)

Fruit or Vegetable	Color	Texture	Any Seeds?	Firmness
apple	outside: red inside: white	smooth	yes	hard

"Apple to zucchini, come take a look. Start eating your way through this alphabet book." No doubt your students have tasted watermelon, which is featured in this book. But how many students have heard of—let alone tasted—dates, endive, or kohlrabi? If the answer is zero, invite your students to eat their way through the alphabet. To do this, have each student bring to school a desired fruit or vegetable that is featured in the book. Ask that the food be ready for consumption and that there be enough of the item so that each child may have a small sampling. Then, for each item that is tasted, complete a section of a chart similar to the one shown. To conclude the activity, have students discuss the similarities and differences among the sampled foods.

Chestnut Cove
written and illustrated by Tim Egan
(Houghton Mifflin Company, 1995)

Cooperation was a way of life in the friendly town of Chestnut Cove until a watermelon-growing contest threatened to change everything. After sharing this story, discuss with students the meaning of the word *cooperation.* Guide students to understand that cooperation among people is imperative when working toward a common goal. Then divide your students into cooperative groups. Provide each group with potting soil, a watermelon seed, and a container suitable for planting. Encourage each group to work together to plant its seed and—in the following weeks—to continue to nurture the tiny plant. (Be sure to tell students that watermelon seeds will not produce melons when grown indoors, but they will yield vines.) Emphasize the fact that there will be no special prize given to the group with the largest plant. Afterward discuss the differences in attitude between the Chestnut Cove residents and your students.

Watermelon Day
written by Kathi Appelt
(Henry Holt And Company, Inc.; 1996)

Jesse finds a special watermelon growing in the corner of her garden. Although she eagerly anticipates eating the watermelon, she realizes she must wait until Watermelon Day when it will be ripe and ready. Lively text and pastel illustrations combine to create a story that celebrates the wonderful pleasures of summer.

To Jesse, Watermelon Day meant cousins and cold peach ice cream, softball and songs. Invite your students to name activities that they would incorporate into their own Watermelon Day festivities. Then, with your students' assistance, plan your own Watermelon Day. When the festivities are over, treat your students to a special snack of watermelon pops.

Watermelon Pops
(Makes 12 three-ounce pops)

Ingredients:
- 1 can frozen concentrated pink lemonade
- 4 cups watermelon, cubed and seeded
- 1 cup ice cubes

Directions:
1. In a blender, mix lemonade and watermelon until well-blended.
2. Add the ice cubes to the blender and pulse until slushy.
3. Pour the mixture into Popsicle® trays and place in the freezer. When the pops are still mushy, insert a Popsicle® stick into each one.

Pattern

Use with "What A Melon!" on page 6, "A Patch Of Graphing Practice" on page 8, "A Perfect Patch" on page 9, and "Melon-Seed Manipulatives" on page 10.

Name _____

Watermelon recording sheet

Melon Math

Predict the outcomes.
Check.

	Guess	**Check**
Does the watermelon sink or float? 1. Place the melon in the tub and observe.		
What is the *circumference* of the watermelon? 1. Use the yarn to measure. 2. Straighten the yarn and measure its length with a yardstick.		
What is the *length* of your watermelon? 1. Use the yarn to measure. 2. Measure the yarn's length with a yardstick.		
How many stripes does your watermelon have? 1. Count.		
How many seeds does your watermelon slice have? 1. Count.		

©The Education Center, Inc. • *Big Book of Monthly Ideas* • TEC1487

Note To The Teacher: Use with "Melon Math" on page 10.

Cooking Up NEW FRIENDSHIPS

Serve up a batch of these fun-filled activities to help your students foster new friendships. Beware, students might just ask for seconds!

ideas by Stacie Stone Davis and Jill Hamilton

Recipes For Friendship

A pinch of humor, a dash of kindness, and a whole lot of understanding are the ingredients needed to ensure a long, lasting friendship! Enlist your students' help in naming characteristics (or ingredients) that help friendships flourish. List students' responses on the chalkboard. Afterward give each child a construction-paper recipe card like the one shown. Using the class-generated list for assistance, have each child write his own recipe for friendship. Then invite interested volunteers to share their recipes with classmates. Mount the recipe cards on a bulletin board that has been decorated with a large construction-paper cooking pot. Spice up the bulletin-board display by mounting students' photographs (or self-portraits) on the board, too. Add the title "Recipes For Friendship" and you've got yourself a mighty fine bulletin board!

Recipe for __friendship__

Ingredients:
1. kindness
2. a dash of humor
3. lots of understanding

Directions:
1. Talk nice.
2. Play with them at recess.
3. Work problems out.

Buddy Boxes

Buddy Boxes will give your students the opportunity to start new friendships. Provide each child with a light construction-paper copy of the box pattern on page 18. To make a Buddy Box, each student completes the questions on the box pattern as desired. Then, to assemble the box, she cuts along the heavy solid lines, folds on the dotted lines, and then tapes the squares together to form a box. (Provide assistance as needed.)

Once the boxes are complete, let the fun begin! Pair students. Instruct one partner to roll his box and read the question that lands faceup; then have the other partner answer the question. Have students repeat this process, as time permits, alternating the roles of roller and responder.

Poetry Pals

This cooperative creative-writing activity is sure to result in some poems with panache. To begin, share some friendship-related poetry of your choice. Then invite students to create their own friendship poems. Pair students and supply each twosome with a copy of the format shown. Have each student pair work together to complete and illustrate the poetry frame. Invite interested volunteers to share their poems with classmates. Then bind the poems between construction-paper covers to create a classroom anthology titled "A Friend To The End."

A friend is someone who _____
and _____.
A friend never _____
or _____.
A friend is _____,
_____, and
_____.

I'm glad that you're my friend!

by _____ and _____
    student   student

We Go Together

Like bagels and cream cheese or peanut butter and jelly, good friends go together! Challenge your students to name other items that go together—such as a baseball and a bat, and bread and butter. To do this, pair students and provide each pair with a sheet of writing paper. On a given signal, instruct each student pair to begin listing things that go together. Allow students to work for a predetermined time period. At the end of the brainstorming session, have each pair share its list with the class. List students' responses on the board.

Then, for a fun variation, use students' list ideas to make a Memory Game. To make the game, select a pair of words from the list. Print one of the words from the pair on an index card, and print the corresponding word on another index card. Repeat this process until you have at least 20 cards. To play, a student pair places all the cards facedown on a playing surface. In turn, each player turns over two cards. If the cards match—or go together—the player keeps the cards and turns over two more cards. If the cards do not match, the player turns them facedown again. Play continues in this manner until all the cards have been matched. The player with the most cards at the end of the game wins!

In A Jam

Survey your students to determine if they've ever found themselves in a sticky situation with a friend. If your students are like most, chances are they have—at one time or another—been in a jam. Use this role-playing activity to help students develop strategies to deal with these uncomfortable situations. To prepare for this activity, cut several strawberry shapes from red construction paper. On each cutout write a situation similar to the ones shown. Store the cutouts in a jelly jar or another suitable container. To begin the activity, have one volunteer select a berry cutout and then read the situation aloud. Working together, challenge the class to list solutions to the situation. After discussing the possible consequence of each solution, have each group decide which solution would work best and why. Model this procedure several times; then divide students into a desired number of groups. Have one member from each group select a berry; then, as a group, have them repeat the problem-solving process practiced earlier. For a fun and educational finale, invite each group to role-play its situation for the class.

You see someone picking on another kid...

You need help...

You want to join a game...

A Tutti-Frutti Friendship Party

Conclude your unit on friendship on an upbeat note: make placemats on which to serve bowls full of Friendship Salad that your students have helped to prepare.

Friendship Placemats

Students will empty their plates in a hurry in order to read these personalized placemats. To make a placemat, a student folds a 9" x 12" sheet of construction paper in half lengthwise. Then she uses a pencil and a ruler to draw parallel lines from the fold. The lines should be about 3 1/2" in length and spaced about two inches apart. Then, starting from the fold, she cuts on each of the resulting lines (taking care to leave a one inch border along the edge). Next she unfolds the paper, and weaves three 2" x 12" construction-paper strips through the resulting slits. She then glues the ends of each strip to the paper mat. To complete the projects, have students write positive comments about their peers on the placemats. To do this, have each student stand behind her desk with her placemat in hand. Next begin playing a musical recording. While the music is playing have each student circulate around the room. Then stop the music. When the music stops, each child locates the nearest student, trades placemats, and writes a positive comment about that student. Repeat this process as time permits. If desired laminate the placemats for durability. After all, these are placemats that children will want to read again and again!

Friendship Salad

This Friendship Salad is sure to be a hit with your youngsters! To make the salad, ask each student to bring to school a resealable bag filled with two cups of his favorite fruit. Ask that the fruit be prewashed and cut into bite-size pieces. Mix all of the fruit into a large bowl; then add two cups of orange juice. Afterward place a bowl of the Friendship Salad atop each child's placemat. When students have had their fill of Friendship Salad, provide each child with a copy of the "Circle Of Friends" reproducible on page 19. Challenge each student to survey her friends and record the findings on her sheet.

Clevell Harris

Books You Can Sink Your Teeth Into

Enjoy this helping of friendship-related books.

Yo! Yes?
written and illustrated by Chris Raschka
(Orchard Books, 1993)

This Caldecott honor book is a simple story about two strangers who meet on the street and become friends. After reading and discussing the story with your students, ask each student to complete a Friendship Diagram. To do this, have each student choose a partner. Provide each student pair with a diagram similar to the one shown. To complete the project, each student analyzes the traits he has in common with his partner and the traits he considers to be uniquely his.

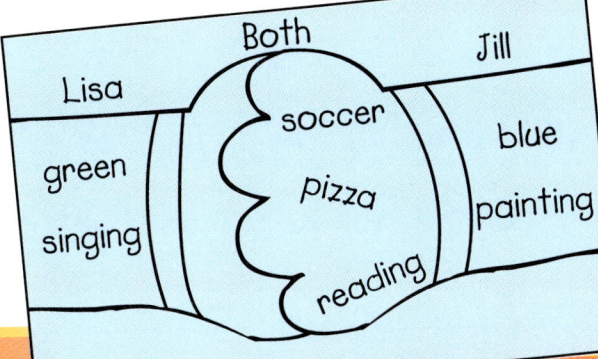

Friends
written and illustrated by Helme Heine
(Aladdin Paperbacks, 1982)

Charlie Rooster, Johnny Mouse, and fat Percy are good friends who always stick together. But when the friends try to plan a slumber party, obstacles get in their way. Finally the friends conclude that sometimes friends can't be together—but they can dream about the next time they will be. After sharing the story, plan a class slumber party. Hold the slumber party during school hours and invite students to wear their pajamas and bring their sleeping bags. During the party ask students to draw pictures of exciting adventures that they would like to take part in with their friends.

Wilfrid Gordon McDonald Partridge
written by Mem Fox
(Kane-Miller Book Publishers, 1989)

Wilfrid Gordon McDonald Partridge is a young boy who lives next door to a nursing home. He likes to visit there, and forms a special bond with Miss Nancy. Although Wilfrid isn't sure what a memory is, he does know that Miss Nancy is missing hers. But during his visits he learns that by sharing his memories with Miss Nancy, he helps her find some of hers.

After reading this story, tell students that friendships can be formed with people of any age. Explain to students that when you make a new friend it's like opening a door to a whole new world. Afterward invite each student to interview an "old friend." This person could be a neighbor, a family friend, or a relative. During the interview, encourage students to ask questions like, "What was your favorite food when you were little?" and, "How did you celebrate the holidays?" Remind students that they should share their memories, too. Ask each child to bring a photograph of his elderly friend to school, if possible.

After the interview process is complete, have each student make one of these special keepsake projects. To make a project, each child turns a 6" x 9" piece of brown construction paper lengthwise, runs a trail of glue along the left edge, and then glues the paper to a 9" x 12" sheet of colored construction paper as shown. Next she decorates the brown paper to resemble a door, then prints "Meet [name of senior citizen]" above the door. Next she folds back the door and glues a photograph (or a crayon drawing) in the resulting space. Finally she writes information about the featured person around the photograph. Mount the completed projects on a bulletin board titled "Opening The Door To New Friendships."

Pattern
Use with "Buddy Boxes" on page 14.

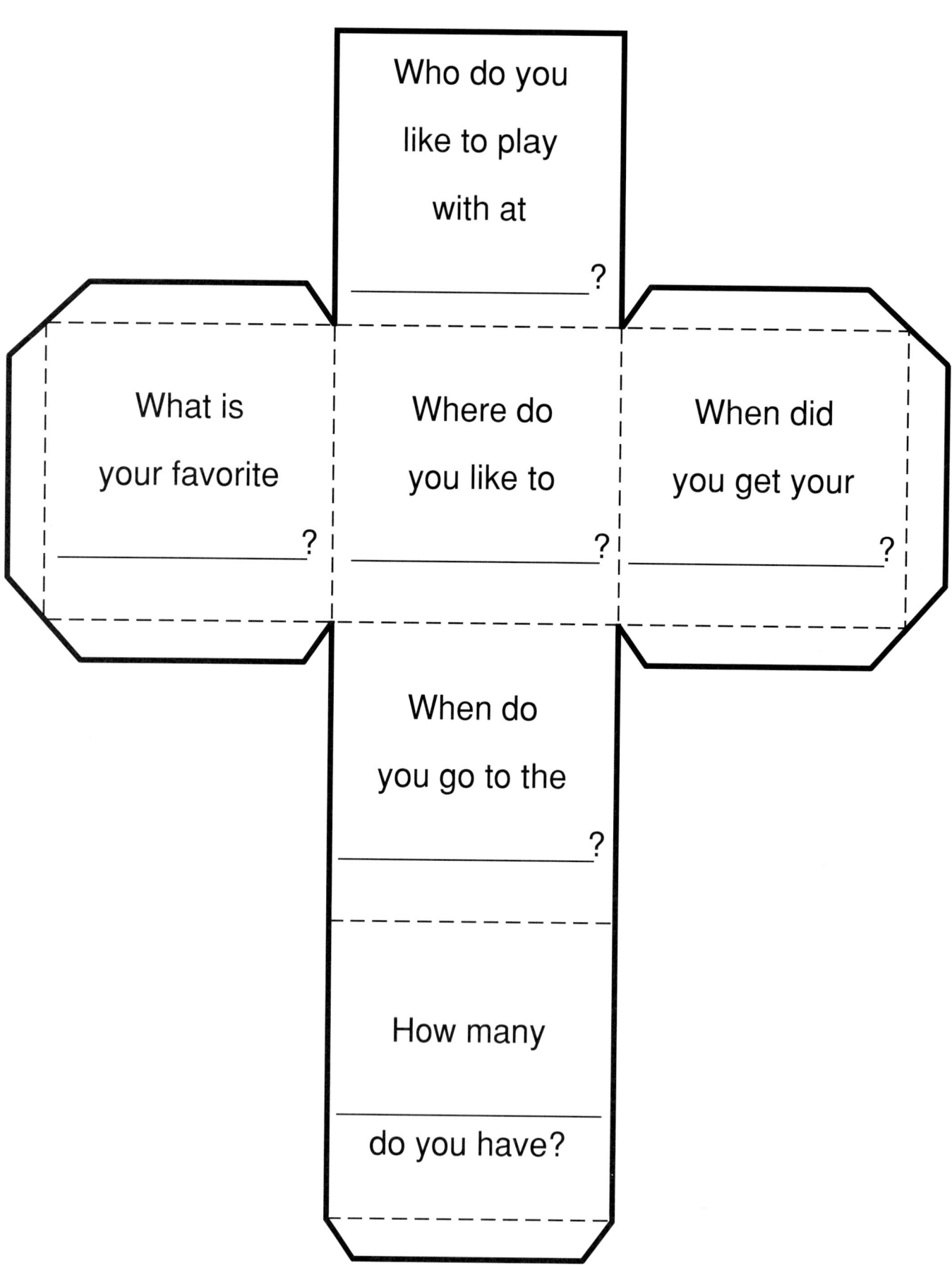

Name _____   *Creating a graph*

Circle Of Friends

Ask each of eight friends which fruit he or she likes best.
Use tally marks to count.

Count the results.

How many friends like apples the best? _____

How many friends like strawberries the best? _____

How many friends like oranges the best? _____

Use the information to make a pie graph.
   Color one pie piece green for each friend who likes apples best.
   Color one pie piece red for each friend who likes strawberries best.
   Color one pie piece orange for each friend who likes oranges best.

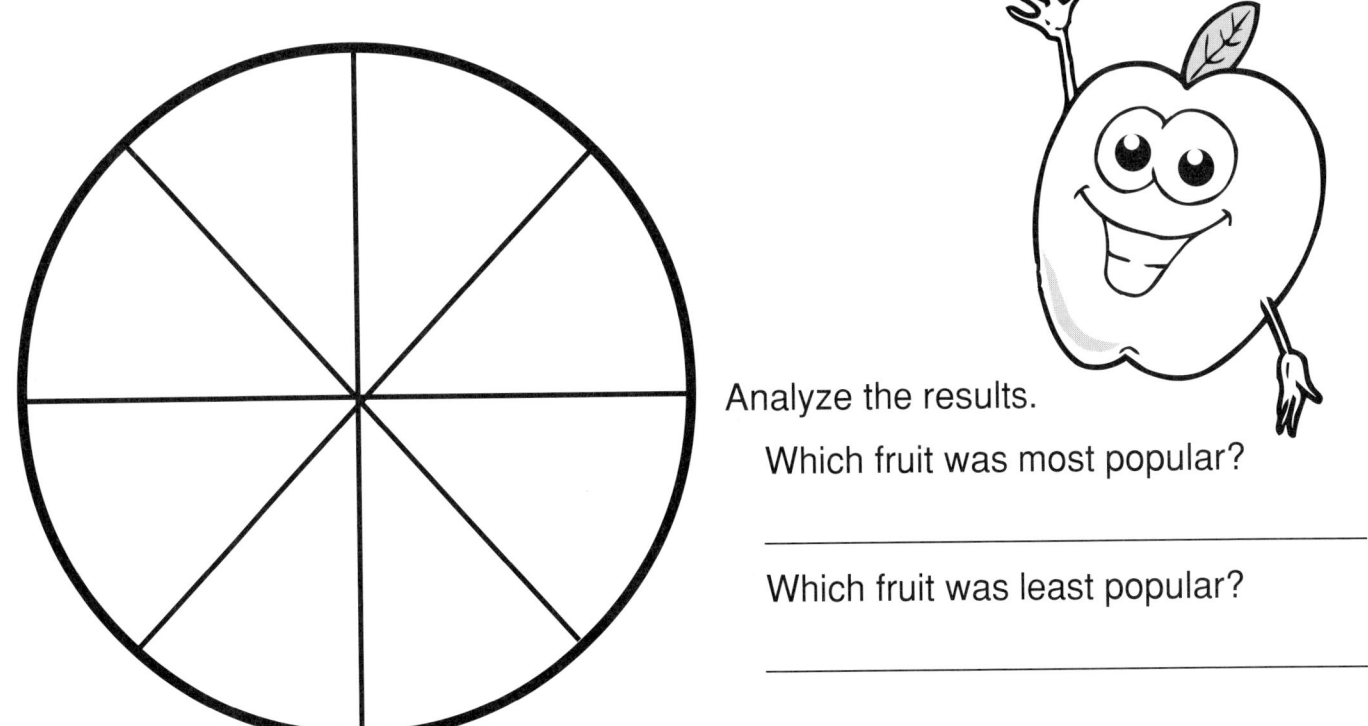

Analyze the results.

Which fruit was most popular?

_____

Which fruit was least popular?

_____

Note To The Teacher: Use after "Friendship Salad" on page 16.

Count On Me!
Math Activities To Start The Year

These getting-acquainted activities add up to loads of fun! Introduce your students to everyday math matters and learn more about your class in the bargain. Students will use dozens of math skills to learn about themselves and their classmates. Now that's "sum" way to launch a school year!

ideas by Amy Erickson and Nicole Iacovazzi

Sort And Tell

Students will have all sorts of fun classifying their favorite stuffed animals in this activity! Ask each student to bring one of his favorite stuffed animals to school on a predetermined day. Be sure to have a few extra stuffed animals available for students who don't bring one. Once everyone has an animal, direct students to place their animals in a designated area of the classroom. Have a student volunteer sort the animals and ask his classmates to guess how he grouped them. Did he sort by size? Outfits? Type of fur? After several students have guessed, ask the volunteer to tell his rule for sorting. Select additional volunteers to take turns sorting the animals into different groups and challenging their classmates to guess the categories. This classified information will surely capture your students' interest!

Sets Of Pets

Millions Of Cats by Wanda Ga'g (Putnam Publishing Group, 1996) is the "purr-fect catalyst" for a math activity on collecting data. This endearing book tells about a lonely couple who think having a pet cat would brighten their lives. After sharing the book, lead students in a discussion about the pets they own. Draw a large Venn diagram on the chalkboard, and label one side "cats," the other side "dogs," and the middle section "both." Ask each student to write her name in the appropriate section. When all of the data has been gathered, have students analyze the diagram to determine how many students have dogs, cats, dogs and cats, and neither dogs nor cats. Then, to assess students' understanding of the information, have each student write sentences about her interpretation of the information. No doubt this activity will be the cat's meow!

Three students have only cats.

The number of students who have only dogs is the same.

More girls than boys have only dogs.

Shapely Names

Reasoning is the name of this math game! Students will put their problem-solving skills to the test when they try to match name shapes with the corresponding people. Lightly writing one letter per square, have each student write his first name on the top line of one-inch graph paper. Ask him to continue by writing his middle name, if any, on the second line. Then have him write his last name on the next line in a similar fashion. Instruct students to conceal their writing by using a crayon to carefully color each block that has a letter. Then have them cut out the resulting colored shapes. Post the shapes on a bulletin board titled "Guess Who!" Challenge students to identify who made each figure. Students will be eager to see how their guesswork scores!

Phone Fun

This activity adds up to a "phon-omenally" good time! Students will familiarize themselves with several useful telephone numbers and call on a variety of math skills as they create personalized telephone directories. In advance, gather a few telephone books for students to use as needed. To create a directory for each student, stack three sheets of duplicating paper, fold the paper in half, and staple on the fold. Invite students to personalize the resulting covers with crayons. On the first page of his directory, have the student write his telephone number. Next have him collect the telephone numbers of nine different classmates, businesses, or emergency services and record and label each phone number on either the front or back of a separate page of his directory. After students have recorded the numbers, explain that they will be adding the digits in each of them. Have each student predict which of the ten telephone numbers will have the greatest sum and which will have the smallest. Then have him add to determine the actual totals and record each sum on its corresponding page. (If desired, provide calculators for this task.) Engage students in a discussion about their results. They're sure to talk about this activity for a long time to come!

"Feet-uring" Remarkable Rulers

Step right up to this idea that reinforces measurement skills! Explain to students that each of them will be measuring with a nonstandard unit: her foot. To begin, have each student trace her foot onto a sheet of construction paper and cut out the resulting shape. Instruct each child to estimate the number of foot cutouts equal to her height and to record and label her estimate on her foot cutout. Then pair students, and ask each child to help her partner use her cutout to determine her actual height. Have her record it below her estimate.

Next have students brainstorm a list of other things that they could measure with their foot cutouts, such as the widths of their desks, the length of the chalkboard, the perimeter of the classroom, and the distance from the classroom to the water fountain. Then have each student estimate and measure several items from the list. Remind students to record their work on their foot cutouts. For an added challenge, have students measure their cutouts with rulers and then convert the previously recorded measurements to standard units. Students will undoubtedly enjoy putting their best feet forward as they work!

It's Time!

Your class will be up-to-the-minute with this approach to teaching the concept of time. Distribute copies of the reproducible on page 25. At five different times during the day, spontaneously declare, "It's time!" Have each child stop what she is doing, draw hands for the actual time on a clock face, and write the corresponding time below the clock. Then direct her to write the activity in which she is engaged on the lines adjacent to the clock. Be sure you make note of the times as well. At the end of the day, announce the times that should be listed on students' papers and invite students to share the corresponding activities. For an added challenge, have each student take home an extra copy of the reproducible to record five weekend activities in a similar fashion. In no time at all, your students will gain a better understanding of how quickly time flies!

Math On A Budget

Cash in on this "toy-riffic" idea for some real-life shopping excitement! Have students brainstorm birthday gifts that they would like to receive. Write their responses on the chalkboard. Choose a few items from the list and ask students to estimate their prices. Write their estimates on the board. Then have students use a variety of catalogs and sales circulars to determine the actual prices of the selected items.

Next send your students on a birthday buying spree. To begin, tell students that they will each have an imaginary budget of $100 to "purchase" birthday gifts. Each student writes his birthday list on a sheet of paper. Then he searches through toy catalogs and sales circulars to find the prices of his items and records them on his list. Next he adds the prices of his gifts to determine their total cost and modifies his list as needed to stay within his $100 budget. Once he has finalized his list, he records each item and its price on a separate 5 1/2" x 8 1/2" sheet of duplicating paper; then he illustrates each gift. After he has recorded and illustrated all of the items, he uses crayons and a gift bow to personalize and decorate one 6" x 9" sheet of construction paper to resemble a gift box. Then he stacks the construction paper atop the other pages and staples the pages. What a profitable way to learn about your students' interests and provide practice with adding money as well!

Nick Greenwood

Math That's Totally Me

This math center adds up to lots of birthday fun! Store a supply of two different colors of birthday candles and a cake cutout in a birthday gift bag. Place the bag, crayons, and a supply of blank paper at a center. A student removes the cake cutout and the candles from the bag. She then uses the cutout and candles to determine number combinations that total her age. For example, four green candles and two yellow ones on a cake could depict six years. Three green candles and three yellow ones is another possibility. After determining each number combination, she sketches a likeness of the birthday cake and writes and solves the corresponding addition problem as shown on her paper. The student continues in this manner until she has determined all the possible addition combinations for her age.

After everyone has completed this center, group students who are the same age and ask them to compare the different combinations that they discovered. Then lead students in a discussion about the individual strategies they used to complete the activity and any patterns they noticed. It won't be long before your students are old hands at working with numbers!

Closet Confusion

Dress your students for success with this problem-solving activity! Ask students if they ever have difficulty deciding what to wear. Then announce that they are going to determine how many different outfits are possible with just two shirts, two pairs of pants, and two pairs of shoes.

Duplicate page 26 onto white construction paper for each student. Have each student personalize, color, and cut out the figure and clothing on his copy. Challenge each child to find eight different outfits. Have the students use the numerals on the pieces of clothing to record the different combinations on their papers. After each student has discovered all possible outfits, ask him to glue one of the outfits on the figure to resemble himself. Provide an opportunity at the end of this session for students to share their strategies for solving the problem and their results. Students will love tackling math in style!

Window On My Week

Schedule some time to bring your students' calendar skills up-to-date. To begin, share the delightful book *Cookie's Week* by Cindy Ward (G. P. Putnam's Sons, 1997). This humorous story summarizes one cat's eventful week. After reading the book aloud, have each student create her own weekly log. To make a log, each child stacks nine sheets of 8 1/2" x 5 1/2" duplicating paper and staples them together on the left side. She then titles the resulting book "Window On My Week," writes an appropriate byline, and draws a window on her cover.

Each student will complete a page in her log each day. To do this, she writes the day, date, and something that happened that day. Encourage all students to illustrate their text. Have students conclude their books with a page titled "About The Author." Students' chronicles of the week will surely become keepsakes that they will read time and again!

Name _____ *Telling and recording time*

It's Time!

11 12 1 / 10 2 / 9 · 3 / 8 4 / 7 6 5 ____ : ____	_____ _____ _____
11 12 1 / 10 2 / 9 · 3 / 8 4 / 7 6 5 ____ : ____	_____ _____ _____
11 12 1 / 10 2 / 9 · 3 / 8 4 / 7 6 5 ____ : ____	_____ _____ _____
11 12 1 / 10 2 / 9 · 3 / 8 4 / 7 6 5 ____ : ____	_____ _____ _____
11 12 1 / 10 2 / 9 · 3 / 8 4 / 7 6 5 ____ : ____	_____ _____ _____

©The Education Center, Inc. • *Big Book of Monthly Ideas* • TEC1487

Note To The Teacher: Use this reproducible with "It's Time!" on page 22.

Patterns
Use with "Closet Confusion" on page 24.

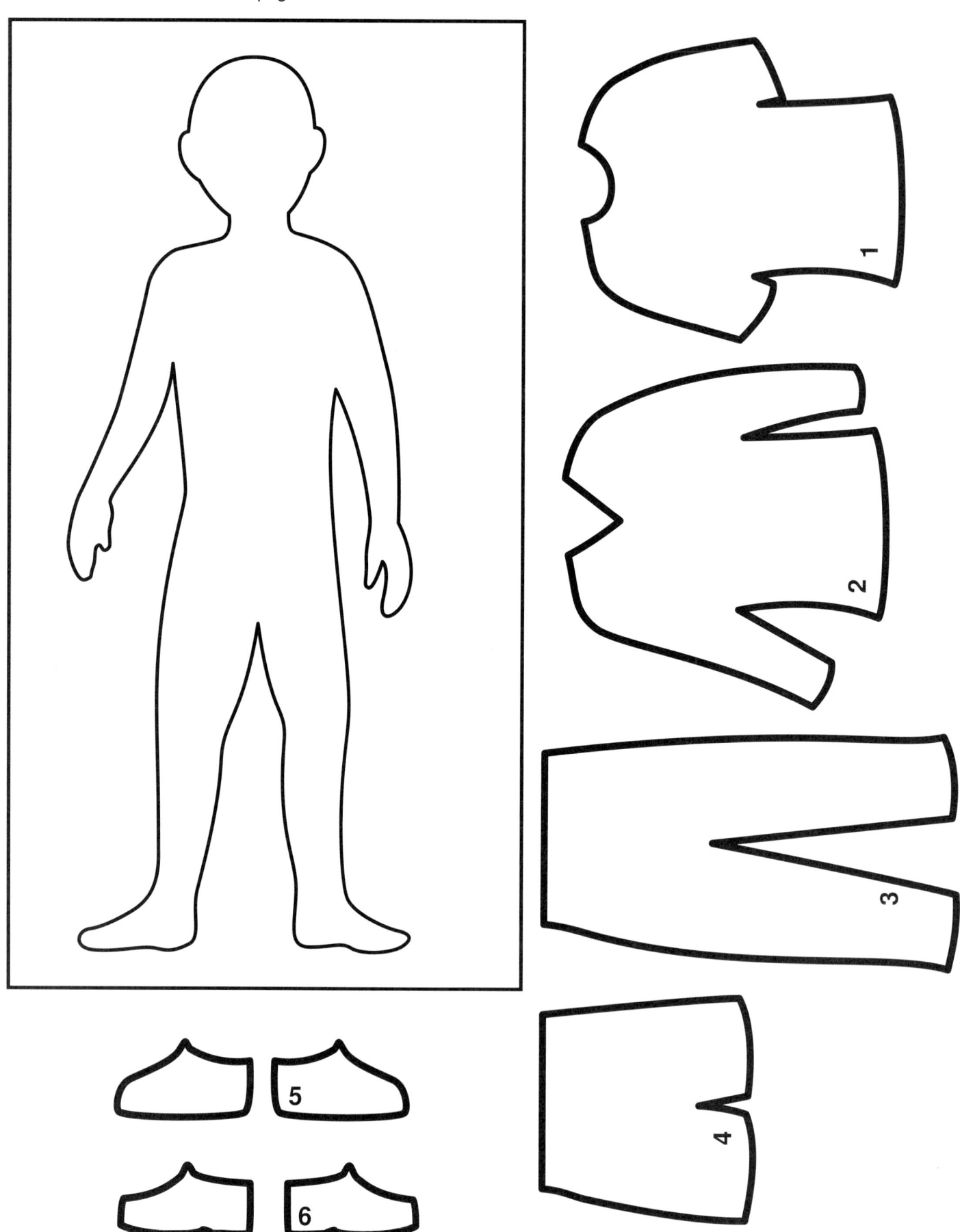

SEPTEMBER

Totally Awesome Autumn

Jump into fall with Sammy Squirrel and this collection of fun fall activities.

Meet Mr. Squirrel

Let Sammy Squirrel scamper across your curriculum to set the mood for autumn studies. To make Sammy Squirrel, duplicate a copy of the squirrel pattern on page 33. Color and cut out the squirrel; then attach him to a ruler to make a stick puppet. Explain to students that Sammy Squirrel will be accompanying them through their autumn lessons. Then share the letter below "written" by Sammy Squirrel with your students. Encourage your students to write responses to Sammy Squirrel. Decorate a cereal box to look like a mailbox. Set the mailbox, along with paper and pencils, at a center so that students can write letters to Sammy Squirrel.

We're Nuts About Fall!

Use this student-made bulletin board to find out why your youngsters like fall. First supply each student with a copy of the squirrel and acorn patterns on page 33, glue, scissors, and some Cheerios® cereal. Instruct each student to color and cut out his squirrel and acorn patterns. Then have the student glue the Cheerios® cereal to the squirrel's tail. Next instruct each student to write on his acorn about why he likes autumn. Have each student glue the acorn between the squirrel's hands. Mount the projects on a bulletin board titled "We're Nuts About Fall!"

Dear boys and girls,
Welcome to fall! Do you like this season as much as I do? For me, fall is a very busy time. I am preparing for winter by gathering nuts. Other animals are getting ready for winter, too. They are getting ready to fly south or they are getting ready to hibernate.

I also like fall because the air is cool and crisp. I love the colorful leaves. Do you like to play in them as much as I do? Well, I need to collect more nuts. You know it gets dark earlier at this time of year, so I need to get back to work. See you later—we'll have fun learning about fall together.

Your friend,
Sammy Squirrel

What A Nut!

Read the story *Squirrels* by Brian Wildsmith (Scholastic Inc., 1994) to help students learn more about Mr. Squirrel and his friends. Remind students that squirrels hide nuts, but they often forget where the nuts are hidden. Then share this poem with students:

>Oh Mr. Squirrel,
>Way up in the tree.
>I see you.
>Do you see me?
>
>Oh Mr. Squirrel,
>Collecting nuts in fall.
>Will you remember
>Where you hid them all?

Then engage students in a nutty scavenger hunt. Allow students to search for acorns that you have hidden in advance around the room. Can your little squirrels find all the nuts?

A Nutty Relay

Engage students in a nutty relay race. Divide children into teams. Have each team line up to prepare for the relay race. Provide the first child in each line with an acorn. That child carries the acorn to a predetermined spot, then turns around and runs back to his team. He passes the nut to the next member of his team, who repeats the process. The team that has all its members complete this activity first wins!

Squirrel Crispies

There's "nuttin" better than a snack of Squirrel Crispies when you come inside after a full day of fall fun. To make Squirrel Crispies you'll need:

1 cup peanuts
1 cup M&M's® candies
1 cup raisins
1 cup Honey-Nut Cheerios® cereal

Mix all the ingredients in a large bowl; then place one-half cup of the mixture into individual resealable plastic bags. Distribute a bag to each student.

Take A Hike!

Share the story *Fall Is Here! I Love It!* by Elaine W. Good (Good Books®, 1994). In the story a young boy details the sights, colors, tastes, and smells as fall arrives at his family farm. Then step into autumn activities with a nature walk around the schoolyard to look for signs of fall. Give each child a clipboard and a copy of a record sheet similar to the one shown. Encourage students to smell and touch the things around them. At some point during the walk, ask each student to stand quietly and listen to her surroundings. Ask each student to list on her record sheet things that she saw, heard, smelled, or touched.

When you return to the classroom, have each student write a "sense-sational" fall poem. Duplicate the leaf poem pattern on page 34; then distribute one to each student. Challenge each student to use her record sheet to assist her in writing a poem. Mount the poems on a bulletin board titled "Fall Is Here! We Love It!"

The Reason For The Season

Read the book *Sunshine Makes The Seasons* by Franklyn Branley (HarperCollins Children's Books, 1985). This book details how sunshine and the tilt of the earth's axis are responsible for the seasons. Then use a globe and a flashlight to demonstrate for students why we have fall. Use the globe to show students that the earth is tilted on its axis. Explain that during the fall months, the sun is not shining as directly on the Northern Hemisphere as it did in the summer, resulting in shorter days and cooler temperatures.

Next ask a student to come to the front of the room. Hold a flashlight directly above his head and ask him to tell what he feels. Then move the flashlight so that the beam of light is not directly hitting the student. Ask the student to name the differences that he felt when the beam of light was aimed differently. Repeat this process with a desired number of students; then explain that this is what happens on the earth. Put this theory into action by having each student record the daily temperature for a predetermined period of time.

I see beautiful leaves
I hear geese honking overhead
I smell the smoke from the chimney
I feel the crunchy leaves
I taste juicy red apples
Fall is here! I love it!
by Kevin

My Autumn Walk

I saw	I heard	I touched	I smelled
geese colorful leaves butterflies	geese honking leaves crunching birds chirping	crunchy leaves bark	apples fresh leaves smoke from a fire

Leaves "A-Weigh!"

Try this measuring activity to demonstrate for students the evaporation of water from fall leaves. In advance collect some newly fallen leaves and place them in a sack. Put the sack on a simple balance scale. Ask students to predict how many Unifix® cubes it will take to balance the scale. Record students' responses on the top half of a chart. Then have students test their predictions by putting Unifix® cubes on the other side of the balance scale. On the bottom half of the chart, record the number of cubes it actually takes to balance the scale. Next ask students to predict what they think will happen to the weight of the leaves after several days. Then repeat the process in a couple of days. Conclude the lesson by discussing students' observations about the weight of the leaves. Guide students to the discovery that as the leaves dry out, they become lighter.

A Fall Wreath

Your students will enjoy making these fall wreaths to present as gifts for their parents. To make a wreath, have each student select several colorful leaves and flowers that she would like to use in her wreath. After the flowers have air dried for several days, provide each student with a paper plate that has had the center portion trimmed away, leaving only the rim. Instruct each student to glue her leaves and flowers to the rim of the paper plate. Supply each student with a raffia bow that she can glue to the top of the wreath.

Planting Bulbs

Surprise students when you tell them that in the fall, many people are already thinking of spring. Explain that the fall months are the time to plant flower bulbs that sprout in the spring. Then provide each student with two or three tulip bulbs to take home and plant. Or ask permission from the school custodian to plant the bulbs somewhere on the school grounds. When the planting is complete, have students estimate when the bulbs will sprout. List students' estimates on a sheet of poster board, display the chart, and then be patient!

Nutty Numbers

This nutty file-folder game will help reinforce basic math facts. To make the game, draw and color ten trees on a file folder. Label each of the ten trees with a sum or a difference. Then duplicate 20 acorns using the pattern on page 33. Color and cut out the acorns; then program each of the cutouts with an addition or subtraction problem. Code the back of each card for self-checking. Laminate the cards and the folder for durability. Put the cards in a zippered plastic bag; then clip it to the file folder. Place the game at a center along with a supply of real acorns.

To play, the student selects an acorn cutout and reads the math problem on it. He then uses the acorns as manipulatives to help him solve the math problem. Next he places the acorn cutout on the correct tree.

Football Fever

Catch football fever with this fun spelling game. In advance use a sheet of poster board to make a football gameboard similar to the one shown. Next program a set of index cards with spelling words. Code the bottom of each index card with a number (divisible by five) between 5 and 50, to represent yardage. Assign the higher values to the more difficult words. Set the gameboard and the index cards at a center, along with a three-inch football cutout.

Begin play by placing the football cutout on the 50-yard line. One student selects a card and asks his opponent to spell the word on the card. If the student spells the word correctly, he moves the football cutout the indicated number of yards toward his end zone. Then it is the opposing player's turn. Play continues until one player gets the football into his end zone and scores a touchdown.

Patterns

Use the squirrel with "Meet Mr. Squirrel" and both patterns with "We're Nuts About Fall!" on page 28. Use the acorn with "Nutty Numbers" on page 32.

Leaf Pattern
Use with "Take A Hike!" on page 30.

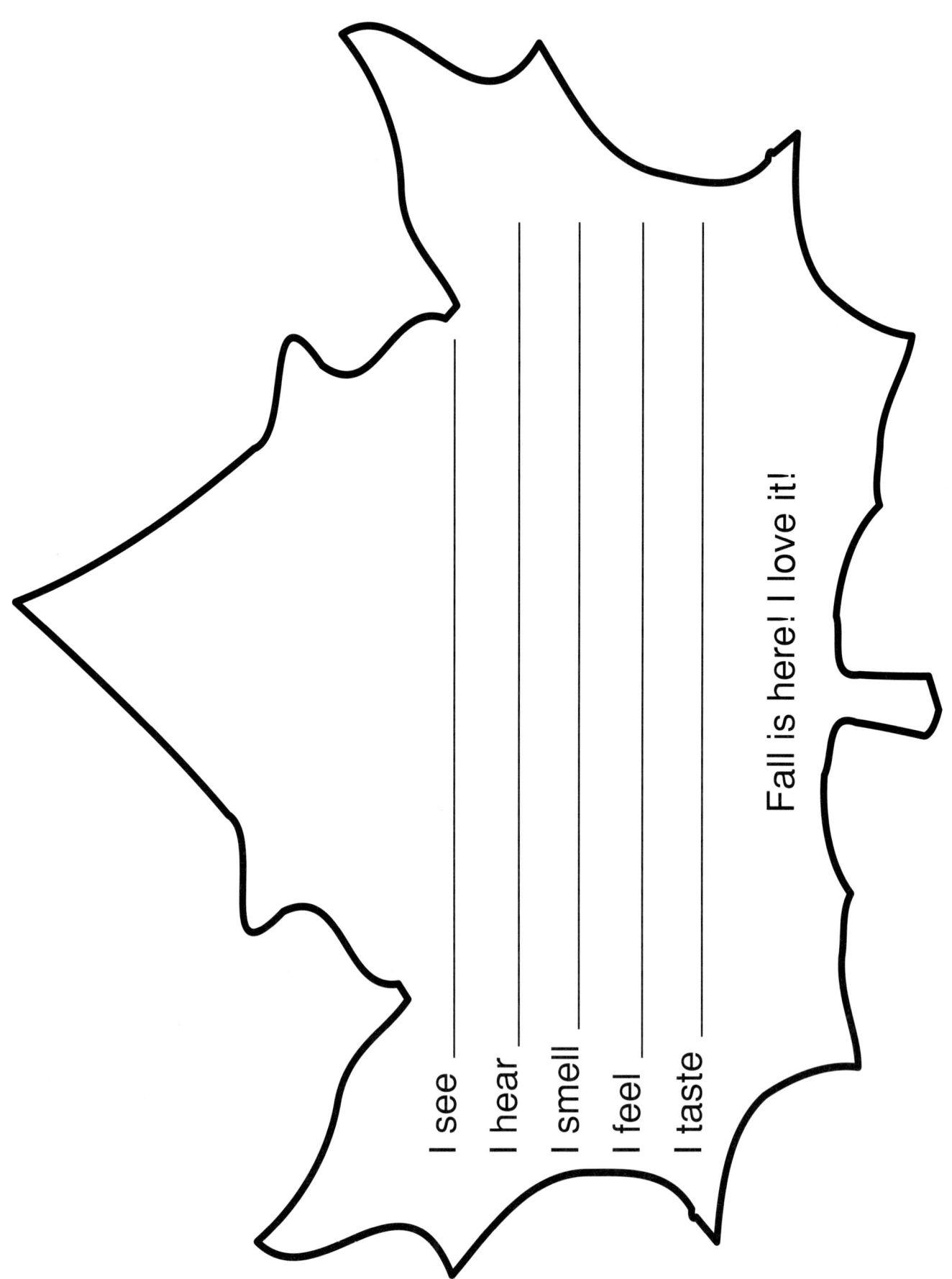

An Open House To Remember

Welcome parents and friends on back-to-school night with creative displays and engaging activities guaranteed to make a lasting impression.

You're Invited!

You're sure to have a full house when you send out these innovative invitations. Duplicate the invitation pattern on page 39 and the ticket patterns on page 40 on white construction paper for each child to complete. Demonstrate how to cut the page in half along the bold line; then cut along the dotted line so the door can open and close. Have each student color and decorate the door to look like your classroom door. Write the information needed to complete the inside of the invitation on the board for students to copy. Check to make sure all information, times, and dates are correct. Show students how to glue the information sheet behind the door as shown. Attach a library pocket to the back of the invitation. Have each child insert a pair of tickets to your classroom.

On Open House night, parents present their tickets to you or to student greeters at the door. (Keep a supply of tickets near the door for parents who forget or additional family members.) Place the tickets in a box so you'll have a record of who visited. At the end of the evening, draw names for a door prize—such as a paperback book or a school T-shirt—for parents to take home to their children. The next day, everyone who participated in the planning will feel like a winner!

The Welcoming Committee

Involve students in your evening Open House by making them tour guides. To distinguish guides from other visitors, have each guide wear a nametag and a red crepe-paper sash. Station student guides at different areas in the classroom such as the math center, reading corner, art area, and computer lab. Rehearse a short presentation with each student so he can explain what goes on at his particular station. This will help familiarize both students and parents with the various materials available.

Video Delight

Show that you're proud of your students, school staff, and fellow teachers by capturing them on film. Before speaking to your group of parents on back-to-school night, play a video showing students and teachers at work in your classroom, at the library, in the cafeteria, or in the gym. If video equipment is not available, play an audiotape of your class singing a song or reciting a favorite poem. This is a nice way to involve your class in your presentation, and parents will be delighted to hear what the students have to say.

We're Back!

Put the *back* in back-to-school night with this display designed to greet parents. Have each student trace the pattern on page 41 or 42 on a sheet of white construction paper. The student colors his pattern to resemble his body from a rear view. Have each student cut out his pattern and write three clues to his identity on the other side such as "I have three people in my family," "I like pepperoni pizza," and "I'm great at baseball." Ask each student to sign his name below the clues.

To display these bodies, attach a string to the top of each cutout and hang it from the ceiling. Or stand the paper dolls up in a chalk tray with their backsides showing. Curious parents will enjoy hunting for their child's back view and flipping the cutouts over to read the clues and discover if they are correct.

A "Classy" Book

Show off the writing abilities of your class and make a great display for Open House at the same time. Read the zany story of a student's daydream about his teacher in *The Teacher From The Black Lagoon* by Mike Thaler (Scholastic Inc., 1989). Then inspire your class to create a book titled "*The Class From The Black Lagoon.*" This time the teacher daydreams she has a class that does the silliest things!

Have the class write the story with you; then divide the class-written story into typed segments for easy reading. Have children work in pairs to draw illustrations for each page. Mount each typed segment and the illustrations on a separate 12" x 14" piece of colored tagboard or construction paper. On the cover, mount a photo of the class and write the title in black marker as shown. Fasten the booklet at the top with two or three metal rings. Visitors will chuckle as they flip their way through the story.

Rustle Up Some Volunteers

Round up your parents to volunteer for activities during the year by displaying "WANTED" posters around the room. On each poster, provide a place for volunteers to sign up for helping with art projects, baking, field trip chaperoning, or being a guest speaker on a particular career or subject. Have students design these posters on 12" x 18" pieces of construction paper. Have them neatly fill in the volunteer information as shown. As an acknowledgment, fill out copies of the reproducible form on page 43 so parents will remember to mark their calendars. The rewards are big smiles and year-round help that's indispensable.

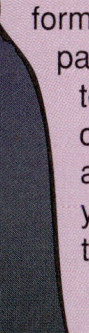

Desktop Surprise

It's always nice to give parents something to take home with them as a reminder of Open House night. Have each student leave his mark—a bookmark that is—on his desk as a welcome gift for his parents. Provide a 5" x 8" unruled index card for each student. Have him fold the card in half to create a 2 1/2" x 8" strip. Demonstrate how to glue the two sides together as shown. Leave three inches at the top of the strip for a school photo. If photos are unavailable, write "Place school photo here." Below the photo, the student can write a message in marker such as "I Love You And Reading Too!" or "Reading Makes You Sparkle." (Many students will enjoy creating their own personal messages.) Student-colored designs on the back of the strip add a nice touch.

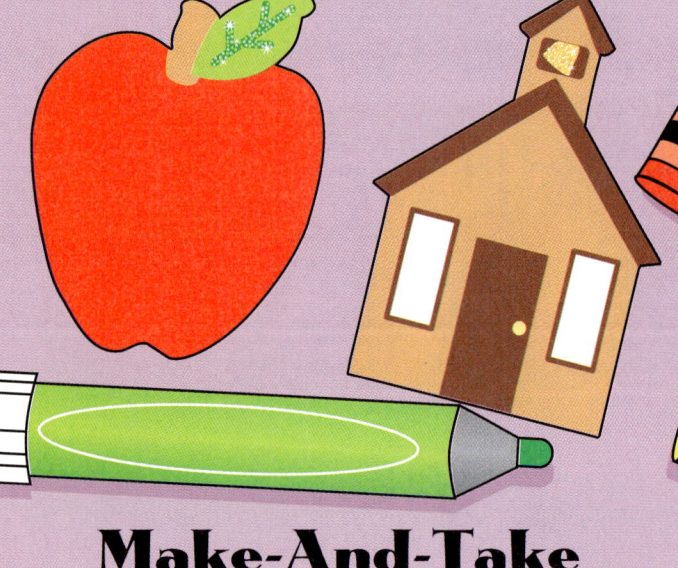

Make-And-Take Magnets

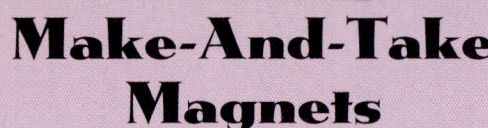

Let your parents become students again as they participate in this activity at your art station. Provide small, wooden cutouts available from your local craft store; markers; pom-poms; adhesive magnetic tape; and glitter pens for parents to use to create refrigerator magnets. Display the directions at the center along with a sample magnet, and encourage parents to work in pairs as they create magnets to take home. Tell them to use the refrigerator magnets to hang your class newsletter or announcements of upcoming school events. This activity is a conversation starter and a sure crowd pleaser as it encourages parents to get acquainted, too.

Noteworthy Students

Students will be thrilled to have notes from their parents on their desks to greet them the morning after back-to-school night. Duplicate the note paper (page 44) and place one on each student's desk before parents arrive. Ask each parent to take a few minutes to write a note to his or her child and leave it on his desk. Encourage parents to comment on how proud they are of their children. If there are some children whose parents were unable to attend, jot quick messages to them, too, so that everyone will get a cheerful note in the morning.

Welcome to room ____!

Glue here.

You are invited to an Open House!

Where: _____

When: _____

Your host for the evening will be _____

Come and see what your child is learning!

Our door is always open!

©The Education Center, Inc. • *Big Book of Monthly Ideas* • TEC1487

Glue here.

Note To The Teacher: Use with "You're Invited!" on page 35.

Patterns
Use with "You're Invited!" on page 35.

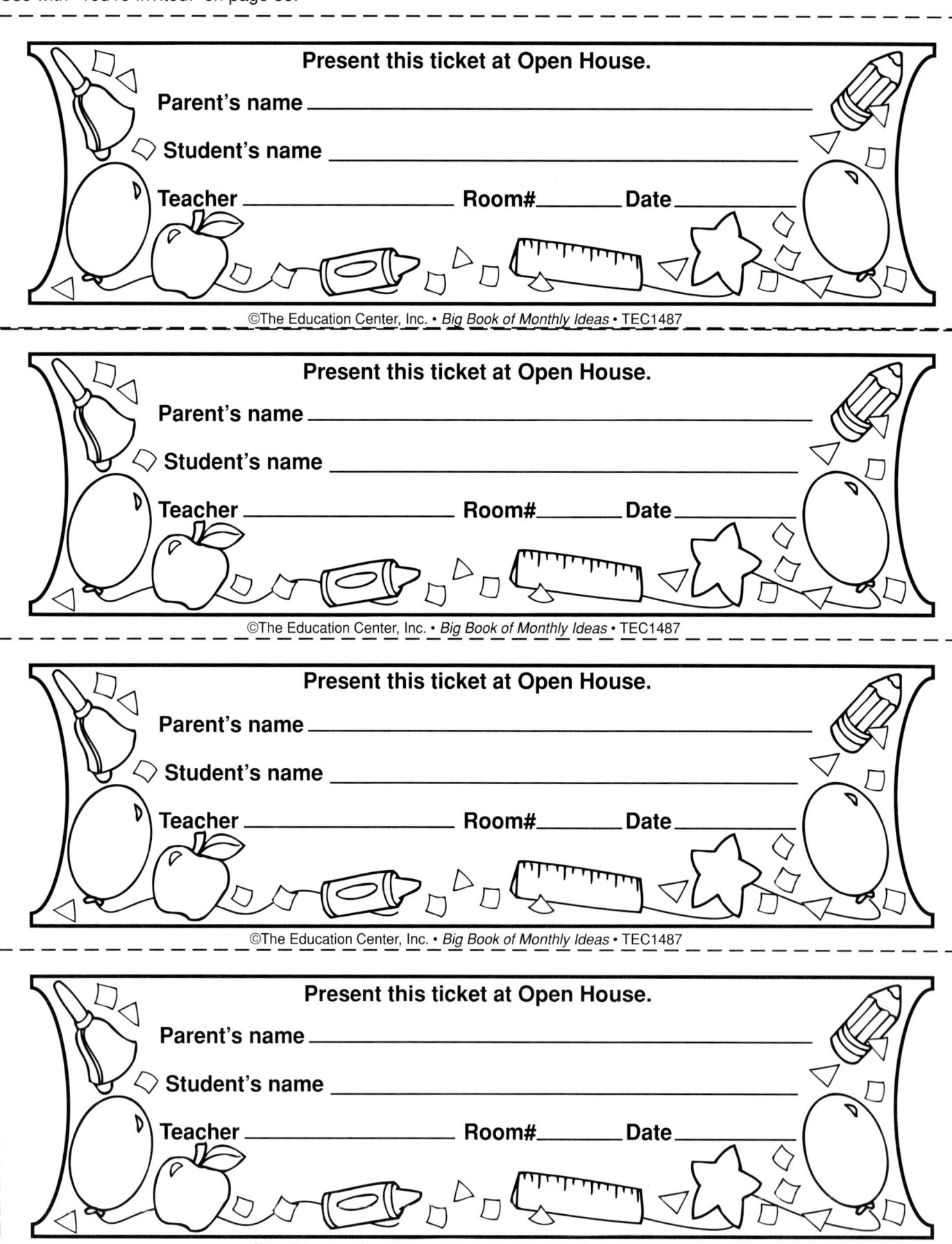

Pattern
Use with "We're Back!" on page 36.

Pattern
Use with "We're Back!" on page 36.

Parent Reminder
Use with "Rustle Up Some Volunteers" on page 37.

THANKS, PARTNER!

Just a reminder that you will be helping _____ at school on _____.
I appreciate your time.

Sincerely,

_____

©The Education Center, Inc. • *Big Book of Monthly Ideas* • TEC1487

THANKS, PARTNER!

Just a reminder that you will be helping _____ at school on _____.
I appreciate your time.

Sincerely,

_____

©The Education Center, Inc. • *Big Book of Monthly Ideas* • TEC1487

Grandparents Are The Grandest People!

Grandparents Day is the first Sunday following Labor Day. Plan to honor grandparents and senior citizens all year long with some across-the-curriculum fun.

A Grand Show-And-Tell

Children will enjoy sharing their grandparents or senior friends by inviting them to show-and-tell. Seniors make great speakers and can be involved with your class in many ways—reading a favorite story, sharing a hobby or interest with the class, showing off a collection, or telling stories of yesteryear. The visitors will enlighten and delight your students with tales of how things used to be, and children will gain an appreciation of the many changes grandparents have seen in their lifetimes.

Today's Special Treat: Inviting Grandparents For Lunch!

On the last day of every month, invite grandparents to lunch! Have each student create a snazzy invitation to invite his grandparent or another special senior to lunch with the class. Provide glitter pens, stamp pads, stickers, and 5" x 8" pieces of colored construction paper at a center. Students fold and decorate the construction paper, then insert a copy of the information as shown. Encourage grandparents who can't make it one month to come the next—or to come more than once!

Grandparent Math

While you have several grandparents in your room for lunch, do some quick math. Hand out a slip of paper to each grandparent and have him write down the year he was born. Collect the slips and, as a class, create a bar graph or a timeline. Discover which years these seniors have in common. Older students, with the assistance of their grandparents, can figure out and share their grandparents' ages—if they don't mind giving up that information!

What's In Grandma's Trunk?

Young children will love to join in as you read a fun-filled *ABC* adventure, *I Unpacked My Grandmother's Trunk* by Susan Ramsay Hoguet (E. P. Dutton, Inc.; 1983). After reading, ask the class to create a new *ABC* story patterned after the book. Start by making a list of objects from *A* to *Z:* anteater…banana…and so on. Use the list to make a "Grandma's Trunk" class book. On a 9" x 12" piece of white construction paper, have each student draw a picture that corresponds to a different alphabet letter. To make the trunk, glue two manila file folders together as shown and cover them with brown bulletin-board paper. Trim the trunk and glue on a three-inch circle cut from gold foil as shown to create a gold lock. Attach a self-stick Velcro® dot to the overlapping flap and another to the folder to close it. Use a black marker to add the title. Assemble the drawings in alphabetical order and store them in the trunk. The children will enjoy unpacking Grandma's Trunk again and again.

What's Cooking?

Many families have favorite recipes which have been passed down from generation to generation. Ask parent and grandparent volunteers to share their cooking secrets by bringing in samples of family favorites. Ask for a copy of each recipe in advance. Have each visitor talk about her recipe, telling where it originated; then enjoy the culinary creations with the class. Reproduce the recipes and bind the pages into a book for each child to take home. Label it "The Gourmet Grandparents' Cookbook." It's guaranteed to stimulate family discussions as well as continue the tradition of good home cooking!

Grandparents And Games Galore

Develop a sense of everyone's worth—regardless of age. Encourage students and seniors to team up together. Ask students to bring in games from home for this activity. Collect games a few days before the event. When seniors arrive, have a variety of game stations set up around the room: checkers, dominoes, lotto, board games, card games, bingo, and skill-related learning centers. Group students with their senior friends to play. Let the groups switch game stations a few times. After the final round of games, treat your class and their senior friends to refreshments. Ask students and seniors to tell what they learned from one another.

Generations Of Helping Hands

Getting grandparents active in your classroom as volunteers can be rewarding for all! To let grandparents know how much they are needed, have students make posters to display in the halls and in the cafeteria when grandparents come for lunch. Encourage students to create eye-catching advertisements for senior volunteers. Whether it's reading to a child, helping with a basic math skill, or just being a buddy, older volunteers will be an asset to your school.

There's A Grandma In My Classroom!

This creative-writing activity is sure to create some humorous tales. Tell your students to imagine that they are sitting at their desks one morning when the principal brings in a new pupil. It's Grandma! This sweet old lady wants to come back to school, so they're letting her repeat elementary school. Ask students to write a story about the grandma in second grade. Would they like having a grandma or grandpa in class all day? Instruct them to describe the elderly person's day, from a trip to the computer lab to an afternoon kickball game. Allow students to illustrate and share their stories.

INTERVIEW

Name: _____
Date of Birth: _____ Age: _____
Who was President of the United States in the year you were born? _____
What were the favorite toys when you were growing up? _____
Movies? Stars? _____
Inventions? _____
Have you ever served in the military? _____
Different jobs you have had? _____
How was school different from today? _____
Events in history? _____
Other? _____

Years Past

To help your class gain an understanding of the differences between generations, share the book *Homeplace* by Anne Shelby (Orchard Books, 1995). It's a story told by a grandma of one family in one house over a period from 1810 to the present. After reading, discuss how life was different for each generation.

As a follow-up activity, ask each child to interview either a grandparent or a special older person. Duplicate an interview form for each child to use. These interviews can be shared with the class a few each day, or can be conducted live with grandparents sharing photos as they tell their stories. Grandparents have so much information to offer us!

It's About Time!

For some intergenerational homework, have students find and record the birth years of three older people they admire. This could be a famous athlete, author, entertainer, or world leader; or a neighbor, a relative, a parent, or an older friend. When the assignment has been completed, have the children compare the different years to see which birthdate is the oldest, which is the most recent, or what years are the same. Make a timeline with the data. Can students tell which lives overlapped? Which people lived generations apart?

A Special Spotlight

To spotlight the special qualities of grandparents, ask each student to bring in a snapshot of his grandparents. If a photo is not available, have the student find a picture of a senior citizen in a magazine. Since pictures come in all dimensions, mount each on colorful paper that's slightly larger than the photo itself. Give each child an index card on which to write a caption about the photo. Display the pictures and captions on a black background. Write adjectives suggested by the students to describe their grandparents on strips of multi-colored construction paper. Use the strips to create a border. Finish the display with the title "Our <u>Grand</u>parents"—underlining the word *"Grand"* for emphasis.

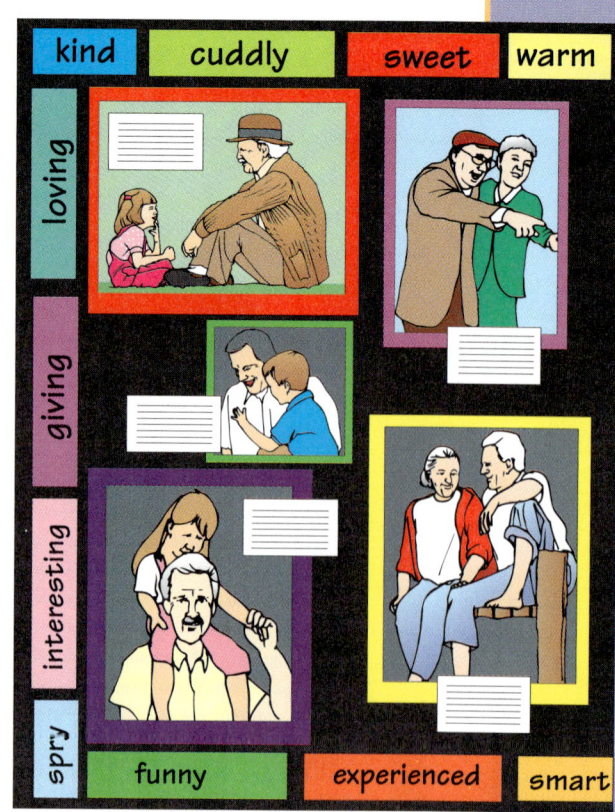

Put a spark in your fire-safety lessons during Fire Prevention Week. These red-hot ideas and reproducibles will ignite students' interest in learning how to be fire-safe and fire-smart!

ideas by Resa Audet

Dalmatian Dan Says...

Use this nifty hands-on display to reinforce fire-safety rules. Enlarge, color, and cut out one Dalmatian Dan and two fire-hydrant patterns (page 54). Label one hydrant "DO" and label the other hydrant "DON'T." Then mount all three patterns on a bulletin board titled "Dalmatian Dan Says."

Have students brainstorm a list of things that they should do to prevent fires. Record their ideas on chart paper labeled "DO." On a second chart labeled "DON'T," record a student-generated list of things they should not do that would prevent fires. Then provide each student with one 9" x 12" sheet of white construction paper. Ask half of your students to each write and illustrate a different fire-prevention idea from the "DO" list. Have each of the remaining students write and illustrate a different idea from the "DON'T" list. Ask students to share their projects aloud; then mount the projects on the bulletin board near the appropriate fire hydrants.

Fire-Fighting Facts

Focus on the evolution of fire fighting by sharing historical facts with students. Duplicate 15 red construction-paper copies of the fire truck pattern on page 55. Using a black marker, program each fire truck with a date and a fact from the list below. Divide your class into pairs. Distribute a fire truck fact to each pair of students. Have pairs share their facts; then mount the fire truck patterns on the wall in chronological order to create a timeline. If desired, have each pair research and write about a different fact from the timeline.

The History Of American Fire Fighting

1608—The first recorded fire in America began in Jamestown, Virginia.
1630—The first fire law was enacted in Boston, Massachusetts.
1648—The first fire prevention act occurred when four fire wardens were appointed.
1658—The first fire alarm system consisted of eight men who patrolled the streets looking for fires. If they saw one, they would shake wood rattles to warn the citizens.
1679—The first paid engine company was formed in Boston, Massachusetts, to manage a hand-carried pumper engine.
1736—The first volunteer fire-fighting company was organized by Benjamin Franklin.
1801—The first fire hydrants were used in Philadelphia, Pennsylvania.
1802—Horses began being used to pull fire engines. Dalmatians or other dogs would run beside the horses to keep them going. The dogs also guarded the horses from robbers while the firefighters were inside burning buildings.
1828—Henry Gratacap created the leather helmet that became a standard part of the firefighter's uniform. Modern helmets look much like Gratacap's original model.
1839—Dr. William F. Channing invented the first fire alarm boxes that could pinpoint the location of a fire.
1853—The first paid fire department was established in Cincinnati, Ohio, to operate the new steam-powered fire engine.
1874—The first sprinkler system was invented by Henry Parmelee.
1878—The first fire pole was designed by firefighter Captain David B. Kenyon of Chicago. This first pole was so successful that firehouses all over the country began to install poles.
1911—The first completely motorized fire department was established in Savannah, Georgia.
1931—Nancy Holst became America's first woman fire chief. She later became the deputy state fire marshal in Rhode Island.

Stop, Drop, Roll

Teach youngsters to act quickly in case their clothes catch on fire. Cut several flame shapes from felt fabric. Demonstrate the "stop, drop, roll" movements used to extinguish flames on a person's body or clothes. Then let students practice the technique by placing the felt flames on a student's clothes. Have the student stop, drop, and roll to remove the flames from his clothing.

Bucket Brigade

Play Bucket Brigade to familiarize students with this fire-fighting method used long ago. You will need ten small paper cups, several gallons of water, a plastic pitcher, and a stick of red sidewalk chalk. Divide your class into two groups: A and B. On a concrete surface, align the groups in two parallel lines that are 50 inches apart. Have opposing team members face one another. At one end of the lines, place a pitcher of water. At the opposite end, use the chalk to write the word "FIRE" in large letters on the concrete.

Now call out the bucket brigade! To begin, pour one cup of water and give it to the first member of Team A. Direct students to pass the cup up the line until it reaches the last student on Team A, who pours the water onto the word "FIRE." This student gives the empty cup to the opposite player on Team B; then the empty cup is passed down that line. As the first cup is making its way down the line, send a second full cup of water up line A. Continue inserting additional cups of water until all ten cups are rotating through the lines simultaneously. The bucket brigade must continue pouring water onto the word "FIRE" until it is erased. After this tiring work, students will begin to understand why their forefathers sought more efficient fire-fighting methods and equipment.

Hats Off To Firefighters!

Young students will love wearing these official-looking fire helmets. Enlarge and duplicate one red construction-paper copy of the pattern on page 56 for each student. Instruct students to cut out the pattern on the solid lines as directed. Then have each student fold up the center portion of the helmet on the dotted lines. Have students wear their helmets during a field trip to the local fire station. Before leaving the fire station, have each child tell the firefighters one thing that he has learned on the tour and thank his hosts for protecting the community from fire.

Fire Escape!

Devising home and school fire-escape plans is a great way to teach children safe behaviors that can protect them in case of a fire. To make a fire-escape plan, draw a basic floor plan of your classroom. Reproduce one copy of the floor plan for each student. Then enlarge a floor plan and display it in a prominent location. Label all windows and doors on the large floor plan, and have students do the same on their copies. As you demonstrate for students, have them draw dotted lines to identify two exit routes from the classroom. Determine a safe meeting place outdoors; then practice following your fire-escape plan. Encourage each of your students to involve his family in drawing a similar fire-escape plan for use at home.

It's In The Cards
Using role-play cards is a good way to help students practice decision-making skills that may help keep them safe if they are ever involved in a fire. To prepare a set of these cards, write fire-related situations on index cards (see the list below). Have individual students or groups of students take turns selecting a card and acting out the situation. After each role-play situation, discuss the students' actions. Ask the class to decide whether or not the students made safe decisions. Encourage students to discuss alternative actions for each situation.

Sample Situations
- The smoke detector wakes you up.
- Smoke is coming into your room under the door.
- There is a fire downstairs and you are upstairs.
- You have left your burning house, but your favorite toy is still inside.
- There is a fire in your kitchen and you want to call for help.
- A small grease fire has started on your stove.

Dalmatian Magnets
These easy-to-make Dalmatian magnets will ensure that emergency phone numbers are easy to find. Each student will need a tagboard copy of the pattern on page 54, a spring-type clothespin, a self-adhesive magnetic strip (2 1/2 inches long), markers or crayons, scissors, and glue. To make a magnet, a student colors and cuts out the pattern. The student glues the pattern to the front of a clothespin. After the glue has set, the student attaches the magnetic strip to the back of the clothespin. Encourage each student to use her magnet to display emergency phone numbers on her refrigerator.

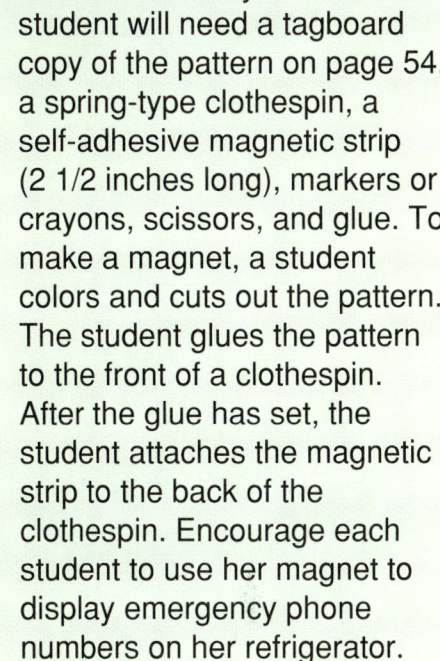

Home Safe Home
Emphasize household fire-safety tips by having each student and his family work together to complete a "Home Safe Home" booklet. Reproduce one copy of the booklet on page 57 for each student to color and cut out. Staple each student's booklet pages in order. Ask each student to take the booklet home and place a check mark in the box beside each activity that he completes with his family. Tell students to return the booklets to school; then sign and date the "Home Fire-Safety Hero" award at the back of each booklet before returning it to its owner. This activity may be a real lifesaver!

Red-Hot Reading
Fire! Fire! by Gail Gibbons (Trophy, 1987)
Fire Fighters: A To Z by Jean Johnson (Walker Publishing Company, Inc.; 1985)
Fighting Fires by Susan Kuklin (Bradbury Press, 1993)
Fire Fighters by Robert Maass (Scholastic Inc., 1992)
The Fire Station by Robert Munsch (Annick Press Ltd., 1991)

Patterns

Use with "Dalmatian Magnets" on page 53.

Use with "Dalmatian Dan Says..." on page 50.

Use with "Dalmatian Dan Says..." on page 50.

Pattern
Use with "Fire-Fighting Facts" on page 51.

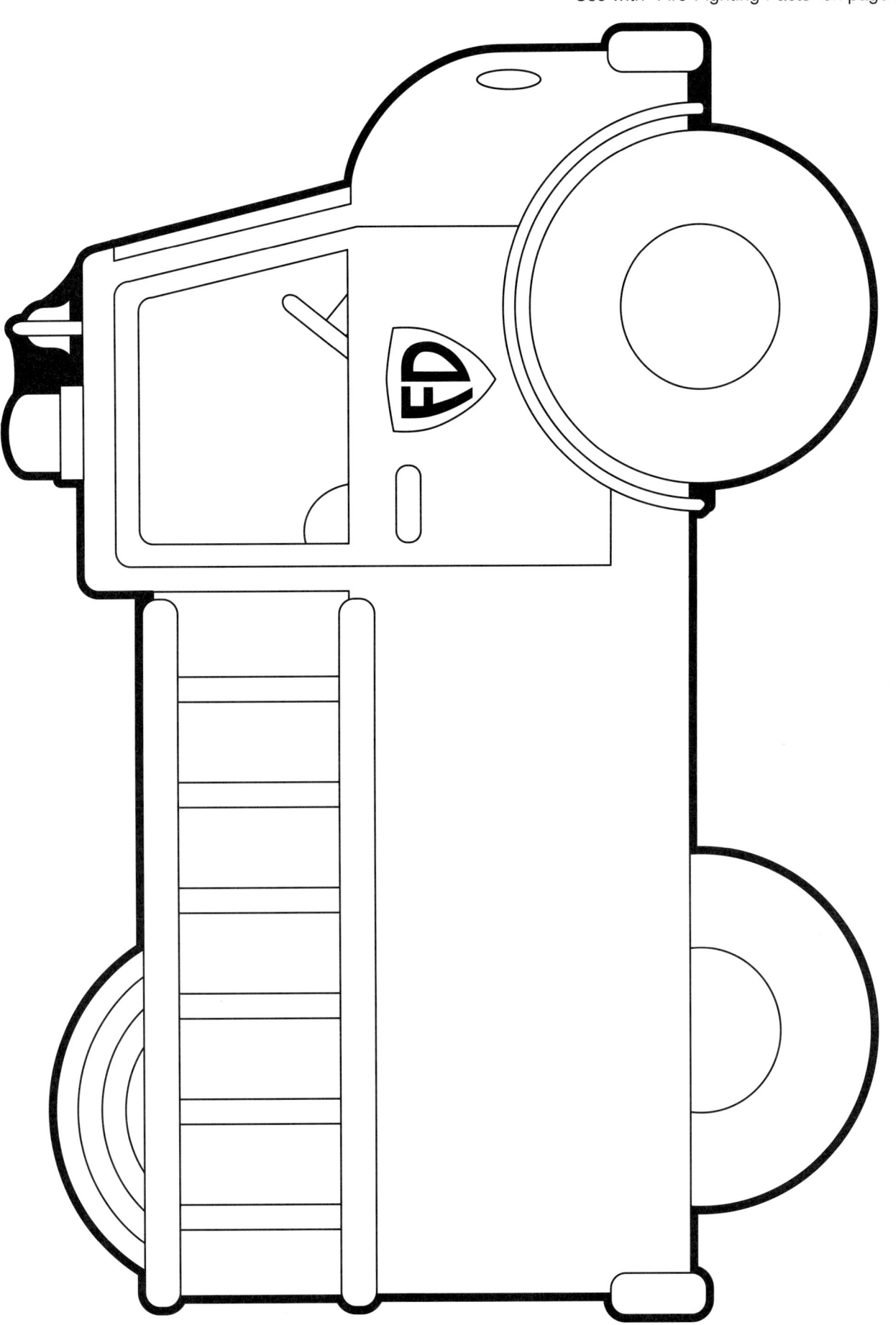

Pattern
Use with "Hats Off To Firefighters!" on page 52.

FIREFIGHTER 1

1. This "Home Safe Home" booklet belongs to:

©The Education Center, Inc.

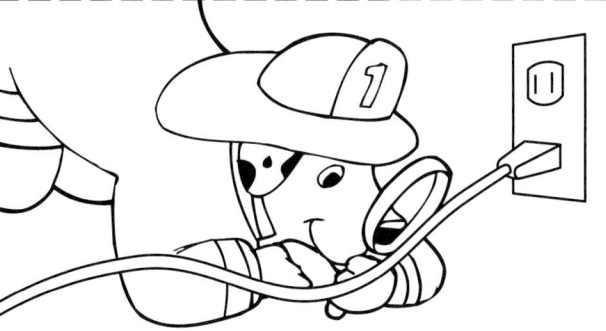

2. Check all electrical cords and outlets.

3. Store flammable liquids in a safe place.

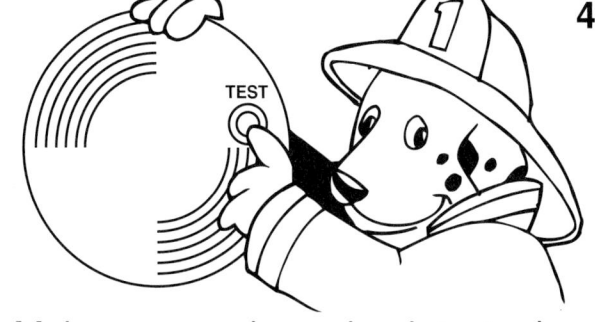

4. Make sure each smoke detector is working. (If not, check the batteries.)

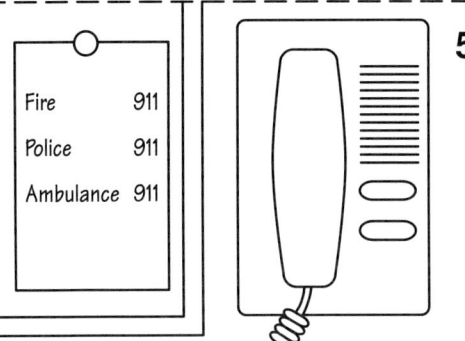

5. Post emergency numbers near all phones.

6. Use a toy phone to practice calling 911.

7. Practice a home fire-escape plan.

8. _____ is a

Home Fire-Safety Hero.

_____
Teacher

_____
Date

©The Education Center, Inc. • Big Book of Monthly Ideas • TEC1487

Note To The Teacher: Use this reproducible booklet with "Home Safe Home" on page 53.

Columbus Day Celebrations

Discover the adventures of the Admiral Of The Ocean Sea while you explore these cross-curricular activities with your students.

Sailing With Columbus

Ahoy, Maties! Sail into learning about Columbus and his explorations with this bulletin board. Cover your board with light blue paper. Cut a length of dark blue bulletin-board paper to resemble waves and staple it along the bottom edge of the board. To make a sailing ship, cut a large boat shape from brown bulletin-board paper and cut three sail shapes from white construction paper. Cut three two-inch-wide strips of brown paper to serve as masts. Assemble the ship on the board as shown. Add the title "Sailing With Columbus." As students learn facts about Columbus and his voyages, print the information on the sails. Continue adding facts to the board throughout your study of Columbus.

- Columbus was looking for a shorter route to the Indies.
- The Niña, Pinta, and Santa María were the names of Columbus's ships on his 1492 trip.
- Columbus was hoping to find gold in the Indies.

A Global Connection

Tell students that Columbus wanted to find a shorter route to the Indies—which at that time included the countries of India, China, the East Indies, and Japan. In Columbus's time, many sailors believed that to get to the Indies, one had to sail around Africa. Show this route on a globe by attaching a length of yarn to the globe with small pieces of Sticky-Tac.

Explain that Columbus believed he could reach the Indies by sailing west. Show Columbus's intended route across the Atlantic to the Indies by fastening another length of yarn to the globe using Sticky-Tac. As students observe the globe, ask them, "Does Columbus have a clear path to get to the Indies?" and "What is in the way?" Guide students to the discovery that Columbus did not have a clear path to the Indies because the islands now called the Bahamas and the land masses of the Americas blocked his route. Explain that when Columbus landed on these islands, he did not know that he had found a New World unknown to Europeans. Columbus believed that he had reached the Indies.

ideas by Nicole Iacovazzi and Stacie Stone

Land Ho!

On August 3, 1492, Columbus set sail heading west from Palos, Spain, with the *Niña,* the *Pinta,* and the *Santa María.* When land was first sighted by moonlight at 2:00 A.M. on October 12, the *Pinta* fired a cannon. Columbus later named this island *San Salvador.* Ask each student to imagine that he's in the crow's nest of the *Pinta* when he is the first to spot land after over two months at sea. Discuss the feelings of joy and apprehension the crew must have had. If possible, bring in a telescope or binoculars, or make cardboard telescopes for students to sight through.

Share the book *The Log Of Christopher Columbus—The First Voyage: Spring, Summer And Fall 1492* by Christopher Columbus with selections by Steve Lowe (Philomel Books, 1992). Then have students make props for creative play. To make a telescope, help each child slide a wide toilet-tissue tube over a narrower aluminum-foil tube. To make a Columbus Day hat, duplicate the patterns on page 63 on brown construction paper for each child to cut out. Instruct the student to glue each strip to one side of his hat. When the glue has dried, assist each student in stapling the strips together to fit his head. Take a full-length photograph of each child wearing his hat and holding his telescope to use with "Captain's Log."

Captain's Log

Explain to students that Columbus kept a log to record events that occurred on his voyage to the New World. Share excerpts from *I, Columbus: My Journal 1492–3* edited by Peter and Connie Roop (Walker Publishing Company, Inc.; 1990). After reading it, have each student make her own log.

To make a log, each student will need several sheets of lined notebook paper and two sheets of 9" x 12" construction paper. Assist each student in stapling the notebook paper between the construction paper. Instruct each student to glue her photo (see "Land Ho!") to the front cover of her log. Have each student title the front cover as shown. Next challenge each student to think of important events in her life and record these events in her log. Older students can imagine that they are sailing to the New World with Columbus. Have students write about their feelings before, during, and after their "voyage" with Columbus.

Old-Meets-New Fruit Salad

When Columbus arrived in the New World, he discovered many unfamiliar foods. He brought the foods back to Spain with him. In return, he introduced the New World to foods that originated in Europe. To develop research skills, share with students the lists of Old World and New World foods that follow. Then divide your class into two groups. Give each group a set of index cards on which you have printed the names of several Old World and New World foods. Challenge the members of each group to use information gathered from reference books to sort its cards into the appropriate categories: From The "Old World" or From The "New World." After each group has sorted its cards, glue the cards on a chart.

To follow up, allow students to make an Old-Meets-New Fruit Salad. Help students mix together chunks of pineapple, peaches, papaya, pears, and watermelon—along with banana slices and blueberries—in a large bowl. If desired, add some chopped peanuts, cashews, and pecans. Serve individual portions in small plastic cups. Give each student a spoon and let him eat the treat while you read aloud *In 1492* by Jean Marzollo (Scholastic Inc., 1991).

From The New World: corn, potatoes, tomatoes, vanilla, beans, pumpkins, avocados, wild rice, chocolate, peppers, pineapples, peanuts, cashews, papaya, pecans, and blueberries

From The Old World: peaches, pears, watermelons, olives, bananas, wheat, barley, sugarcane, lettuce, onions, chickens, cattle, pigs, sheep, okra, and honeybees.

Message In A Barrel

Tell students that Columbus had a very difficult return voyage. On Christmas Eve the *Santa María* wrecked near present-day Haiti. Later the ship that Columbus was sailing on—the *Niña*—almost sank. Columbus was determined to leave an account of his findings—in case he should be lost at sea or unable to return to Spain. So Columbus wrote an account of his discoveries, sealed it in a cask, and threw the cask overboard. To date, no one has ever reported finding the message. Ask students what they think might have happened to the cask. Brainstorm with students what they think Columbus may have included in his message. List students' responses on the board.

For a creative-writing activity, ask each student to imagine that she is with Columbus on the *Niña* after the *Santa María* wrecked and to think of a message to put in a barrel. Provide each student with a copy of the barrel pattern on page 64. Then ask each student to use their brainstormed list to write her own message on the barrel. Allow each student to share her message; then bind the stories into a classroom collection titled "Messages From Columbus."

Creative Coats Of Arms

Tell students that when Columbus returned to Spain from the New World, he was given a hero's welcome. His title—Admiral Of The Ocean Sea—was confirmed and he was given a reception by the king and queen of Spain. They also granted him the right to have his own coat of arms. Explain to students that a coat of arms has symbols on it, and each symbol has its own special meaning. The most basic part of any coat of arms is the shield. Then show students a picture of Columbus's shield (above) that you have duplicated in advance. Explain that the castle and lion symbols found on Columbus's shield are also used on the Spanish shield. Ask students to name reasons why they think the same symbols are found on both shields. Then discuss how the island and the anchor symbols reflect Columbus's interests and accomplishments.

To follow up, have each student design his own coat of arms. Give each student a copy of the shield pattern on page 65. Encourage each student to draw symbols on his shield that reflect his interests and achievements. Have student volunteers share their shields with classmates, explaining why they chose to illustrate them as they did. Mount the shields on a bulletin board titled "Class Heraldry."

Cultural Encounters

To encourage a discussion of how different cultures view history and the voyages of Columbus in particular, share the book *Encounter* by Jane Yolen (Harcourt Brace Jovanovich, Publishers; 1992) with students. This story is told through the eyes of a native boy who watches Christopher Columbus and his men come ashore and occupy his homeland. The Taino natives trade gifts and share a feast with "the pale strangers from the sky," but the boy is afraid. When the strangers leave, they take Taino natives—including the boy—with them as slaves. The boy escapes and tells his story of the day his language, religion, customs, and dreams were taken from him by the white man. At the end of the story, Jane Yolen explains that a few Taino were taken to Spain and used as slaves. The 300,000 native Taino diminished to fewer than 500 by the year 1548. Today no pure Taino exist.

After reading the book, discuss why Native Americans may feel that Columbus is no hero to them. Ask students to name good and bad things that came from Columbus's voyages and those of explorers who followed him. Name items from the story that were traded between Columbus and the Taino. (The Taino offered fish darts, balls of cotton thread, and parrots. Columbus brought Venetian glass beads, little brass bells, and red caps.) Explain that these items represented each culture's customs and lifestyles. Then ask students, "If you met someone from another land, what would you trade?" List students' responses on the board.

The Life And Times Of Christopher Columbus

Use this timeline to give your students a visual reminder of the important events in Columbus's life. Share the following information on individual sheets of 12" x 18" construction paper:

—Columbus is born in Genoa, Italy, in 1451.
—Columbus leaves Genoa in 1470 or 1471 to head to sea.
—Columbus marries Felipa de Perestrello in 1479.
—Columbus requests supplies for his journey to the Indies from King John II of Portugal in 1482. He is denied.
—In 1485 Columbus asks the king and queen of Spain to finance a trip to the Indies. His request is denied.
—In January of 1492, King Ferdinand and Queen Isabella of Spain decide to finance Columbus's voyage to the Indies.
—On August 3, 1492, the *Niña, Pinta,* and *Santa María* set sail from Palos, Spain.
—On October 12, 1492, Columbus and his men spot land. Later that day Columbus steps on land. He names the island *San Salvador*.
—Columbus returns to Spain on March 15, 1493.
—In the years 1493–1496, Columbus makes a second voyage to the New World.
—Columbus makes a third voyage to the New World in the years 1498–1500.
—A fourth voyage is made to the New World in the years 1502–1504.
—Columbus dies on May 20, 1506.

Then divide students into pairs. Ask each pair to select a fact that it would like to illustrate. After each pair has finished its illustration, enlist students' help in sequencing the events in Columbus's life. Then mount the pictures in sequence on a bulletin board titled "The Life And Times Of Christopher Columbus." Conclude the lesson with a discussion about Columbus. Ask students, "How many years did Columbus wait before King Ferdinand and Queen Isabella decided to finance his trip?" and "How many years did Columbus wait from the year his first request for supplies was made until the actual first voyage occurred?" Discuss how determination and patience can help us reach our goals.

Explore A Good Book

Pedro's Journal: A Voyage With Christopher Columbus (August 3, 1492– February 14, 1493) by Pam Conrad (Boyds Mills Press, Inc.; 1991)
Christopher Columbus by Stephen Krensky (Random House, Inc.; 1991)
Christopher Columbus by Ann McGovern (Scholastic Inc., 1992)
Three Ships For Columbus by Eve Spencer (Raintree Steck-Vaughn, 1992)
Columbus Day by Vicki Liestman (Carolrhoda Books, Inc.; 1992)

Patterns: Columbus Day Hat

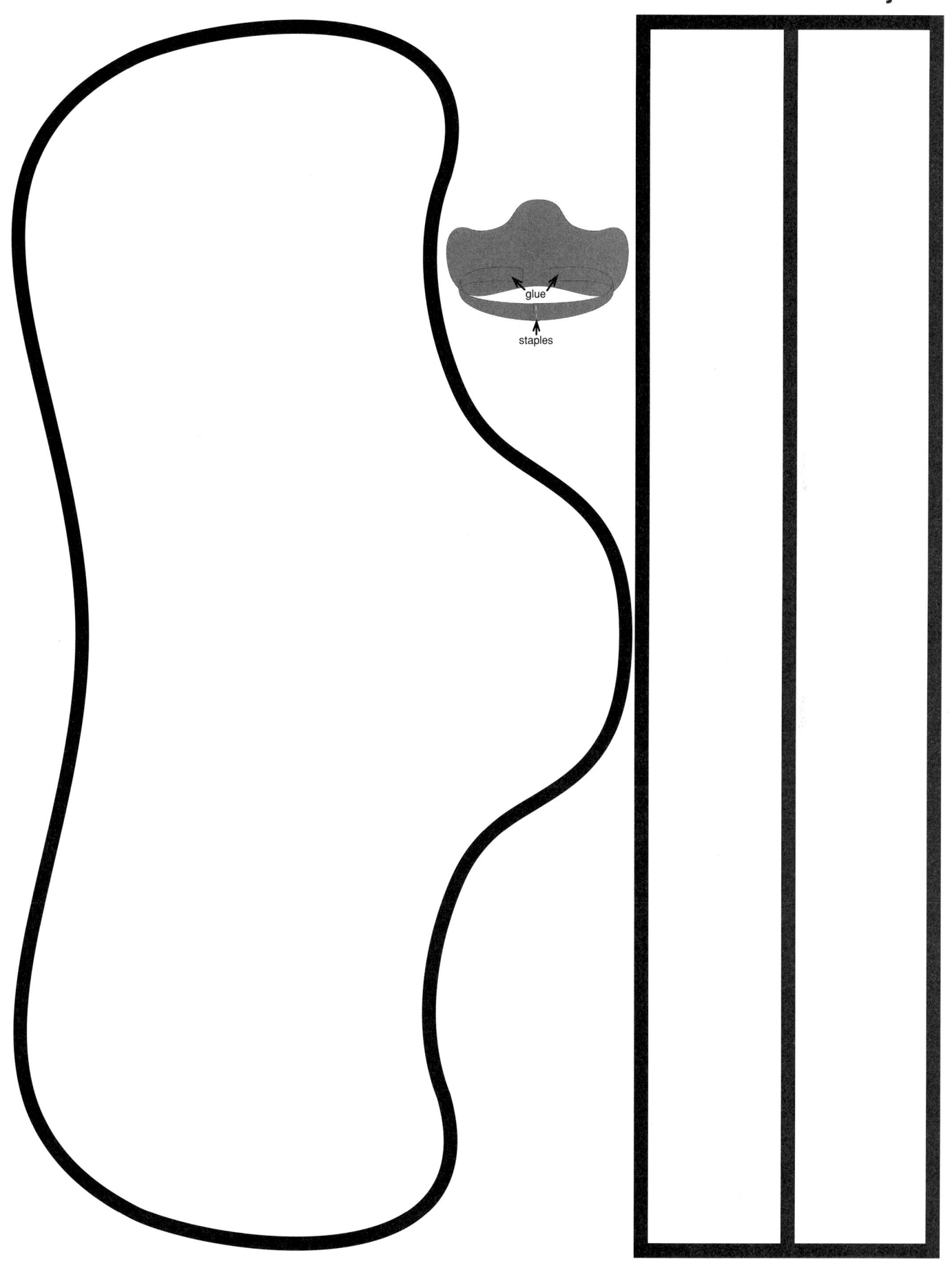

©The Education Center, Inc. • *Big Book of Monthly Ideas* • TEC1487

Note To The Teacher: Use with "Land Ho!" and "Captain's Log" on page 59.

Name _____ Creative writing

Message In A Barrel

Shield Pattern
Use with "Creative Coats Of Arms" on page 61.

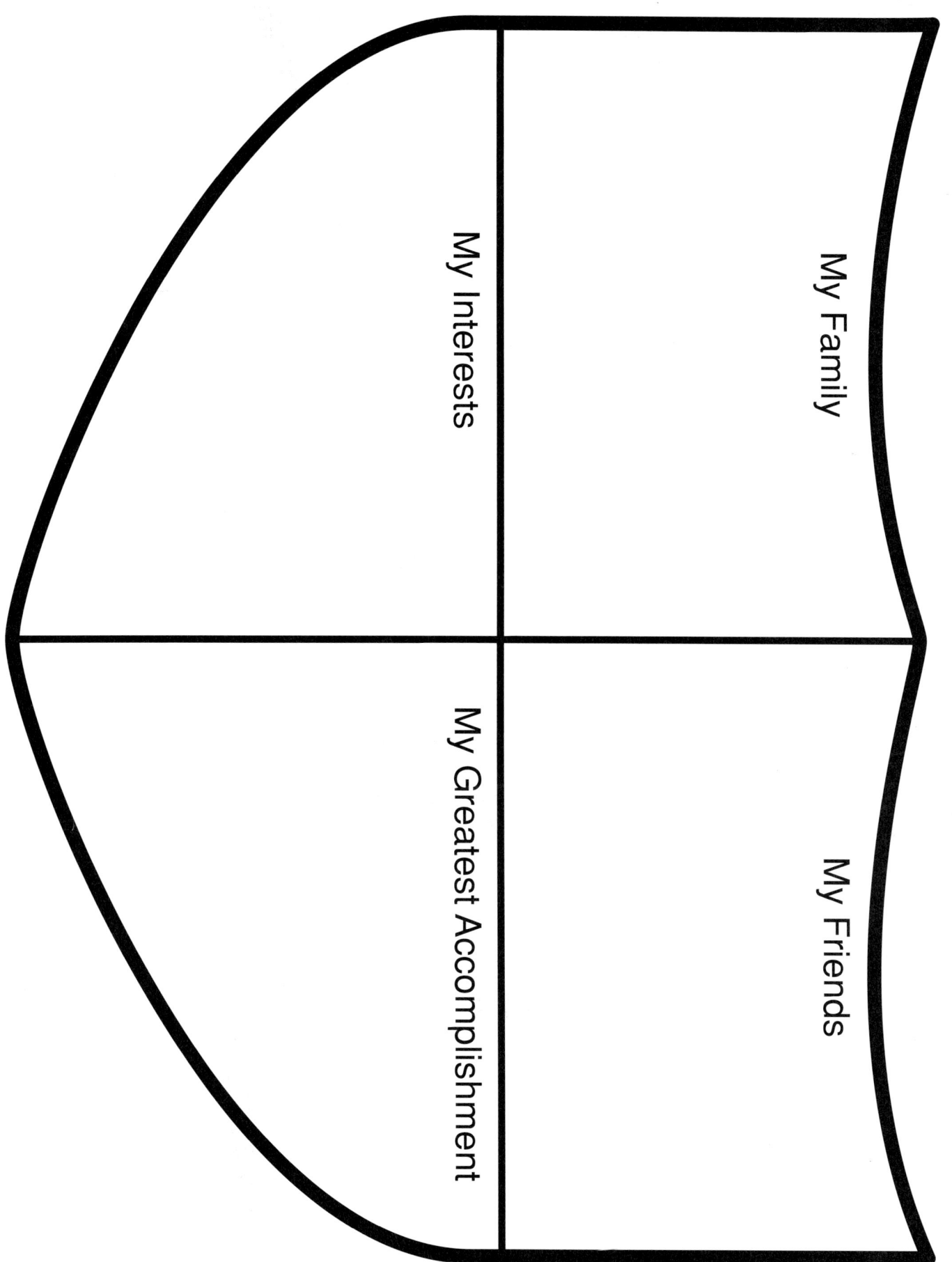

Happy Halloween!

Creeping spiders, screeching owls, and swooping bats are just a few of the things that will haunt your classroom with this collection of Halloween ideas.

ideas by Nancy Matthews

When people think of Halloween, bats often come to mind. Most people fear being bitten, but bats really are our friends. Share the following books and find out why bats are beneficial: *Zipping, Zapping, Zooming Bats* by Ann Earle (HarperCollins Publishers, 1995) and *A First Look At Bats* by Millicent E. Selsam and Joyce Hunt (Walker And Company, 1991). Have students list the physical characteristics of bats and discuss how the bat's wing is similar to a human's hand. Discuss the benefits of bats and list them.

Then create this bulletin board to reinforce facts about bats. Cover your bulletin board with brown paper. Using another strip of the same paper, tear a jagged edge and attach it to the top of the bulletin board. This will give the effect of a cave. Trace several bat patterns (page 71) on black paper and cut them out. Fold the wings of each bat in toward the body. On the back of one wing, write a fact or myth about bats. On the inside (body), write the corresponding answer—fact or fiction. (See the steps to make the bat on page 71.) To display these bats, hang them upside down from fish line on the bulletin board. Use paper clips to secure them. The student chooses a bat, reads the wing, and decides if the statement is fact. He then checks his answer by unfolding the wings and reading whether it is a fact or just a myth.

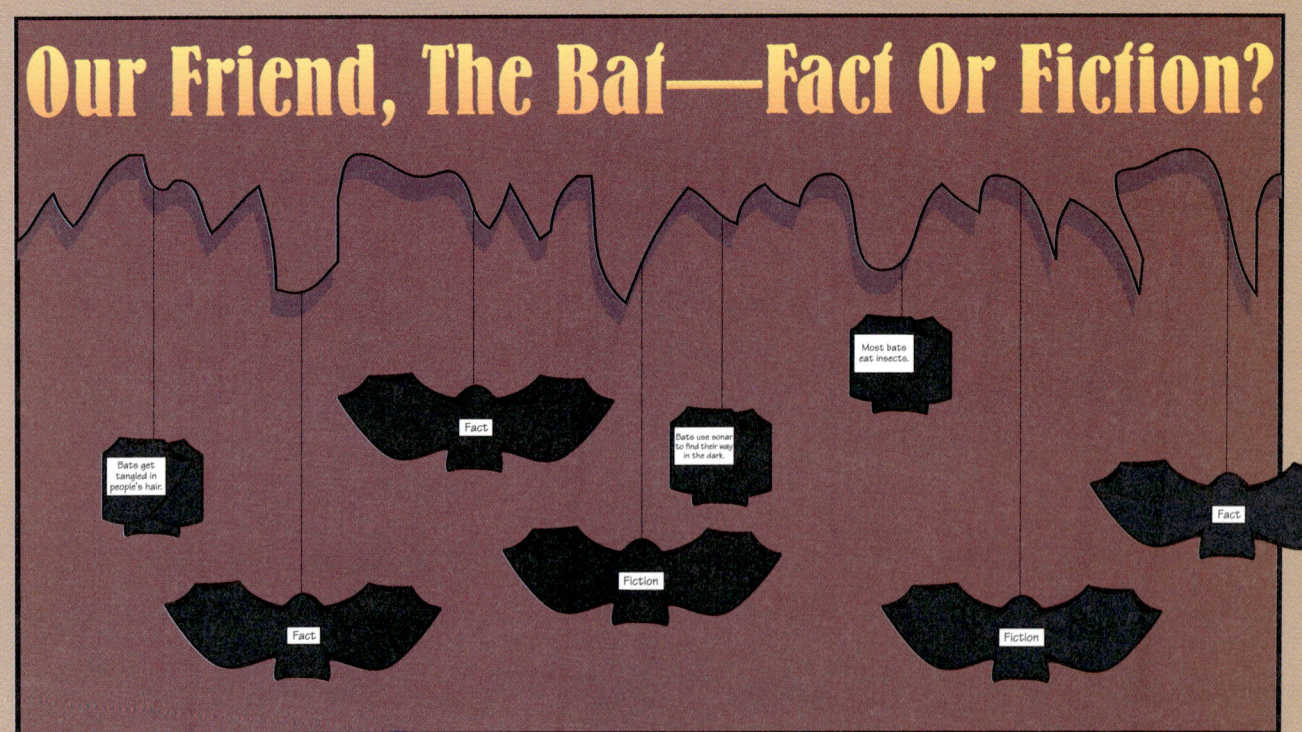

Pumpkin Magic

Plump Pumpkins

Share the book *The Biggest Pumpkin Ever* by Steven Kroll (Holiday House, Inc.; 1984) with students. Discuss why the pumpkin grew so large and beautiful. As a group, write directions for caring for a pumpkin plant. Discuss the elements that a plant needs to grow and compare them to the directions the students came up with.

Distribute a large sheet of orange construction paper to each student. Using markers, pencils, and scissors, have students create their own jack-o'-lanterns. When each student has finished drawing and cutting out the face, tape a piece of aluminum foil over the back of the pumpkin so the shiny side shows through. Glue each jack-o'-lantern on black construction paper and mount it on a board titled "Pumpkin Magic."

Creepy Crawlies

No Halloween is complete without a few spiders hanging around. Pour black tempera paint into a small Styrofoam® or plastic cup for each student. Distribute a paper plate, a paintbrush, scissors, glue, and one piece each of white and black construction paper to each student. Have the student paint the entire back side of the paper plate black. While it dries, have each student fold his black construction paper in half (across), then in half again (the same direction), and then again a third time. Unfolded, the paper should have eight equal sections. Instruct the student to cut the sections apart on the folds. These will be the eight legs for the spider. To make the legs curved, have each student hold his pencil under a strip (with his thumb on top) and curl the paper like you would curl ribbon. Glue the eight legs to the plate and create the face by gluing on pieces of white construction paper. When completed, hang the spiders from the ceiling or lights with fishing line. You'll have creepy crawlies descending toward students' desks. EEK!

Shining Jack-O'-Lanterns

Make these pumpkin viewers to demonstrate that jack-o'-lanterns are most beautiful when light shines through them. Distribute an empty toilet-tissue or paper-towel tube, a 5" x 5" piece of black construction paper, a 4 1/2" x 5 1/2" piece of orange construction paper, and a tack to each student. Have each student lightly trace around the end of the tube on the black paper, cut out the circle, and then draw a jack-o'-lantern face inside the resulting circle. Tape the black paper over one end of the tube so that the face is centered. Using the tack, gently poke holes to outline the face. Wrap the orange paper around the tube and secure it with tape.

Have each student hold the tube up to his eye to look through the "telescope" at the jack-o'-lantern "constellation." Try darkening the room and holding a flashlight in the open end. Walk toward a flat surface or the wall until the jack-o'-lantern appears. Spooky!

Halloween Treat Bags

Students will walk proudly when carrying their handmade trick-or-treat bags home. Distribute a brown paper lunch bag, a paper plate, glue, green yarn, markers, and scissors to each student. Cut apples in half as shown. Give each student one half. Instruct the student to fold his bag flat and cut the top of the bag to make handles as shown. Pour orange tempera paint on each student's plate. Have the student dip the cut side of the apple into the paint and then press it onto the paper bag to make a pumpkin shape. (This can be repeated in any pattern or as many times as wanted.) Students add details and faces to their pumpkins with the markers after the paint has dried. Using green yarn, glue curly vines among the pumpkins. Let the glue dry, and then fill the bags with Halloween treats from the teacher such as stickers, bookmarks, or plastic spiders.

A Halloween-Candy Hodgepodge

Halloween candies make good math manipulatives. Distribute a lunch bag containing a handful of assorted, wrapped candies to each student. Have each student feel the bag from the outside and estimate how many pieces of candy are in it. Have the student record her estimate on a piece of paper, pour the candy out, and count. Record the answer. Ask students, "How many pieces off was your estimate? Add or subtract to find the difference."

Next have students group their candies in their work areas. Ask each student what characteristics she used to sort and group the candies (size, shape, color, texture, wrapper, etc.). Then have each student sort them according to another characteristic. Give each student a copy of the blank graph worksheet on page 72 to graph the results. Each student labels the groups along the bottom of the graph and then numbers the left side of the graph. Students color each column to show the number of candy pieces. Discuss who had the most or least of each kind. Then munch away!

Witches' Brew

Let students stir up some Witches' Brew for creative writing. Write the following recipe on the chalkboard and have students read what to do. You will need ginger ale, red Hi-C® punch, green Hi-C®, and lime sherbet. Pour all the ingredients in a large bowl over construction-paper flames on a table.

Recipe For Witches' Brew

1 bottle of snake venom (ginger ale)
1 bottle of bat blood (red Hi-C®)
1 bottle of eel juice (green Hi-C®)
Several spoonfuls of green mold
    (lime sherbet)

Stir up in a cauldron and drink,
    but BEWARE!

After serving this potent concoction, have students write their own recipes for Witches' Brew on recipe cards. Display the cards on a board around a large cauldron cutout labeled "Witches' Brew!" Add cut-out bubbles, black cats, spiders, and bats.

The Candy Trail

Children look forward to dressing up on Halloween, but what they look forward to the most is trick-or-treating. Brush up on following directions and using mapping skills while on the trail of Halloween candy. On a large piece of tagboard or an overhead transparency, draw a simple town map complete with a compass rose in the corner. Include a house for each student in the class and label each with a student's name. Glue a piece of candy to each house. Also write each student's name on an index card.

Begin the activity by discussing the compass rose showing north, south, east, and west. Next shuffle and hand out the index cards randomly. Tell students that the name on their card is the house where they will trick-or-treat. The only twist is, they need to give directions telling how to get there. Each student takes a turn telling where the house is and giving directions (using north, south, east, and west) on how to get to the treat house on his card. Students may write the directions first and then read them aloud. Have each student follow the trail with his finger while giving directions. Once the student arrives at his destination, he can remove the piece of candy and enjoy.

Bat Pattern

Use with "Our Friend, The Bat—Fact Or Fiction?" on page 66.

1. Glue "fact" or "fiction" here.

2. Fold here.

3. Glue sentence here.

©The Education Center, Inc. • *Big Book of Monthly Ideas* • TEC1487

Name _____ Graphing

Counting Candy

Number of pieces

Kind of candy

1. I grouped my candy by _____.

2. I had the most _____.

3. I had the least _____.

4. My favorite of these candies is _____.

NATIONAL CHILDREN'S BOOK WEEK

Worm your way into reading with this collection of activities to celebrate National Children's Book Week.

ideas by Shari Abbey and Kathy Wolf

BOOKWORM BOOKMARKS

Begin a week of celebrating children's books by supplying your students with the necessary tools—bookmarks! Duplicate the bookmark and bookworm patterns from page 78 on white construction paper for each student. Have each student cut out the bookmark along the solid line and fold along the dotted line so that it makes a small book. Next have her cut out and color her bookworm and add two wiggle eyes. After the student has decorated the front cover of her bookmark, have her glue the bookworm to the inside so that it peeks over the top. Each time the student finishes a book, she writes the title on the back of the bookmark and colors in a bookworm. Present the "Bona Fide Bookworm" award on page 78 to those readers who color in all five worms. These bookmarks are sure to wiggle their way into children's books!

TAKE A BITE OUT OF READING!

Encourage students to read some deliciously good books with this wonderfully wormy reading-incentive program. Create a bulletin board of bookworms to motivate students to take a bite out of reading each day. Cover your bulletin board with yellow background paper. Duplicate the leaf pattern on page 80 on green construction paper for each child to cut out. Duplicate the worm patterns on page 78 on different colors of construction paper. Give one worm to each student to cut out and label with his name. Supply each student with a pair of wiggle eyes to glue to his worm cutout. Have students glue the worms to their leaf cutouts. Pin the worms on the board as shown. Each time a student finishes reading a book, he punches a hole at the edge of his leaf with a hole puncher. Students will love watching their progress as their leaves disappear. How many good books can your little bookworms devour?

GRAND ENTRANCES

Get students involved in a schoolwide celebration of books with a grand entrance for every classroom. Prior to National Children's Book Week, ask each of your colleagues to select an author to promote with a display on her classroom door. Provide the sign-up sheet on page 81 or ask your librarian to create a sign-up list of best-known children's authors to ensure that each class will feature a different author and title.

Enlist the help of your class in selecting a favorite book from the list. Read the book aloud and ask students how they would convince others to read the book using an eye-catching door display. Divide your class into groups and have each group help with the design of the grand entrance on or around the door. During Book Week allow students to take a book walk through the halls and vote on the best grand entrances. Award books donated by local stores to the winning classes.

BOOK BARTERING

Here's a sure way to get your students to browse their bookshelves. Hold a used paperback book exchange in your classroom. Several days ahead of the exchange, inform parents of your plan and invite students to bring in at least one paperback book from home. Give each student a ticket (page 80) for each book he brings. On the day of the exchange, display all the books in a special area and allow students to browse the titles. Students may exchange their tickets for "new" used books. You may want to have a Book Barter Day every month!

ADOPT-A-BOOK PROJECT

Oh, those poor, unattractive books that sit on the library shelves all year. No one ever checks them out because of their dusty, lackluster appearance. Help your students remember the saying, "You can't judge a book by its cover" with this spiffy idea. Ask your librarian for help in choosing several of those seldom-checked-out books that would be suitable for your grade level. Give each student a book to adopt. Have the student read the book and then design a new book jacket. In addition to a beautiful new front cover, have the student include author and illustrator information and a summary of the book on the inside flaps. Then, with your librarian's help, display the new and improved books in a special area of the library. Those adopted books will be checked out again in no time.

BOOK WEEK BOOK TOUR

Explain to students that publishers often send authors on book tours to promote their titles and sell more books. You may indeed entice an author to visit your school for a book talk by contacting the publisher. If this is not possible, your students can still simulate a book campaign to generate support for reading.

Divide your class into pairs and have each pair decide on a favorite book to promote. Give each pair the choice of promoting its book by writing an ad, drawing a poster, creating a song, dressing up as characters from the story, or making the book into a movie. Older students can also do research to report about the author and illustrator and then display other titles by the same author. Arrange for your students to visit other classrooms or the library to present their books on tour. As the students embrace their favorite authors, they will encourage others to read them, too!

WHO ARE THESE CHARACTERS?

Celebrate your favorite books in a big way. Brainstorm a list of your students' favorite fictional characters such as Ms. Frizzle, Amelia Bedelia, Clifford, etc. Then pair students to create larger-than-life book characters. Have each pair choose one character to illustrate. Tell students that their characters should be two to three feet tall. Supply each pair with a large sheet of bulletin-board paper, various colors of construction paper, and markers. Next give each pair one 8 1/2" x 11" sheet of construction paper to fold in half like a card. Ask each pair to list five adjectives that describe its character on the outside of the card and write the character's name on the inside. Display each character in the hallway with the descriptive card beside it. Add the title "Who Are These Characters?" As they walk past these fictional folks, teachers, students, and visitors will enjoy trying to guess the characters.

GET PUBLISHED!

Motivate your would-be authors to write about their favorite books. Duplicate the book-review form on page 79 for each child to complete. Share samples of book reviews published in newspapers or book catalogs; then help students choose books to write about. Practice filling out a book-review form together; then allow students to complete their copies. Submit the student reviews to your local newspaper for publication. With some notice, most small newspapers will gladly publish student-written material. Some papers may even have limited space for artwork. To spur community awareness, write up an introduction for the submission stating that this project was done to celebrate National Children's Book Week.

A PARADE OF CHARACTERS

What's a celebration without a parade? Take your celebration of National Children's Book Week schoolwide with this showstopping idea. Several weeks in advance, send a note home to parents explaining that children are going to dress up as book characters on a specified date. Plenty of notice will be appreciated by parents in order for them to help their children decide upon characters and create costumes. A week or two before your scheduled parade, have each student announce the character he is going to portray and write three to four sentences telling about his character—including whom he is, what story he is in and what he does in the story, the author who created him, and books in which others could read more about him. Older students may be encouraged to memorize these lines. Be sure to allow time for students to practice. Direct your youngsters to say their lines loudly and clearly. Arrange to visit other classrooms with your parade of characters during National Children's Book Week.

On the day of the parade, have several volunteers on hand to help students get into their costumes. Line children up in single file, and march from room to room so students can show off their costumes and say their lines. This is one parade that is sure to get rave reviews!

LITERARY LUNCHEON

End the last chapter of your celebration of books with a surprise twist in the plot. Ask your students to bring a sack lunch on the last day of National Children's Book Week. With approval from your librarian, take your students to the library to eat lunch among the literature. If possible, invite a storyteller, local celebrity, or community leader as a guest reader to provide entertainment while your kids munch on their lunches.

Bookmark Pattern
Use with "Bookworm Bookmarks" on page 74.

Get between the covers  of a good book!

National Children's Book Week
November
_____

Books I've read this week:

_____   _____

_____   _____

_____   _____

Bookworm Pattern
Use with "Bookworm Bookmarks" and "Take A Bite Out Of Reading!" on page 74.

Award
Use with "Bookworm Bookmarks" on page 74.

Name _____

Is A Bona Fide Bookworm!

_____
Signed

A KID'S REVIEW OF A KID'S BOOK

Book Reviewer: _____ Age: _____

Title: _____

Author: _____

Illustrator: _____

Publisher: _____

Copyright Date: _____

I give this book ☆☆☆ : _____

because: _____

_____

_____

_____

_____

_____

©The Education Center, Inc. • Big Book of Monthly Ideas • TEC1487

Note To The Teacher: Use with "Get Published!" on page 77.

Pattern
Use with "Take A Bite Out Of Reading!" on page 74.

Tickets
Use with "Book Bartering" on page 75.

CHOOSE A FAVORITE CHILDREN'S BOOK AUTHOR!

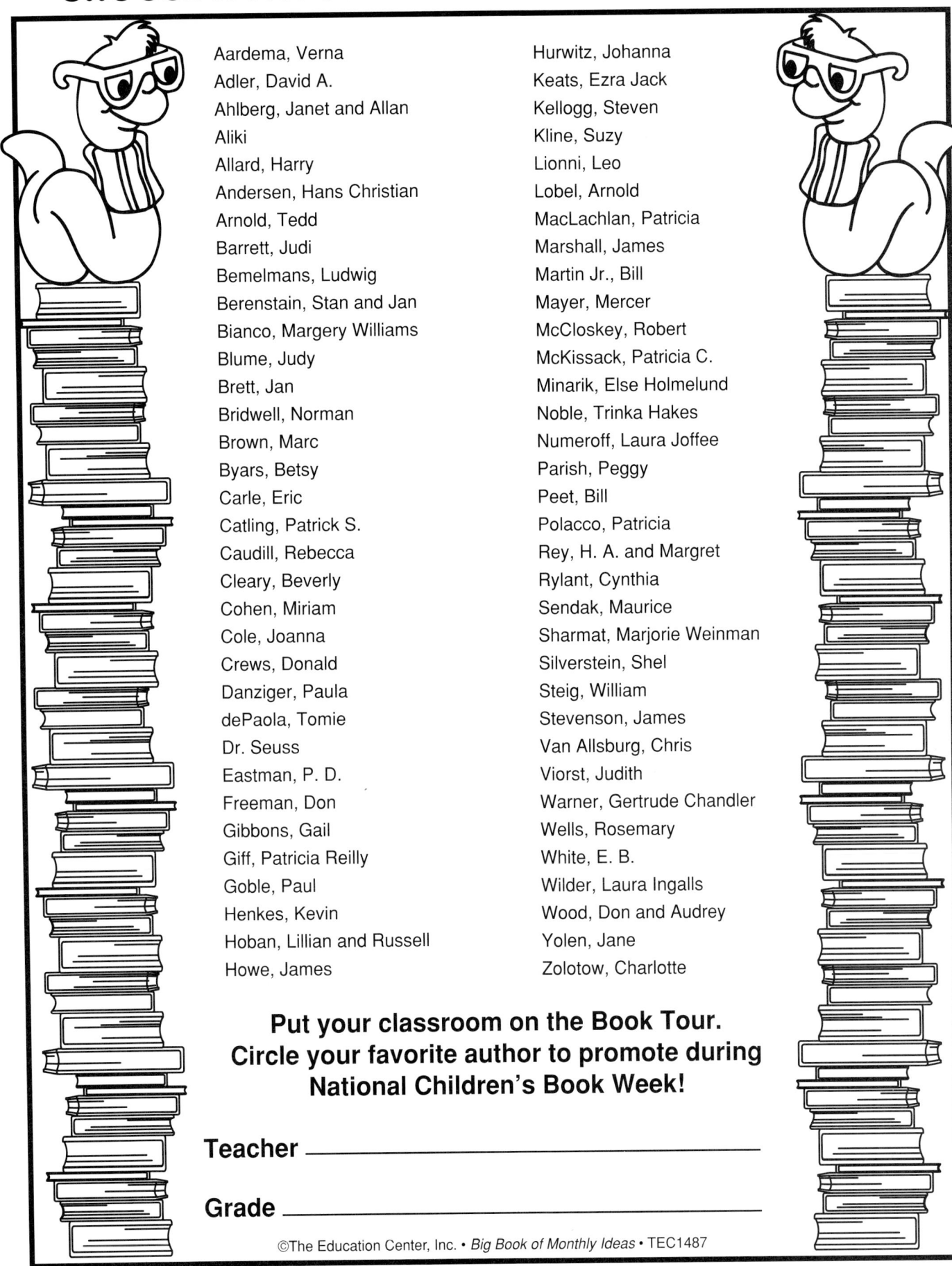

Aardema, Verna
Adler, David A.
Ahlberg, Janet and Allan
Aliki
Allard, Harry
Andersen, Hans Christian
Arnold, Tedd
Barrett, Judi
Bemelmans, Ludwig
Berenstain, Stan and Jan
Bianco, Margery Williams
Blume, Judy
Brett, Jan
Bridwell, Norman
Brown, Marc
Byars, Betsy
Carle, Eric
Catling, Patrick S.
Caudill, Rebecca
Cleary, Beverly
Cohen, Miriam
Cole, Joanna
Crews, Donald
Danziger, Paula
dePaola, Tomie
Dr. Seuss
Eastman, P. D.
Freeman, Don
Gibbons, Gail
Giff, Patricia Reilly
Goble, Paul
Henkes, Kevin
Hoban, Lillian and Russell
Howe, James

Hurwitz, Johanna
Keats, Ezra Jack
Kellogg, Steven
Kline, Suzy
Lionni, Leo
Lobel, Arnold
MacLachlan, Patricia
Marshall, James
Martin Jr., Bill
Mayer, Mercer
McCloskey, Robert
McKissack, Patricia C.
Minarik, Else Holmelund
Noble, Trinka Hakes
Numeroff, Laura Joffee
Parish, Peggy
Peet, Bill
Polacco, Patricia
Rey, H. A. and Margret
Rylant, Cynthia
Sendak, Maurice
Sharmat, Marjorie Weinman
Silverstein, Shel
Steig, William
Stevenson, James
Van Allsburg, Chris
Viorst, Judith
Warner, Gertrude Chandler
Wells, Rosemary
White, E. B.
Wilder, Laura Ingalls
Wood, Don and Audrey
Yolen, Jane
Zolotow, Charlotte

**Put your classroom on the Book Tour.
Circle your favorite author to promote during
National Children's Book Week!**

Teacher _____

Grade _____

©The Education Center, Inc. • *Big Book of Monthly Ideas* • TEC1487

Note To The Teacher: Use with "Grand Entrances" on page 75.

A Feast Full Of Thanksgiving Ideas

Here's a cornucopia of ideas to help you incorporate skills with your Thanksgiving festivities.

Ideas by Nancy Matthews

Welcome To America!

Today, when reflecting on Thanksgiving, students think of turkey dinners, Thanksgiving Day parades, football games, and family and friends coming together. Explore some of the similarities and differences between Thanksgiving today and Thanksgiving centuries ago by reading *Thanksgiving Day* by Gail Gibbons (Holiday House, Inc.; 1983) to your students. This is a short story about the origin of Thanksgiving and how it is celebrated today. Summarize the story by telling students that the Pilgrims sailed from England to America to find a new life with religious freedom. The Pilgrims were met by Indians who lived in the area. At first, they were suspicious of each other. But the Indians taught the Pilgrims how to plant, hunt, and gather food. After their first harvest, the Pilgrims were thankful for a bountiful crop and for the help of the Indians in producing it. They invited the Indians to celebrate with them in the first Thanksgiving feast.

Compare the two cultures by having students think of ways the guests were different from their Pilgrim hosts. Some examples are clothing, language, appearance, eating habits, and skills. Divide the class into two groups. Have students in each group imagine they are either Pilgrims or Indians. Have each group tell what its thoughts or suspicions might be about the other group. Ask students to compare these fears to how they think a new student might feel in a new school. Together list ways that students might make new students feel welcome. Wrap up with a discussion about how we can help people from other lands feel welcome in America today.

A Bountiful Basket

Most of us are fortunate enough to enjoy a Thanksgiving feast. Remind students to be thankful for the food on their tables with this class project. At the beginning of your unit on Thanksgiving and continuing until the holiday, encourage students to think of those less fortunate by bringing in food for the needy. First decide as a class who will benefit from the collection. Students can prepare a holiday basket for a needy family, or they may choose a church or homeless shelter to receive their Thanksgiving gift. Encourage students to bring in canned fruits and vegetables; canned or bottled juices; bags of rice, raisins, and nuts; etc. Students may supplement the basket by bringing in spare change to buy a turkey for the recipient of the gift. No rewards or incentives should be given to students who participate. The good feeling of giving is reward enough.

Living In Plymouth Colony

Students learn about the Pilgrim houses of Plymouth Colony by reading the books *Oh, What A Thanksgiving!* by Steven Kroll (Scholastic Inc., 1988) and *Sarah Morton's Day* by Kate Waters (Scholastic Inc., 1989). Point out the illustrations and reproductions of houses of the 1620s, and discuss how they compare to the houses of today. The typical Pilgrim cottage was a small, one-room shelter made of wooden posts covered by sticks and straw mixed with clay. Wooden clapboards were used on well-to-do homes. Each cottage had a steep, thatched roof and a chimney made of clay and sticks.

To make a Pilgrim cottage, provide a clean, empty, half-pint milk carton for each child. Cut lengths of craft sticks to glue to all sides of the milk carton. After students glue on their clapboards, help them cover the roofs. Paint the top of each carton with a layer of thick white glue. Dip each roof into a bowl of crumbled shredded wheat cereal to cover as shown. Next have each student glue on doors, windows, and a chimney cut from brown construction paper. Display the cottages in a village arrangement atop a table. Label the display "Plimoth Plantation," after the living-history museum in Plymouth, Massachusetts.

Sail With The *Mayflower*

The Pilgrims fled from England to find religious freedom. One hundred two passengers traveled across the ocean on a ship called the *Mayflower*. Share *The First Thanksgiving* by Jean Craighead George (Philomel Books, 1993) with students and then discuss the conditions the Pilgrims had to endure on their journey. Have students imagine they are passengers on the Mayflower and tell what they like or dislike about the voyage.

Make individual models of the *Mayflower* for creative dramatics. Enlarge the pattern on page 85 and duplicate a copy for each student on tagboard. Provide students with markers and crayons to decorate their ships. Cut out each ship and tape two 18-inch pieces of yarn or heavy string parallel to each other across the back of the ship cutout. Have each student tie the *Mayflower* around his waist and dramatize a scene from the journey.

Gobblin' Good Vocabulary

Brainstorm vocabulary words that have a Thanksgiving theme to use with a week full of tasks. Write the words on feather cutouts and mount them, along with three turkeys, on the bulletin board as shown. (See the patterns on page 86.) Add the title "Gobblin' Good Words." Place a shoebox and a roasting pan nearby. Students use the words to complete the following daily tasks:

• Choose a word from the board and come up with other Thanksgiving words that begin with each of its letters.

    Ex: **G**iving
           Others
           Berries
           Bread
           Love
           Eating

• Write the words in ABC order.
• Write and illustrate a story about the turkey that came to your house for dinner. Use as many of the words as possible.
• Look up one word in the dictionary and write it on a feather cutout. Write its definition on another feather cutout. Put the feathers in the shoebox near the board. After all your classmates have contributed to the shoebox, take turns matching definitions to vocabulary words.
• Use as many words from the display as possible to create a word-search puzzle. Put your puzzle in the roasting pan. Once the pan is full of puzzles from the class, choose one and solve it.

Mmmm! Mmmm! Math

This activity includes a little homework over Thanksgiving as well as a follow-up class math activity. Explain that the majority of families serve turkey for Thanksgiving dinner. Discuss the average size of turkeys. Guide the students to understand that the more people who will be sharing a Thanksgiving meal together, the bigger the turkey will probably be. Have each student estimate how many people will be eating Thanksgiving dinner with his family. Next have each student estimate how much their turkey will weigh. Over the holiday, have each student find out the actual weight of the turkey and count how many people are at the Thanksgiving celebration.

After the holiday, have students compile this information for a class math activity. Write all the students' names on the board or on a transparency. Give each student the opportunity to record his information about the turkey's actual weight and number of people. Then each student compares the actual and estimated weights of his turkey to find out how close the estimation was. Then repeat this process with the number of people. Who had the biggest turkey? The most people? Was it the same person?

Pattern
Use with "Sail With The *Mayflower*" on page 83.

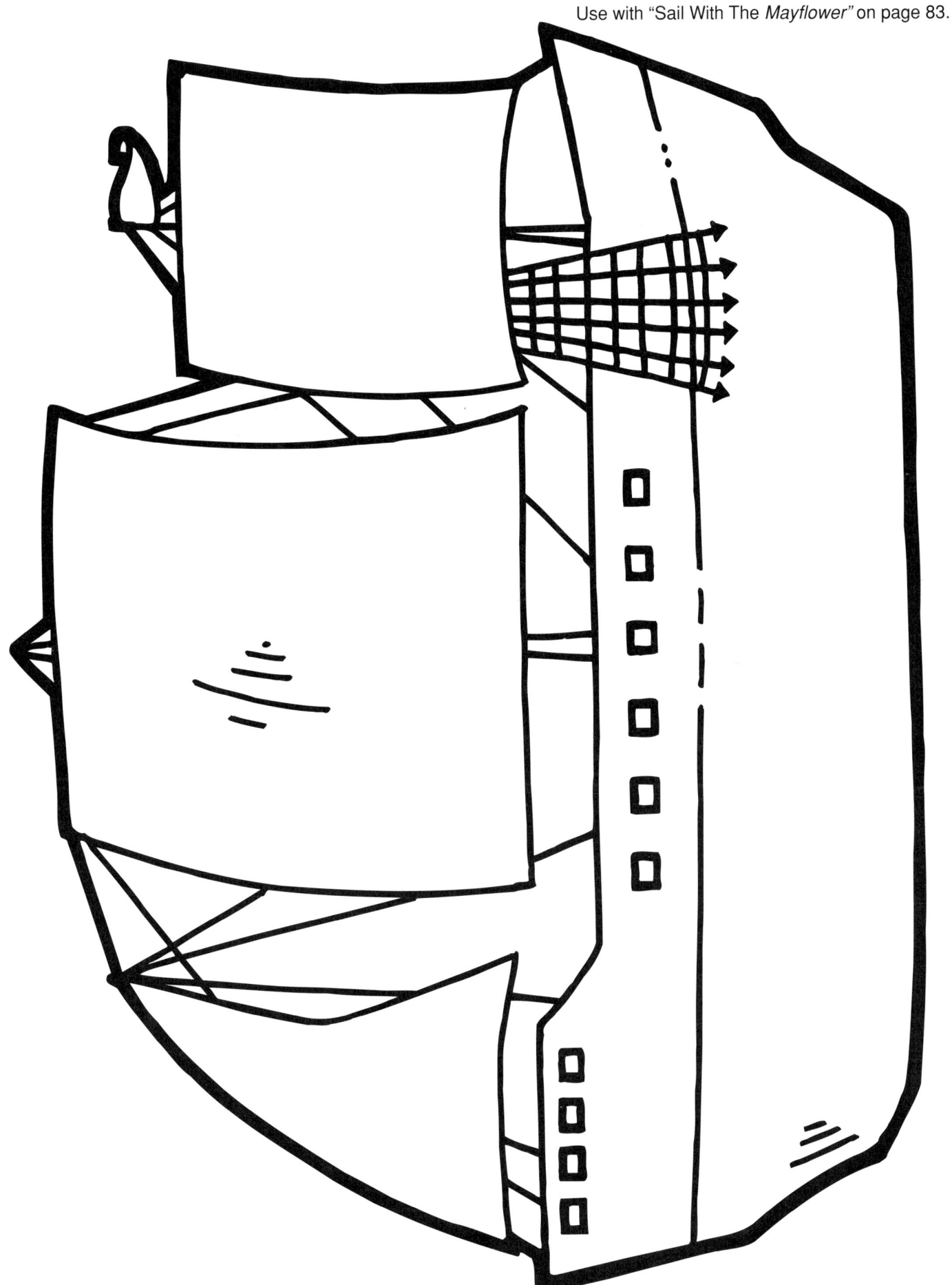

Patterns
Use with "Gobblin' Good Vocabulary" on page 84.

HANUKKAH LIGHTS

This Jewish festival of lights is celebrated for eight days by lighting candles, eating special foods, singing songs, playing games, and giving gifts to the children in Jewish families. The celebration begins at sundown each night, since the Hebrew calendar is based on the moon instead of the sun. Share in the history and traditions of Hanukkah with these activities that are sure to light up faces in your classroom.

ideas by Carolyn Kanoy and Kathy Wolf

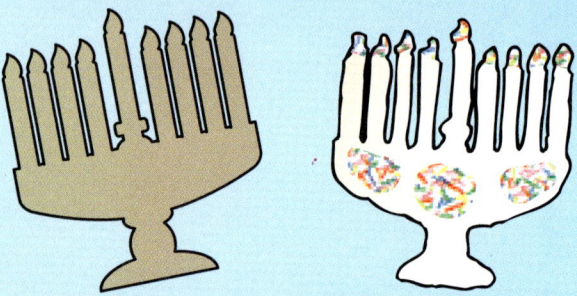

Making A Menorah

A very special candleholder is used each night of Hanukkah. It is called the *menorah*. There are varied designs and shapes of menorahs, but each shares common characteristics. All menorahs have a place for eight candles and the leader candle, called the *shamash*. The shamash stands taller than the other candles and is used to light each of the other candles. On the first night, the shamash is used to light one candle. One additional candle is lit each night until all eight candles are lit on the last night. A special blessing in Hebrew is recited when the menorah is lit each night.

If possible, have a Jewish person bring in a menorah and explain the symbolism of the eight candles. Duplicate a class supply of the reproducible on page 91 so each student can read about the history of Hanukkah. Then have each student make a menorah out of dough. Provide the pattern on page 92 for each child to trace and cut out a menorah from cardboard. Prepare salt dough by mixing 4 cups all-purpose flour, 1 cup salt, and 1 1/2 cups cold water. Give each child a portion of dough. Demonstrate how to mold the dough into the shape of a menorah cutout. Add candy sprinkles if desired, and allow the dough to dry.

Lots Of Latkes!

Potato pancakes, called *latkes*, are a favorite traditional food at Hanukkah. They are fried in oil—symbolic of the tiny amount of oil found in the temple. Help children prepare latkes following the recipe below. Then let them sample the mini latkes as you read *Latkes And Applesauce* by Fran Manushkin (Scholastic Inc., 1990). This story is about a family who grows their own potatoes and apples for their Hanukkah latkes and applesauce. One year a blizzard covers up their food. It looks like there will be no latkes and applesauce, but a stray dog and cat save the day.

To make mini latkes, peel and grate five medium potatoes. Grate one medium onion. Add 1/2 teaspoon salt and 1/4 teaspoon of pepper. Add one egg. Mix all together and add three tablespoons of flour or matzo meal. Drop spoonfuls of this mixture into very hot oil in a frying pan. Turn and cook until crisp on both sides. Drain on paper towels. Have children top their latkes with applesauce if desired.

Dreidel Days

A favorite Hanukkah game is played with a top called a *dreidel*. According to legend, the Jews used the dreidel game to trick the Syrian soldiers long ago. The Jews were forbidden to practice their religion and had to hide their holy books from the Syrian soldiers. If they heard soldiers approaching while they were studying, the Jewish boys would hide their scriptures and pull out a dreidel.

Today children enjoy playing the dreidel game with peanuts, pennies, nuts, or *gelt* (chocolate coins wrapped in gold foil). If the dreidel lands on the נ *(nun)*, the player gets nothing. If the dreidel lands on the ג *(gimmel)*, the player gets the pot. A ה *(hay)* signifies that the player gets half the pile and a ש *(shin)* means you add a piece to the pot. Each letter stands for the first letter in the four Hebrew words meaning "A great miracle happened there." The miracle, of course, occurred when the Maccabees recaptured their temple in Jerusalem, and the oil burned for eight days.

Have students play with a dreidel for math practice. Duplicate the pattern on page 93 on construction paper for each child to cut out and assemble. Have students print the numerals 6, 5, 4, and 3 on the dreidel instead of Hebrew letters. To play, pair students and provide peanuts in the shell. Each student in turn spins two times and adds (or multiplies) both numbers. Spin 6 + 6 or 3 x 4 to win instantly!

Light The Candles!

To culminate your study of Hanukkah, have students participate in choral speaking and candle making. Duplicate the rhyme on page 90 for each child. Divide the class into eight groups and assign verses to recite. Allow time to practice.

Then have each group create a candle to light during the choral speaking. Purchase the following materials from a craft store: paraffin wax, stearine crystals, wire wicking, and candle scents or colors, if desired. You will also need a hammer, a nail, newspapers, clean milk cartons, an old coffee pot or an empty three-pound coffee can, scissors, and a roll of duct tape. Cover your work area with newspaper and have pot holders handy.

Use the hammer to break the block of paraffin into smaller pieces. Place pieces of wax in the pot and heat on low heat until melted. Discuss the appearance of the wax before and during the heating. Introduce the words *solid* and *liquid*. Point out that scents and colors can be added to the wax in its liquid state. Allow students to add the crystals, a few drops of scent, and colors to the wax. (Tell students to use caution because the pot and wax are hot.)

Give each group a carton and a three-inch piece of wire wicking. Have one student in each group reinforce the carton by wrapping a length of duct tape around the middle. Another student uses a nail to poke a small hole in the center of the carton bottom, inserts the wick, and secures it by taping it on the bottom. Help the students pour two inches of the melted wax into each carton. Allow the candles to set overnight. Peel off the cartons to reveal the eight candles. Have a *shamash* (helper candle) and a lighter ready.

Now you're ready to invite another class for a choral presentation! Darken the room and have each group in turn recite its verse and light its candle with a shamash. Students will glow with pride as their candles burn brightly for a Hanukkah remembrance.

Eight Candles Burning Bright

Candle 1   The time has come.
　　　　　We've waited all year.
　　　　　It's finally sundown
　　　　　And Hanukkah is here!

Candle 2   There are presents to open
　　　　　And so much to do.
　　　　　There are prayers to recite
　　　　　On night number two.

Candle 3   We're standing very proudly,
　　　　　Our flames burning bright.
　　　　　Our lights stand for hope
　　　　　On this, the third night.

Candle 4   The children play with dreidels
　　　　　In a circle on the floor.
　　　　　They try to win the gelt.
　　　　　It's night number four!

Candle 5   On the fifth night of Hanukkah,
　　　　　Songs fill the room.
　　　　　Voices are singing
　　　　　A very familiar tune.

Candle 6   Latkes are cooking;
　　　　　In oil they will fry.
　　　　　It's hard to believe
　　　　　Six nights have gone by.

Candle 7   Lots of presents
　　　　　Are wrapped in blue.
　　　　　On this seventh night of Hanukkah,
　　　　　They may be for you.

Candle 8   We're all burning proudly.
　　　　　The eighth night is here.
　　　　　We'll put away the menorah
　　　　　Until this time next year!

—Carolyn Kanoy

©The Education Center, Inc. • *Big Book of Monthly Ideas* • TEC1487

Note To The Teacher: Use with "Light The Candles!" on page 89.

A Miracle Happened There!

At Hanukkah, we remember a **miracle**. It happened more than 2,000 years ago. The king of Syria named **Antiochus** tried to make everyone pray to Greek gods. The Jewish people wanted to worship their one God. The king's army attacked the Jewish holy place. They took the holy things from the **temple**. They put Greek **idols** in the temple instead.

A small group of Jews led by **Judah Maccabee** fought bravely against the Syrian soldiers. Finally the Maccabees won. They had to clean up their temple. They had to find oil for the holy light that always burns in the temple. The Jews found a small amount of oil. But it was only enough to burn for one day. Then a miracle happened—the oil burned for eight days!

Today Jewish people celebrate Hanukkah by lighting eight candles in a holder called a **menorah**. The menorah has eight candles plus a helper candle called a **shamash**. The shamash is used to light the other candles. Hanukkah is also called the **Festival of Lights** because the candles shine brightly for eight nights.

Draw lines to match the words to the meanings.

1. shamash   pray to, honor
2. worship   helper candle
3. temple   fighters, army
4. soldiers   holy place, church
5. miracle   the leader of a small band of Jews
6. idol   the Syrian king
7. menorah   a statue, a god
8. Hanukkah   a wonderful event, a blessing
9. Antiochus   Festival of Lights
10. Judah Maccabee   a special candleholder

Menorah Pattern
Use with "Making A Menorah" on page 88.

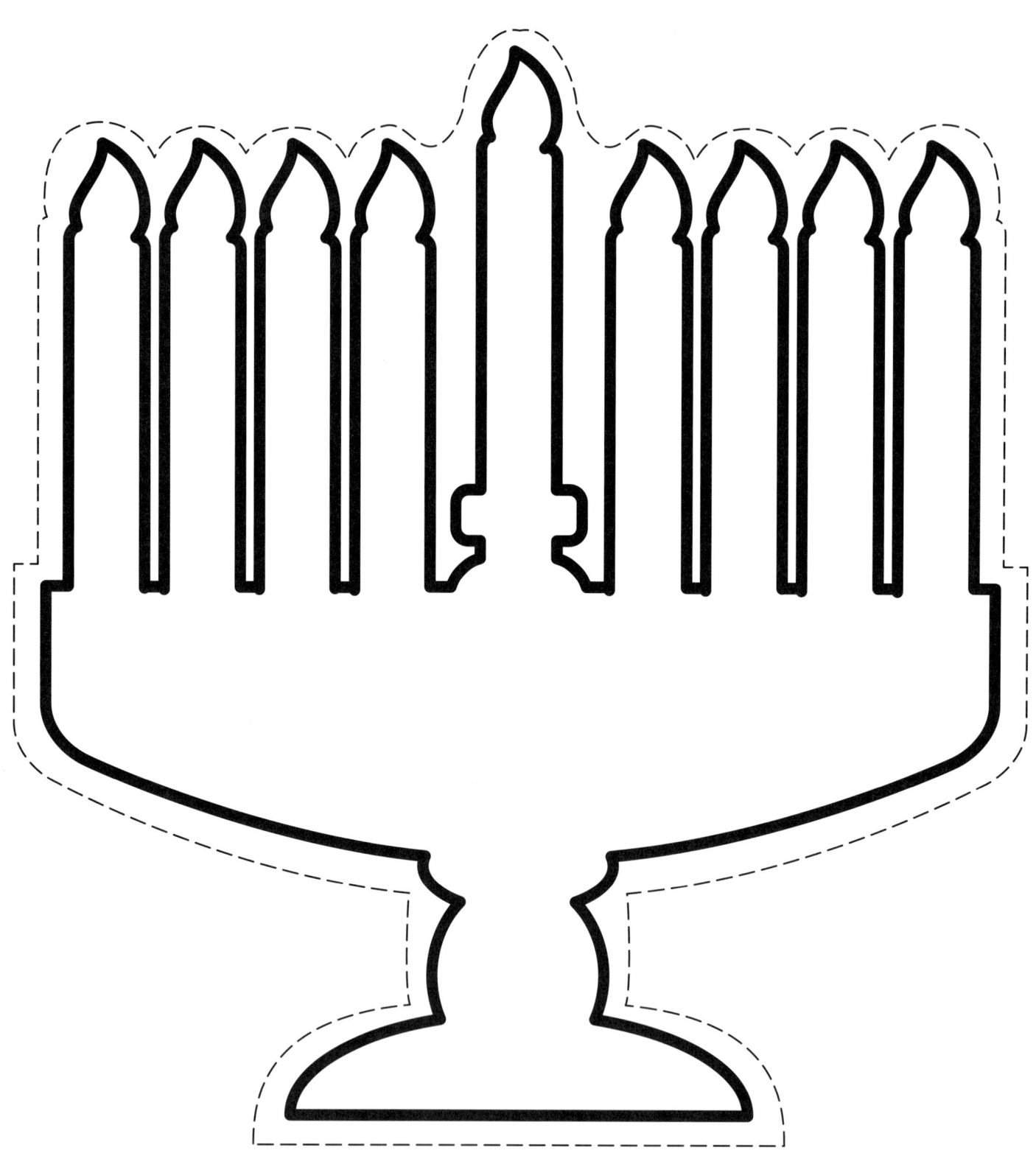

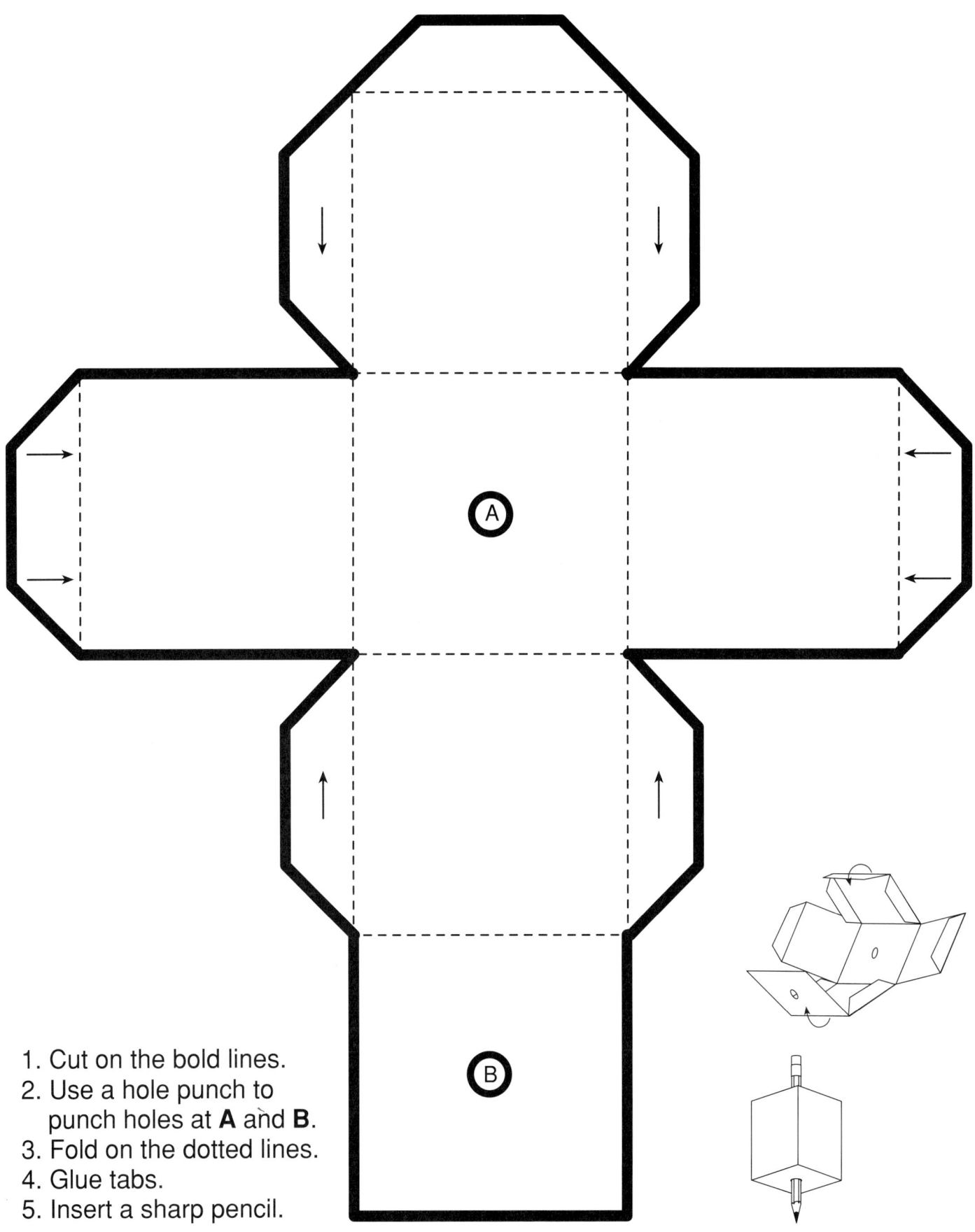

A Christmas World Tour

Pack your bags and grab your passports. Take off on a whirlwind holiday tour to learn about Christmas customs around the world. Your world travelers will be visiting six countries: Sweden, England, France, Germany, Italy, and Mexico.

ideas by Karen Ciampa and Kathy Wolf

Hop On Board The Holiday Express!

For a lesson in geography, have students trace their world travels on a holiday bulletin board. Cover your board with blue background paper. Enlarge, color, and cut out the airplane pattern on page 95. If desired, glue students' school photos to the airplane windows. Cut out several clouds from white paper. Mount the airplane, clouds, and title along with a world map. Duplicate six copies of the suitcase pattern on page 95 on brown construction paper to cut out. Label and number each of these six suitcase cutouts with one of the countries above. Have students locate their destinations and pin the suitcases to the map. Bon voyage!

Plan Your Travel Itinerary

To prepare for each stop on your Christmas tour, duplicate the world map on page 106 for each student. Ask students what they already know about each country on the itinerary. List their responses on a chart. On another chart list some things students would like to find out about each country. When you introduce each new country, have the students color that stop on their maps and map keys. Students may keep small travel diaries or journals in which they write facts about each country.

Apply For Your Passports

Explain to students that obtaining a passport is one of the first steps in planning any international travel. Travelers must present their passports for identification to enter each foreign country. Provide each student with a copy of the passport application on page 107. Help students fill in the blanks. After the applications are complete, provide a copy of page 108 for each student to fold into a passport booklet. Have each child complete the information and affix a photocopy of his school photo to his passport.

As you complete the study of Christmas in a country, allow each student to get his passport stamped. Assign a "passport agent" to affix a colorful Christmas sticker in the appropriate box on each passport. At the end of the unit, your students will have six stamps in their passports to show they are world travelers!

Pack Your Bags!

Here's a clever way for students to keep their passports, travel maps, and travel diaries and journals handy. Have them create suitcases from 9 1/2" x 12" brown file folders. Have each student cut out handles from tagboard, glue them to the insides of the folder, and staple the two sides of the folder closed. Add details with a black marker, as shown. Laminate the suitcases for durability if desired. Provide an airline address label for each child to fill out and attach to his suitcase.

Have students place their passports, maps, and journals inside and hang their suitcases on the bulletin board for easy access. After they have visited each country, your tourists may decorate their suitcases with symbols of the country or with Christmas stickers.

Airplane Pattern
Use with "Hop On Board The Holiday Express!" on page 94.

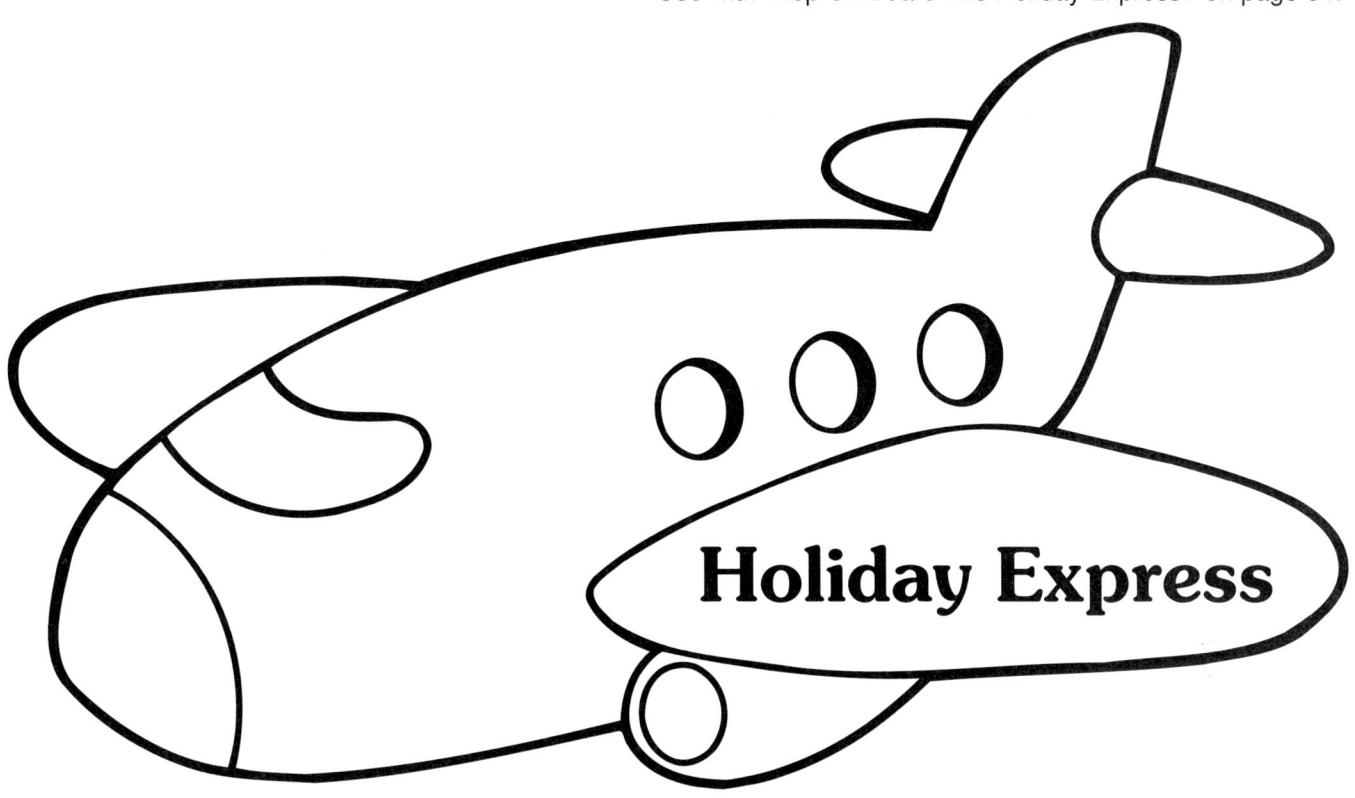

©The Education Center, Inc. • *Big Book of Monthly Ideas* • TEC1487

Suitcase Pattern
Use with "Hop On Board The Holiday Express!" on page 94.

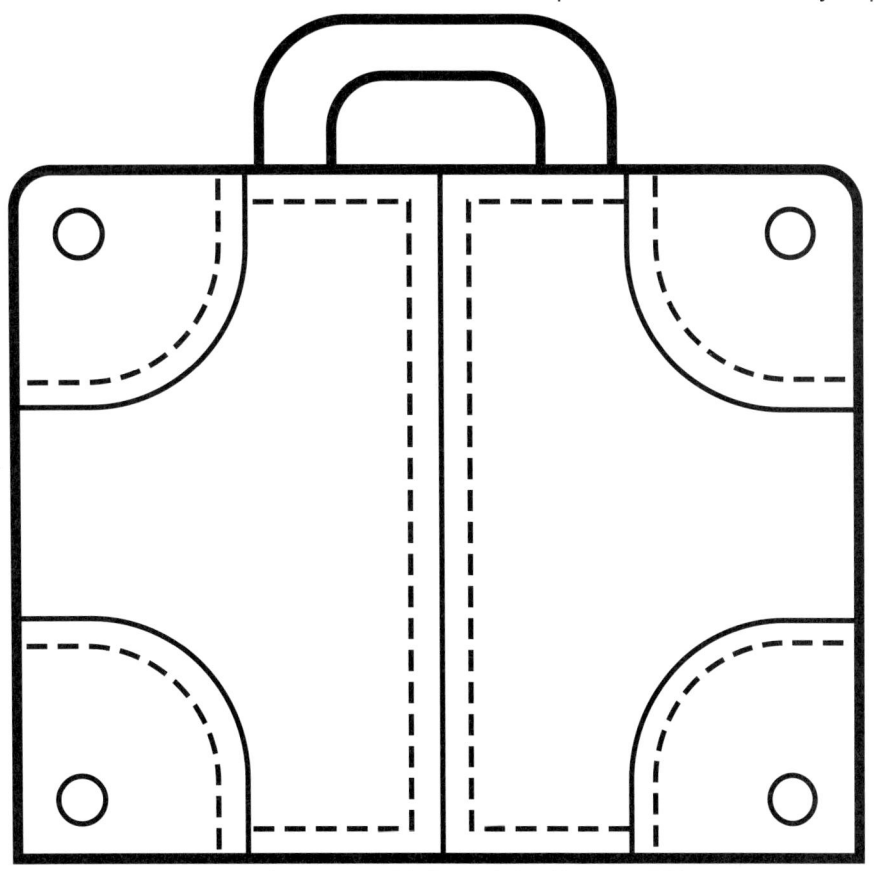

©The Education Center, Inc. • *Big Book of Monthly Ideas* • TEC1487

ENGLAND

Welcome To Merry Olde England

Have students arrive in England to the sounds of recorded Christmas carols as you serve warm, spiced apple cider from a large punch bowl. Play "Deck The Halls"; "God Rest You Merry, Gentlemen"; "Wassail Song"; and "We Wish You A Merry Christmas." Printed words and music for all of these can be found in *Tomie dePaola's Book Of Christmas Carols* (G. P. Putnam's Sons, 1987). Then locate England on the world map. Explain that England, Wales, and Scotland make up Great Britain. On Christmas Day, many British families tune in to hear the queen give a Christmas message on the *tellie.*

Explain that caroling is one of our Christmas customs that originated in England. On the days before Christmas, carolers go from house to house singing joyful songs. The singers are invited inside to partake of a warm fruit punch or *wassail* from a large wooden bowl. *Wassail* comes from the old Anglo-Saxon greeting *waes hael* and translates as "what hail" or "here's to your health!"

Father Christmas

Sending Christmas cards is another tradition that began in England. The first cards, similar to postcards, were printed in the 1840s. By the 1870s, the custom had spread throughout Britain. To encourage critical thinking, display Christmas cards with pictures of Father Christmas and Santa Claus. Have students compare the two characters. *(English children hang their stockings by the fireplace for Father Christmas who—wearing a red suit and hat like our Santa Claus—delivers gifts to children.)* Then have students create original Christmas cards showing Santa. Allow students to exchange cards with classmates. Ho, ho, ho! It's jolly good fun!

Celebrate Boxing Day

December 26 is a national holiday in England called *Boxing Day.* Long ago on this day, noblemen gave boxes of gifts to their servants. Today collection boxes in churches are opened and the contributions are distributed to the poor. Explain this English tradition and have students decorate a collection box for donations for a needy family. Encourage students to bring in canned foods or contribute change, if possible, to buy a fruit basket or frozen turkey.

Create A Christmas Cornucopia

Christmas trees in English homes often include cornucopia ornaments to symbolize the spirit of sharing the plenty with others. Have students make miniature cornucopias to decorate their family Christmas trees. Duplicate the pattern below on colored construction paper for each child to cut out. Have each child form a cone and staple or glue it together. Have students decorate their cornucopias with ribbon, sequins, glitter, stickers, and lace or rickrack. Attach a piece of gold cord to each cornucopia, as shown, for hanging. Fill the cornucopias with wrapped Christmas candies, and allow students to take them home.

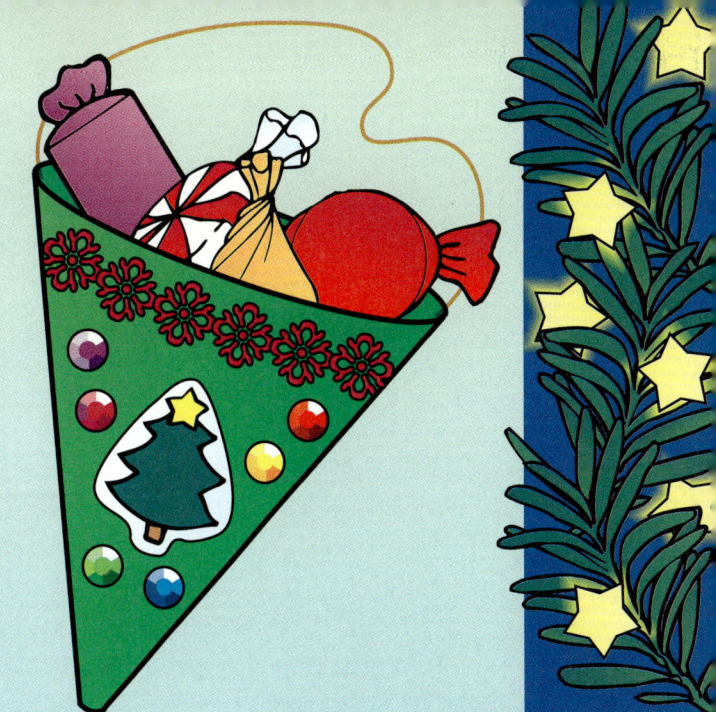

Cornucopia Pattern

Use with "Create a Christmas Cornucopia."

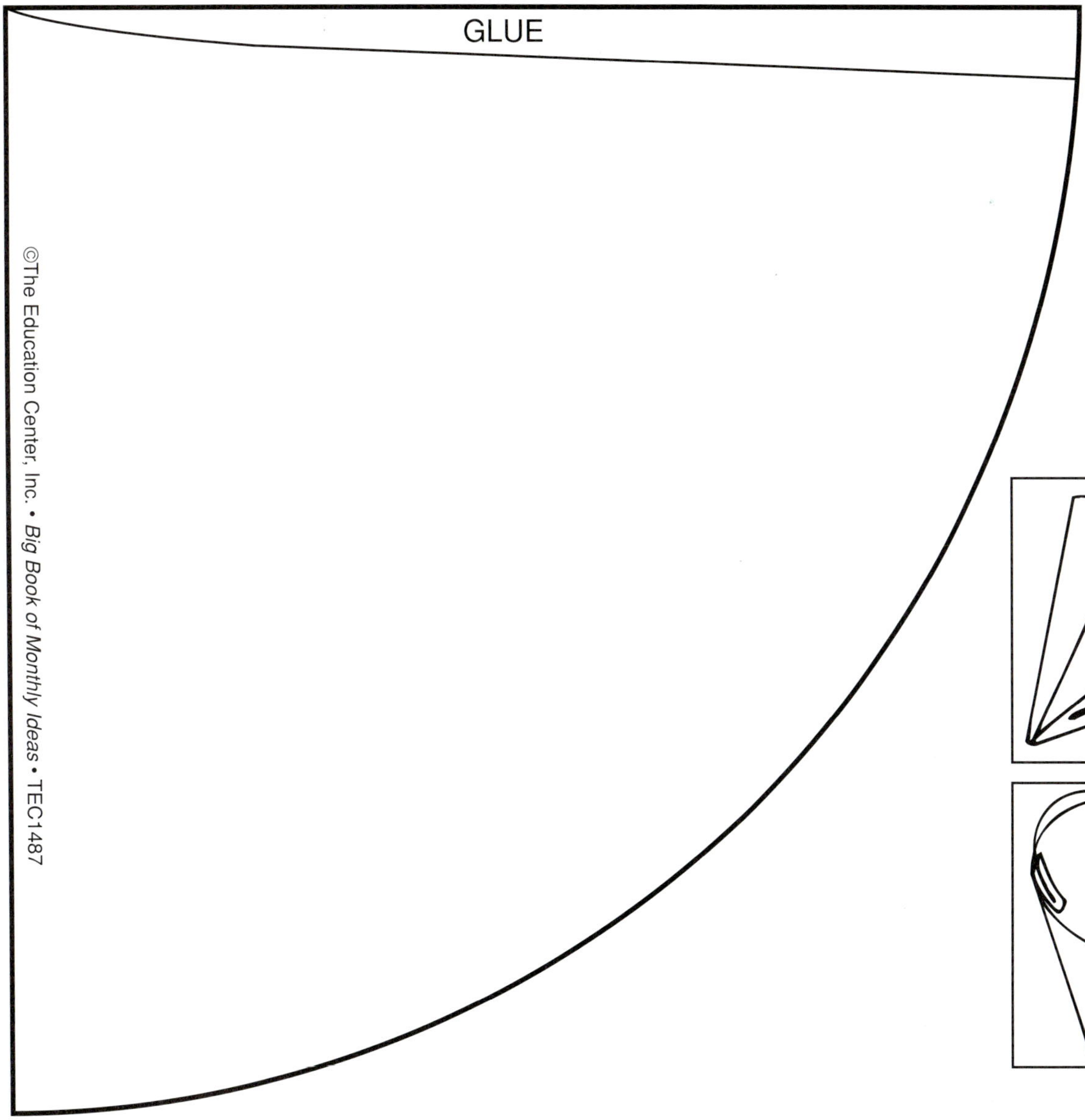

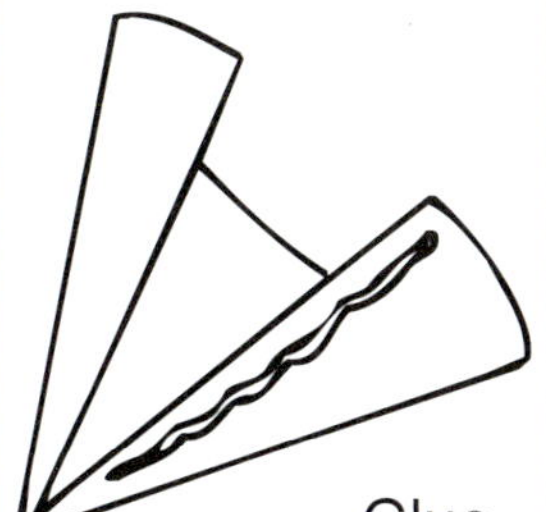

Glue.

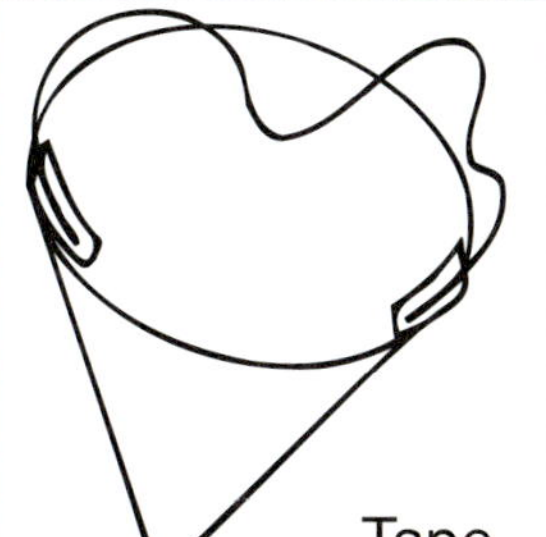

Tape.

Bring In A Bûche De Noël

On Christmas Eve, many French families attend midnight Mass and then have a festive, late-night supper called a *réveillon.* To create the atmosphere of a French Christmas, darken the classroom, light several candles, and serve the traditional French dessert called *bûche de Noël,* or Christmas log. This cake roll is frosted to look like a yummy Yule log—a large piece of tree trunk. In ancient times, people thought an unburned Yule log had magical powers. Today people burn Yule logs to bring good luck.

Play recorded versions of the traditional French carols "The First Noël" and "Bring A Torch, Jeannette, Isabelle!" For printed words and music, see pages 10 and 60 of *Tomie dePaola's Book Of Christmas Carols* (G. P. Putnam's Sons, 1987). Explain that these traditional French Christmas songs are hundreds of years old. Print the following vocabulary words on individual cards and ask students to match the French to the English words: l'enfant—the baby, un flambeau—a torch, la mère—the mother, belle—beautiful, beau—handsome. Locate France on the tour map and have students color it on their maps. Don't forget to stamp their passports!

Joyeux Noël, Babar!

In France children put their shoes in front of the fireplace on Christmas Eve. Father Christmas, also known as *Père Noël,* fills the shoes with candies and nuts. Read aloud *Babar And Father Christmas* by Jean de Brunhoff (Random House, Inc.; 1968). In the story, Babar gets a magical red suit that enables him to fly so he can help Father Christmas deliver presents to the elephant children. After reading the book, discuss why this famous French elephant was looking for Father Christmas.

For creative-writing practice, have students "send" postcards showing Babar and his dog Duck looking for Father Christmas. Provide each student with a blank 5" x 7" index card and have him draw Babar on one side. Have each student write a message on the back telling where Babar is and address the postcard to his family. Provide Christmas stickers for students to use as stamps.

A Noël Welcome

At Christmastime the French hang door decorations on their front doors to welcome friends and neighbors. Have your students create a Noël door hanger to take home. Each student will need a 12" x 5" piece of colored construction paper, a six-inch dowel, Christmas gift wrap, scissors, glue, sequins, rick-rack, ribbon, and glitter.

To make a hanger, cut a V at the bottom of the construction paper as shown. Fold the top edge over and glue it in place to form a casing for the dowel. Trace the word *NOEL* on wrapping paper. Cut out the letters and glue them vertically on the construction-paper banner. Decorate the banner with sequins, glitter, and rickrack. Insert the dowel and tie a piece of ribbon to each end. Help each student tie the ribbon in a bow. Allow students to take their banners home.

FRANCE

Oh, Tannenbaum!

To introduce your study of German customs, read *An Early American Christmas* by Tomie dePaola (Holiday House, Inc.; 1987). Discuss how the tradition of the lighted Christmas tree came to America from Germany. The trees once were decorated with lighted candles, paper roses, cookies, and fruit. Today glass ornaments, straw stars, little gingerbread men, hand-carved wooden angels, and tinsel are common.

Locate Germany on the world map. Then have students help you decorate a small Christmas tree in your classroom. Invite a craftsperson to demonstrate the art of German paper cutting called *scherenschnitte* (SHEAR-en-scnhit-tah). Provide templates (available at craft stores) for students to trace and then cut out ornaments from white paper. As you decorate the tree together, play the song "Oh, Tannenbaum" ("Oh, Christmas Tree"). See page 66 of *Tomie dePaola's Book Of Christmas Carols* (G. P. Putnam's Sons, 1987) for the words and music.

Have your "passport agent" affix a Christmas-tree sticker to each passport to represent Germany and say, *"Fröhliche Weihnachten!"* (FROY-likh-eh vy-NAHCK-tehn), which means "Merry Christmas!"

More Horsepower For St. Nick

St. Nicholas was a beloved Christian bishop who died long ago in the AD 300s. He is remembered for his kindness to children. On December 5, the eve of St. Nicholas Day, St. Nick brings gifts to children in parts of Germany. Children fill their shoes with straw and carrots for St. Nick's horse and place their shoes beside the fireplace. In return St. Nick leaves candy and presents for the children. Sometimes St. Nicholas may have his assistant *Kris Kringle* deliver the gifts. In other parts of Germany, *Christkindl*, the Christ Child, sends *Weihnachtsmann* (Christmas Man) with gifts for the children on Christmas Day.

For critical-thinking practice, ask students to compare St. Nick and Christmas Man to Santa Claus. Discuss the need for more horsepower for St. Nick. Then have students write letters to St. Nick telling why they think he should trade in his horse for eight reindeer and a magic sleigh. Or have each student design an even faster means of transportation for Santa and include an illustration with his letter. Share their letters before mailing. What's faster than a speeding bullet? A supersonic Santamobile!

GERMANY

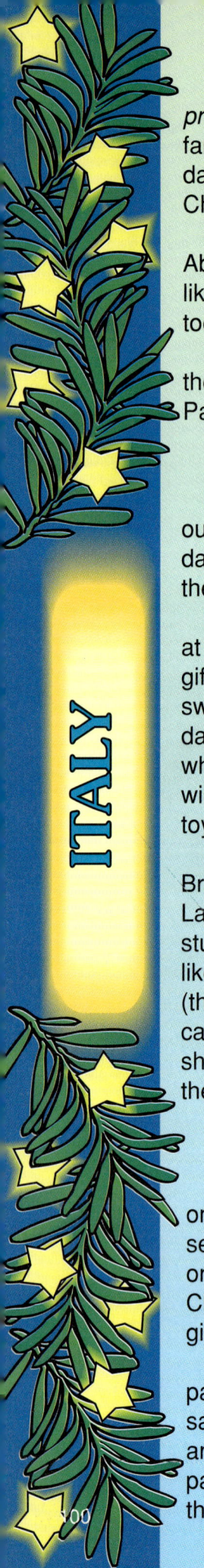

Buon Natale!

In Italy, Christmas is a religious and family holiday. Before Christmas a *presepio,* or nativity scene, is set up in every church and in many homes. Some families gather at the manger scene to say prayers each evening of the nine days before Christmas. Distant family members travel home for the holidays. On Christmas Day, families go to church together.

Before Christmas small groups of musicians from the mountains of the Abruzzi region travel from town to town. These fellows, called *zampognari,* look like shepherds in traditional sheepskin jackets and laced sandals with pointed toes. The zampognari go from house to house playing hymns on their bagpipes.

If possible share a nativity scene with your class and discuss the role of the shepherds. Read *The Little Drummer Boy* by Ezra Jack Keats (Aladdin Paperbacks, 1987) and provide musical instruments for students to play.

Introducing La Befana

Italian children may receive gifts from *Babbo Natale,* the Italian version of our Santa Claus, on Christmas morning. Traditional gift giving comes 12 days later on Epiphany, January 6, when families remember the journey of the Three Wise Men to Bethlehem to present gifts to the *Bambino Gesù.*

Italian legend has it that the three kings rested on their way to Bethlehem at the home of an old woman. They asked her to join them in bringing gifts to the Baby Jesus, but the old woman said she was too busy sweeping her house. Later she reconsidered but lost her way. To this day she is looking for the Christ Child. *La Befana,* the kind old witch whose name derives from *Epiphania,* flies on a broomstick through windows and down chimneys. She fills the shoes of good children with toys and candy. Bad children receive pieces of coal!

Read *The Legend Of Old Befana* by Tomie dePaola (Harcourt Brace & Company, 1980); then have students model a story about La Befana. Duplicate the reproducible on page 101 for each student to complete. Then help each child decorate a broom like La Befana's. Purchase a small broom for each child (these are available at craft stores). Each child makes a gift card, punches a hole in it, and ties it with a red ribbon as shown. Tell students to take their brooms home to grace their holiday hearths.

A Taste Of Italy

On Christmas Eve, Italians fast from sunset on December 23 to sunset on December 24. Traditionally for Christmas Eve dinner, fish or baked eel is served. On Christmas Day, an Italian feast may include pasta, roast turkey or veal, fish, vegetables, cheeses, and pastries. A traditional loaf-shaped Christmas cake made with raisins and citron called *panettone* is given as a gift to the hostess—much like fruitcakes are given as gifts in America.

Italian chefs are famous for gracing holiday tables with delicious filled pastries called *cannolis.* Provide these Italian pastries for students to sample. Or have your little bambinos prepare some. Purchase pastry shells and the ingredients for instant vanilla pudding. Have students help you prepare the pudding following the directions on the box. Fill a pastry bag with the pudding and allow each student to fill his shell. Buon!

LA BEFANA IS SPECIAL IN ITALY

La Befana is a special person in Italy.

Shall I tell you why?

Because _____

Because _____

Because _____

Because _____

Just because—that's why!

La Befana is a special person in Italy.

SWEDEN

Say Hello To Saint Lucia!

Welcome your students to your classroom dressed as Saint Lucia. Introduce yourself and explain that Lucia's lighted crown reminds us that the long, winter nights will soon be replaced with days of longer sunlight. Help students locate Sweden on your world travel map. Point out its proximity to the North Pole.

Explain that in Sweden the Christmas season begins with St. Lucia Day, December 13. On that morning, the oldest daughter—or the mother if there is no daughter—dresses as Saint Lucia in a white dress with a red sash and wears a crown of greenery with seven lighted candles. She awakens the family and serves coffee and sweet buns to family members in their beds.

Have students create St. Lucia crowns of paper to wear. Duplicate the pattern on page 103 on white construction paper for each child to color and cut out. Provide a strip of green construction paper for each child, and have him glue on his candles as shown. Fit and staple each strip to make a headband. Have both boys and girls wear their crowns as you serve a snack of sweet buns and warm cocoa.

Meet A Swedish Christmas Elf

Swedish families give gifts wrapped in paper and sealed with wax. Gift tags are attached with riddles or verses giving hints to what is inside. The gifts are put in a wicker basket and distributed on Christmas Eve. In addition, a gnomelike gift-giver called *Jultomten* or *Tomten* leaves gifts for the children. Children in Swedish farm families believe that these beneficent gnomes live in their barns. Read aloud *The Christmas Tomten* by Viktor Rydberg (Coward, McCann & Geoghegan, Inc.; 1981). After reading, ask students what they would say to the tomten if they discovered him.

To encourage creative writing, have students discover a gift-wrapped box from the Christmas tomten. Use the pattern on page 103 to make a Christmas gnome cutout or purchase a gnome doll and place it in a gift-wrapped box. Write a riddle on the gift tag, as shown. Place the box where students will find it. Have students read the riddle and guess the contents; then open the box to reveal the gnome cutout or doll.

Next have each student create a gift for the Christmas gnome and write a corresponding riddle. Provide each student with a 9" x 12" piece of construction paper, a 9" x 6" piece of gift wrap, ribbon, a paper scrap, and a copy of the gift tag on page 103. The student writes his riddle on the gift tag and cuts it out. He folds the construction paper in half and draws his gift inside. To complete the project, the student glues the wrapping paper and a ribbon to the front to resemble a present and attaches his gift tag. Display the mystery packages on a bulletin board. Allow students to read the riddles and lift the flaps to find the answers.

Christmas Gnome Pattern
Use with "Meet A Swedish Christmas Elf" on page 102.

©The Education Center, Inc. • Big Book of Monthly Ideas • TEC1487

Gift Tag Pattern
Use with "Meet A Swedish Christmas Elf" on page 102.

WHAT'S INSIDE?
I am _____ and _____
I sound _____
I feel _____
You find me in (on, at) _____
_____
Can you guess what I am?

©The Education Center, Inc. • Big Book of Monthly Ideas • TEC1487

Pattern
Use with "Say Hello To Saint Lucia!" on page 102.

©The Education Center, Inc. • Big Book of Monthly Ideas • TEC1487

MEXICO

Feliz Navidad!

Welcome students to Mexico with a display of real poinsettias. Explain that Dr. Joel Roberts Poinsett, the American ambassador to Mexico from 1825 to 1829, introduced this plant to the United States. The poinsettia is also known as *flor de la noche buena,* or the "flower of the holy night." Have students examine a poinsettia more closely. Point out that the red, pink, yellowish, or white petals are really *bracts,* or special leaves that surround the actual tiny flowers. Caution students that, if eaten, the leaves and stem of the poinsettia can cause a severe stomachache. In addition the plant's sap can irritate the skin and eyes.

Read *The Legend Of The Poinsettia* retold and illustrated by Tomie dePaola (G. P. Putnam's Sons, 1994). Then have students make a beautiful basket of paper poinsettias to decorate your classroom bulletin board. To make a ten-inch, pinwheel-shaped bloom, each child will need the following:

— a ten-inch square of red bulletin-board paper
— a small square of yellow construction paper
— pieces of green bulletin-board paper for leaves
— glue, scissors, and a hole puncher

Demonstrate how to make a paper poinsettia and have students follow along as they make their own flowers.

1. Fold the square in half diagonally and crease.
2. Open and repeat the folding from the other corners.
3. Cut on each fold about three-fourths of the way toward the center.
4. Glue each corner to the center of the pinwheel.
5. When all four corners are glued, cut and glue a small yellow circle to the center.
6. Glue two red leaves and two green leaves to the back of each pinwheel.

To make a bulletin-board display, cut a large basket from brown paper, adding woven details with a black marker. Staple the ten-inch poinsettias close together as shown and add the title "Feliz Navidad."

To make individual poinsettia ornaments, provide each child with a five-inch square of red bulletin-board paper to make a paper poinsettia as above. Provide him with a piece of gold cord to glue to the back. Students can hang these bright ornaments on their family Christmas trees as remembrances of your trip to Mexico.

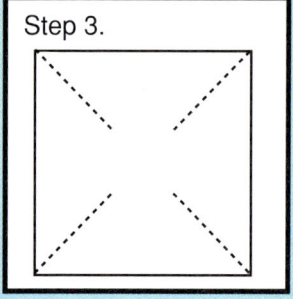
Step 3.

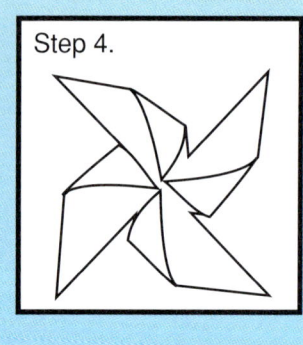
Step 4.

Las Posadas And Piñatas

The nine days before Christmas are called *Las Posadas* in Mexico. Each evening beginning on December 16, processions make their way through the village streets to reenact the journey of Joseph and Mary to Bethlehem. The travelers, led by a boy and girl carrying figures of Joseph and Mary, go from house to house looking for *posada,* or shelter, each night until Christmas Eve. Each posada is followed by a feast at a participant's home where the children try to break a papier-mâché, candy-filled container called a *piñata.* Read *Pancho's Piñata* by Stefan Czernecki and Timothy Rhodes (Hyperion Paperbacks For Children, 1994) and discuss this old Mexican legend of the Christmas Star. If possible hang a piñata for students to break open.

For a lesson in geometry and following directions, provide templates and colored paper. Have each student cut out one four-inch circle and five triangles. Have the student assemble the pieces as shown and glue them onto a 9" x 12" piece of blue construction paper. Next provide small squares of colored tissue paper for the student to glue onto his star shape to resemble a piñata. Have him add foil star stickers as shown. Hang these piñata pictures on a line strung across the room.

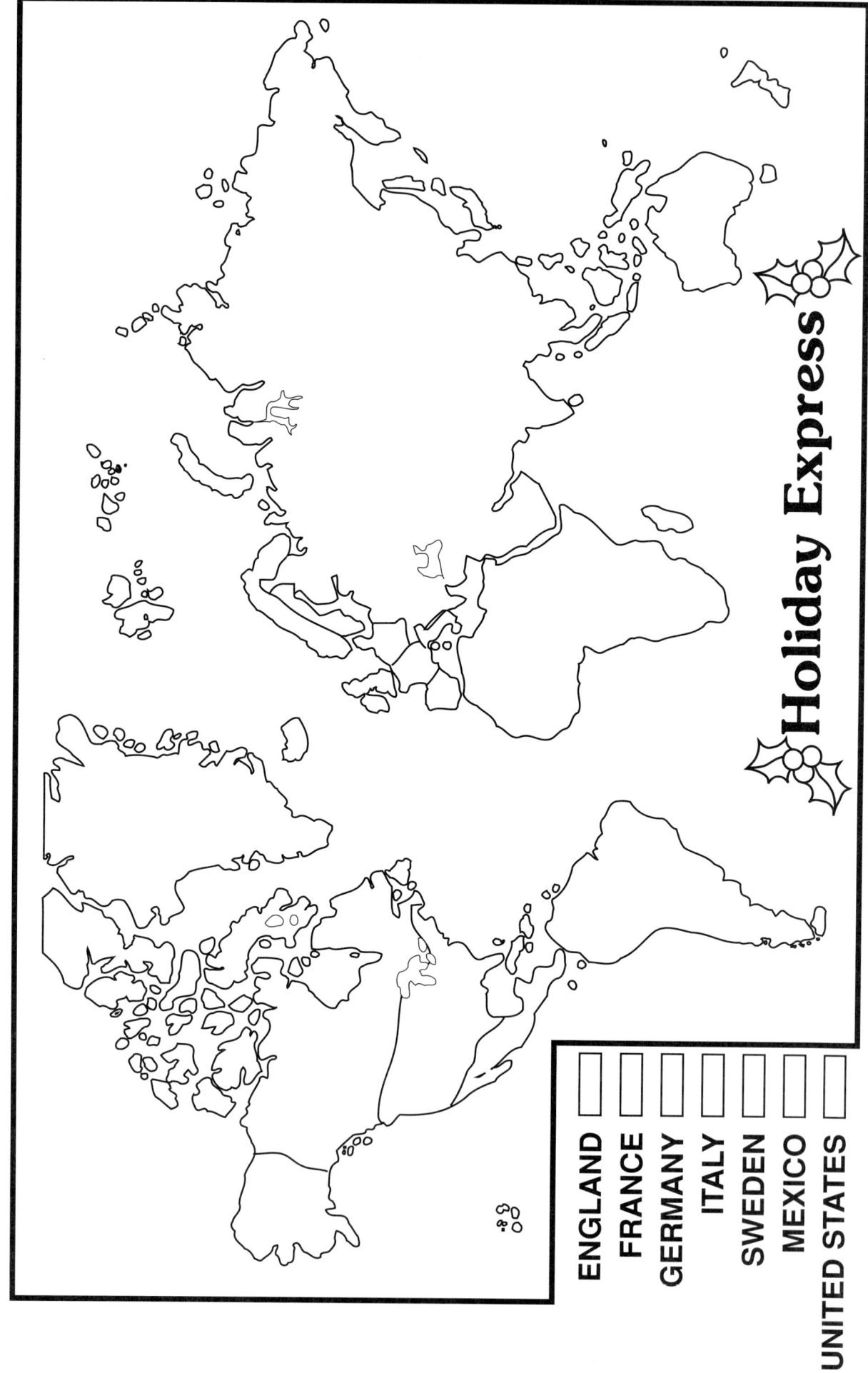

Passport Application
Christmas Around The World

Last name _____

First name _____

Street address _____

City _____ State _____

Date of birth _____

Place of birth _____

Height _____ Weight _____

Color of hair _____ Color of eyes _____

Citizen of what country? _____

Signature _____ Date _____

Passport Approved

☐ yes   ☐ no

Glue photo here.

Official Seal

Note To The Teacher: Use with "Apply For Your Passports" on page 94.

Passport Pattern
Use with "Apply For Your Passports" on page 94.

HOLIDAY EXPRESS
PASSPORT TO THE WORLD

Fold here.

		ITALY	SWEDEN
		PLACE STAMP HERE.	PLACE STAMP HERE.

This passport certifies that the bearer is a citizen of the world. The bearer is entitled to travel and enjoy, but must always learn and respect the cultures of others.

Glue your photograph here.

Fold here.

ENGLAND	MEXICO
PLACE STAMP HERE.	PLACE STAMP HERE.

Name _____
School _____
Birth Date _____
Hair Color _____
Eye Color _____

GERMANY	FRANCE
PLACE STAMP HERE.	PLACE STAMP HERE.

©The Education Center, Inc. • Big Book of Monthly Ideas • TEC1487

KWANZAA

Kwanzaa is an African-American holiday celebrated for seven days each year from December 26 to January 1. Kwanzaa is not a religious holiday. It was created in 1966 by Dr. Maulana Karenga to promote awareness of traditional African customs and family values. It is a time for people of African descent to celebrate their kinship and evaluate their lives.

ideas by Pam Kucks

The Seven Principles Of Kwanzaa

NGUZO SABA (en-GOO-zoh SAH-bah)

The seven-day celebration is centered around seven Kwanzaa principles. On each day of Kwanzaa, a candle is lit to highlight one of the seven principles. Share these principles with your class by writing the words and definitions on a chart. Add a geometric border of red, green, and black—the colors for the holiday.

- UMOJA—(oo-MO-jah)—*Unity.* We help each other.
- KUJICHAGULIA—(koo-jee-cha-goo-LEE-ah)—*Self-determination.* We decide things for ourselves.
- UJIMA—(oo-JEE-mah)—*Collective work and responsibility.* We work together to make life better.
- UJAMMA—(oo-jah-MAH)—*Cooperative economics.* We support our community.
- NIA—(NEE-ah)—*Purpose.* We have a reason for living.
- KUUMBA—(koo-OOM-bah)—*Creativity.* We make things with our minds and hands.
- IMANI—(ee-MAH-nee)—*Faith.* We believe in ourselves, our forefathers, and the future.

For each day of the celebration, teach the meaning of a principle with an activity:

1. Gather your students to set the mood for a day of unity. Have the class sing a favorite song or recite a special poem together in the morning.
2. To practice self-determination, have students vote on a free-time activity.
3. To demonstrate collective responsibility, provide a task that requires cooperation to complete. Divide the class into groups. Send each group on a scavenger hunt to find Kwanzaa-related items such as a straw mat *(mkeka)*, ears of corn *(muhindi)*, or fruits and vegetables *(mazao)*.
4. To encourage awareness of community, provide telephone books and have students look in the Yellow Pages™ for local businesses. Have each student list one for each of the following categories: a movie theater, a restaurant, a grocery store, a doctor.
5. To emphasize that each person has a purpose, have each student write down on an index card what he would like to accomplish that day. At the end of the day, have students pull out their cards for self-evaluation. Allow each student who determines he has accomplished his goal to choose a sticker to affix to his card.
6. To motivate creativity, provide materials at a center so each student can create a Kwanzaa bracelet or necklace by stringing red, green, and black beads in a unique pattern. Allow students to wear their creations as reminders of Kwanzaa.
7. To emphasize faith in the future, have each child think of a career or job he or she aspires to; then have each student draw a picture of himself in this role.

Dance To The Beat

One of the seven principles of Kwanzaa, *Kuumba* (koo-OOM-bah), means "creativity." Part of the celebration on the day observing this principle involves music and dance. Invite students who play musical instruments to share their talents at an African Dance Festival.

To prepare, look in a local library or ask the music teacher for a collection of African dance music or folksongs on album or cassette. Play the music for the class and have the students listen for different instruments. Play the music again and have them move to the music.

As a culminating activity for the festival, obtain a bongo-type drum, some shakers, and some wood blocks from the high-school music department. Have the class stand in a circle. Select a few students to stand in the middle of the circle and play these instruments along with the recorded music while their classmates move around them. Alternate so every student gets a chance to play an instrument. This is one movement activity that just can't be beat!

Children Count!

At each Kwanzaa table one ear of corn, or *muhindi,* is placed on the mkeka mat to represent each child in the family. (To learn more about the mkeka, see "Mkeka Mats" on page 111.) Create a class chart to show the number of ears of corn each family would need for its mat. Duplicate the corn patterns on page 112 for each child. Have the student cut out the number of ears of corn he needs to represent the number of children in his family. Then have each student attach the ears of corn to the chart in a column. Have students compare, add, and subtract using the information on the chart. Challenge the students to make up word problems using the chart.

A Gift Of Love

Handmade gifts, or *zawadi* (zah-WAH-dee), are given to family members on the sixth night of Kwanzaa. Allow each student to make a special necklace to show love for a family member. Provide ziti- or rigatoni-type noodles and red and green tempera paint. Have students paint the noodles red and green. Allow the noodles to dry overnight. Have each student cut two 2-inch circles from black tagboard. With a large hole puncher, make a hole in each circle as shown. Give each student a 24-inch piece of black yarn. The student threads the noodles, alternating colors and adding the black circles. Help each student tie his necklace and wrap the gift in red and green tissue paper. Tie the packages with black ribbon or yarn. Encourage students to present the zawadi at a family gathering.

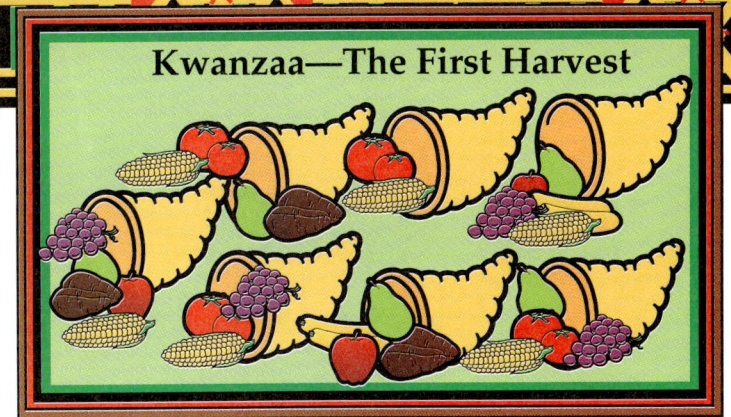

First Fruits

The word *Kwanzaa* comes from Swahili, an East African language. It is derived from *kwanza,* which means "the first." (The extra *a* gives the holiday name seven letters—one for each of the seven Kwanzaa values.) The phrase *Matunda ya kwanza* means the "first fruits," referring to the yearly harvest. To create a bulletin-board display for the celebration of Kwanzaa, have students make cornucopias.

Enlarge and duplicate the cornucopia pattern on page 114 on brown construction paper for each student. Have each student cut out his cornucopia. Next distribute colored tissue or construction paper from which students can cut out fruits and vegetables. (See patterns on page 114). After students have glued the fruits and vegetables to their cornucopias, collect the cornucopias and mount them on a bulletin board as shown. Add the title "Kwanzaa—The First Harvest." To create a border, use 1 1/2-inch strips of red, green, and black paper as shown.

To reap the rewards of this colorful display, ask students to bring in real fruits to make a Friendship Fruit Salad. Younger students can select, identify, and wash the fruits. Help older students peel and cut the fruits into bite-size pieces. Have each student sample one piece of each fruit before mixing the fruits together. Discuss why fruits are good for us and create a graph to show students' favorites.

Mkeka Mats

The *mkeka* (em-KAY-kah) is a mat, usually made of straw, displayed on the family's table at Kwanzaa time. Have your students weave African tradition into their school day by creating their own mkekas. Provide each student with three sheets of 12" x 18" construction paper in the three colors that represent the holiday: red, green, and black. Cut 1 1/2" x 12" strips for weaving from two of the three colors. Each student will need ten strips in all. Let each student use the third sheet to be the background color of his mat.

To prepare the background mat for weaving, fold the paper in half. Next, using a paper cutter, make long, vertical slits starting at the fold of the paper and ending at least one inch from the edge of the paper to prevent tearing. (Make the slits about 1 1/2 inches apart, leaving one inch from the top and bottom of the paper.) The students then weave in an over-under pattern, alternating the two colored strips. Secure each woven strip with a glue stick. When weaving has been completed, have students make small cuts along the sides of their mats to look like fringe. Have the students use their woven creations at snacktime.

Corn Patterns
Use with "Children Count!" on page 110.

Kinara Pattern
Use with *My First Kwanzaa Book* on page 113.

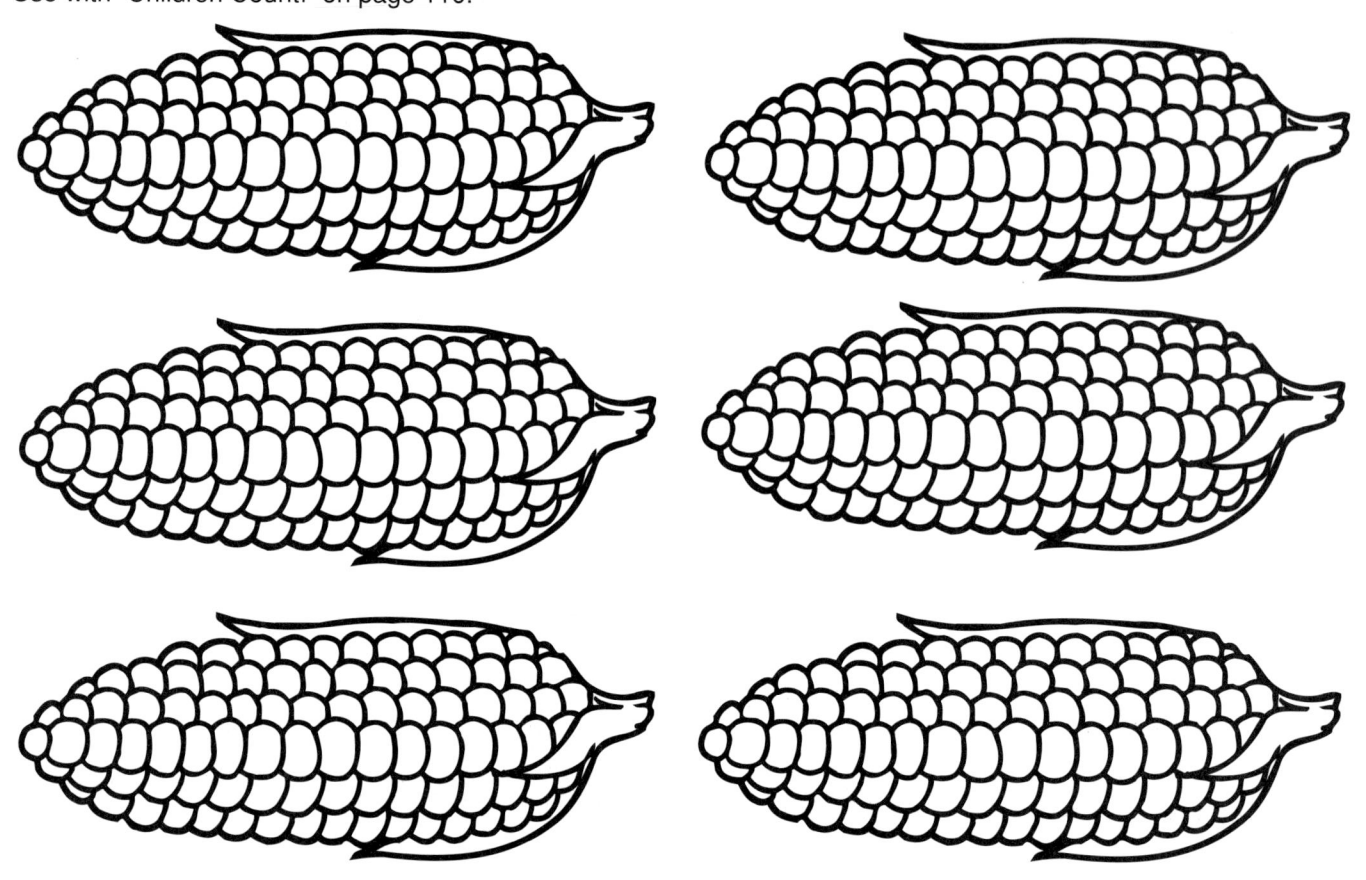

Seven Candles For Kwanzaa
by Andrea Davis Pinkney
(Dial Books For Young Readers, 1993)

This colorful book about Kwanzaa helps to explain the weeklong celebration. It highlights the African words used during the holiday and gives the phonetic spellings. The detailed pictures show the family preparing for each day of the celebration.

After reading, have your students brainstorm a list of family-related activities. Next have each student draw a picture of his family doing one of the activities listed. Label each picture with each family's name. Put all the pages together in a book. Give the book a colorful cover with a geometric border. In the center, write the word "FAMILY" with a black marker and add a red paper heart on each side of the word. Put the book on display at the reading center in your classroom for everyone to enjoy.

My First Kwanzaa Book
by Deborah M. Newton Chocolate
(Scholastic Inc., 1992)

This story of the Kwanzaa celebration is told by a young boy. He celebrates this African-American holiday with his family and learns about his heritage. The author takes the reader through the holiday one day at a time. Brightly colored pictures help to explain what is happening on each day. When reading the story aloud, point out the *kinara* (kee-NAH-rah) pictured at the bottom right-hand corner of each page. Explain that a kinara is a candleholder usually made of wood. Each night of Kwanzaa, one candle is lit and the principle for that day is discussed.

Have students light a large bulletin-board *kinara.* Enlarge, color, and cut out the pattern on page 112. (The center candle is black, the three candles to the left are red, and the three to the right are green.) Mount the kinara on the bulletin board. To "light" the candles use either orange chalk or construction paper to make little "flames." The black candle is the first lit; then on each following day, alternate lighting the red and green candles until all seven are lit on the final day.

Each morning, have one student light the appropriate candle and another student say, *"Habari gani"* (hah-bar-ee gah-nee)—the Kwanzaa greeting that asks, "What is the news?" The answer given by the whole group should be the principle for the day. Lead the class in a discussion on the principle for that day.

Patterns
Use with "First Fruits" on page 111.

A PARADE OF PENGUINS

Grab your parka and head for the Antarctic for a parade of perky penguin ideas! Urge your students to "chill out" with wintry, penguin-related literature and activities.

by Susie Kapaun and Susan Hohbach

PENGUIN PARTNERS

Introduce your students to penguins by reading the story *Solo* by Paul Geraghty (Crown Publishers, Inc.; 1995). The endearing main character, Solo, leads students on an Antarctic adventure. The story describes an amazing penguin quality—the ability to locate a chick or mate by recognizing its distinctive voice.

After reading, engage students in this selective listening activity. In advance gather a class supply of small index cards; then sort the cards into pairs. Program each pair of cards with the same animal, such as "cat," "lion," "dog," "frog," "sheep," etc. Combine all the prepared cards in a container. Have each student randomly choose a card from the container. Explain to the class that each student is to walk around the room and make the sound of the animal he has selected. When he finds a classmate making the same sound, he stops and waits quietly with his newfound partner. As groups form, the room becomes quiet and your students are sorted penguin-style for a partner activity of your choice.

FASCINATING PENGUIN FACTS

Fascinate your students by sharing these fabulous facts.
- Penguins are speedy swimmers—averaging speeds between four and six miles per hour.
- Penguins can stretch their mouths, throats, and stomachs to swallow their prey whole.
- Penguins are known to walk in lines—as if playing Follow The Leader.
- Penguins eat seafood such as fish, krill, and squid.
- The largest penguin—the emperor penguin—can be as tall as four feet high and may weigh up to 100 pounds.
- During the breeding season, penguins gather on land or ice in large colonies called *rookeries*.
- Penguins group together for protection while swimming, but most work alone while hunting.

PENGUINS ON PARADE

Students will line up to take part in this penguin painting project. Enlarge the penguin pattern on page 120 to fit on a 9" x 12" piece of paper. Duplicate one copy for each student on white construction paper. Provide the students with small containers of black paint and orange paint and cotton swabs. Using a cotton swab, each student dabs orange paint onto the penguin pattern—filling in the beak and feet areas only. Next have him use a second cotton swab to apply black paint onto the penguin's body and wings using the same technique. Emphasize that the stomach is left white. To present a pleasing array of penguins on parade, staple the finished penguins to a bulletin board in rows as shown.

DIVE INTO PENGUIN FACTS!

All penguins live in the Southern Hemisphere, but only seven species live on the shores of Antarctica—the *emperor, king, Adelie, gentoo, chinstrap, macaroni,* and *rockhopper.* Add a splash of excitement to researching penguin facts by having students create life-size penguins. Divide your class into seven groups and assign each group the name of one Antarctic species. Provide resource books or computer references, and have each group research facts about its penguin, determine the penguin's height, and find a picture showing its features and coloring. Supply each group with a piece of bulletin-board paper that will accommodate the size of its penguin. Have each group measure, draw, and color a life-size picture of its penguin. Then create a small poster stating the penguin's name and a short list of facts. Display the finished projects and posters in a hallway. The whole school will dive into penguin facts with this unconventional display!

PROGRAMMABLE PENGUINS

Emperor penguins lay and care for one egg at a time. Your students will enjoy matching these adult penguins with their eggs while practicing an important skill. Reproduce 10–15 copies of the penguin pattern from page 120 on white construction paper. Cut an equal number of egg shapes from white construction paper. Color the penguins and program them with contractions, math facts, or opposites. Print a matching answer on each egg. Place the penguins and eggs in a string-tie envelope with directions and an answer key to make a Penguin Pocket Pal. The penguins and eggs will generate lively conversations about penguins and teach valuable skills at the same time.

Directions:
1. Match each emperor penguin to his egg.
2. Check the answer key.

BRRRR!!!!!

Students will love reading their way through these chilly choices about penguins!

TACKY THE PENGUIN
by Helen Lester
(Houghton Mifflin Company, 1988)

Single out this activity to highlight each student's individuality! After reading this comical tale about Tacky, discuss how Tacky is unique. Emphasize that each person is special in his own way; then give each student a copy of the "Uniquely You!" form on page 120. Have each student read and answer the questions. At the bottom of his form, the student writes something unique about himself. The student may choose a special talent, an unusual place he has visited, or a description of a collection of which he is proud.

Collect the forms from the students and have all of them stand. Select one form to begin the activity. Choose a numbered item from the form and make a statement such as "Remain standing if your favorite pet is a cat," or "Continue to stand if baseball is your favorite sport." A student sits down if his answer does not fit the statement. Continue making statements in this manner until only one special student is left standing. Return the form to that student and have him read aloud what makes him unique. Draw a new form from those that are left and ask students to stand before you repeat this one-of-a-kind activity.

CINDERELLA PENGUIN OR THE LITTLE GLASS FLIPPER
by Janet Perlman
(Puffin Books, 1995)

Your students will love the transformation of this story. In a parody of the classic, *Cinderella*, this retelling portrays the characters as penguins instead of people. As a class, brainstorm other favorite fairy tales. Read original versions of these classics; then have students change the main characters to penguins. An example might be "Goldilocks Penguin And The Three Polar Bears."

Have students work in groups to write a new version of their favorite tale. Bind the various stories and keep them in your classroom library. These funny fairy tales are sure to be among your students' favorites.

PERFECT PENGUIN PICKS!

Antarctica
by Helen Cowcher
(Scholastic Inc.,1990)

Cuddly Dudley
by Jez Alborough
(Scholastic Inc.,1993)

Little Penguin's Tale
by Audrey Wood
(Scholastic Inc.,1989)

Pattern

Use with "Penguins On Parade" on page 117.
Use with "Programmable Penguins" on page 118.

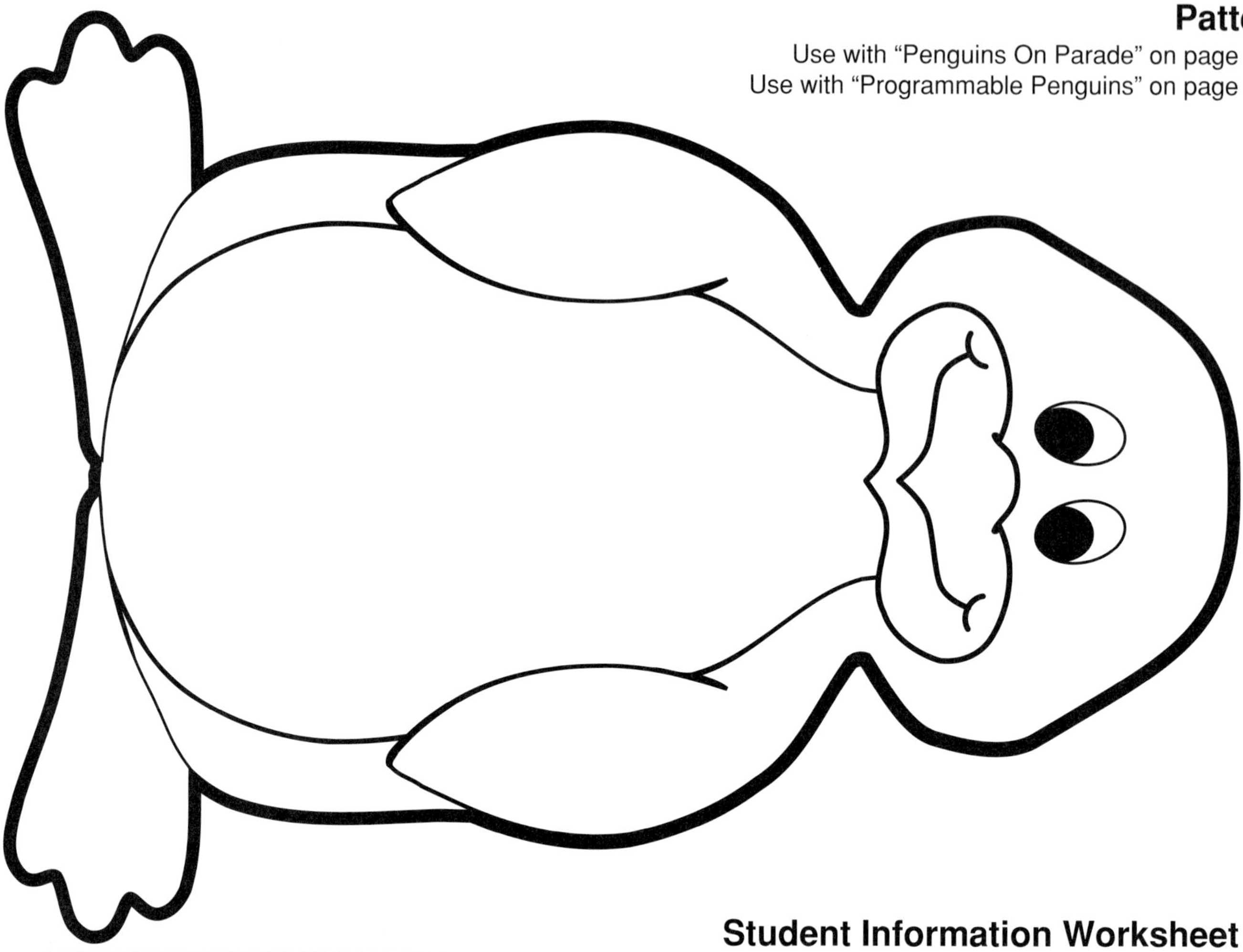

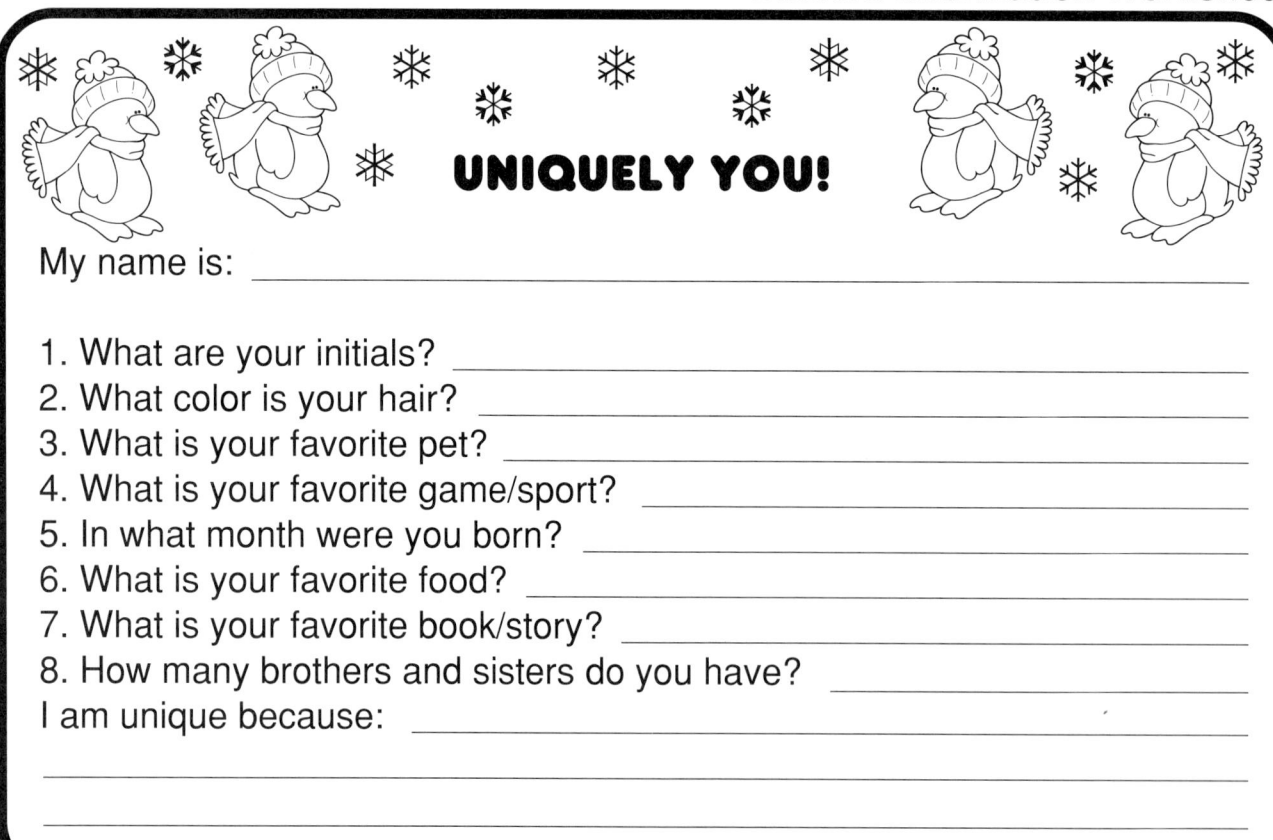

Student Information Worksheet

UNIQUELY YOU!

My name is: _____

1. What are your initials? _____
2. What color is your hair? _____
3. What is your favorite pet? _____
4. What is your favorite game/sport? _____
5. In what month were you born? _____
6. What is your favorite food? _____
7. What is your favorite book/story? _____
8. How many brothers and sisters do you have? _____
I am unique because: _____
_____
_____

©The Education Center, Inc. • Big Book of Monthly Ideas • TEC1487

Note To The Teacher: Use with *Tacky The Penguin* on page 119.

Remembering Martin Luther King, Jr.

Lead your students down the road to freedom with these cross-curricular activities to celebrate Martin Luther King, Jr. Day!

ideas by Doug Poage and Sharon Murphy

Happy Birthday, Martin Luther King, Jr.

Your students are sure to look forward to studying Martin Luther King, Jr., when you begin your unit with a birthday party in his honor. Have them figure out how old Dr. King would be on this birthday (see the timeline on page 122). Then encourage your students to join in as you sing "Happy Birthday" to him.

Next share *Happy Birthday, Martin Luther King* by Jean Marzollo (Scholastic Inc., 1993) with your students. This easy-to-read book gives a brief account of the life of Martin Luther King, Jr. Be sure to emphasize Dr. King's dream "that people everywhere would learn to live together without being mean to one another." Ask students how Martin Luther King would want everyone in the class to treat each other. List students' responses on the board.

After discussing the book, ask your students to think of something nice they could do for their classmates or something that would help make the classroom a more pleasant place. Tell students that they are each going to write down this good deed and then wrap it as a present for Martin Luther King's birthday. Each student will need an 8" x 8" sheet of lined paper, colored construction paper, glue, and birthday wrapping paper. First have students write their good deeds on the lined pieces of paper. Next have each student glue his piece of wrapping paper to the piece of construction paper, as shown, to make a flap. Then each student staples the wrapping paper on top of the good deed at the top to make a present. As an extra touch, have each student tie a bow from yarn and glue it to the top of the present where the staple is located. Then display these beautiful presents on a bulletin board titled "Happy Birthday, Martin Luther King, Jr." Your class will enjoy lifting up the wrapping-paper flaps to reveal the good deeds.

In Step With Martin Luther King

Motivate your students to work on both their map and sequencing skills as you let them follow in Martin Luther King's footsteps. First write each of the years listed below on a sentence strip. (Be sure to include the event and location.) Provide a U.S. map and a world map large enough for all students to view at one time.

To begin the activity, mix up the sentence strips so they are not in sequential order. Next read each of the sentence strips to the class and ask your students to help you put the events in the order in which they happened. Tape the sentence strips to a piece of chart paper as students give them to you. After the class has placed the events in sequence, older students can find the locations on one of the maps.

1929 MLK was born. *(Atlanta, Georgia)*
1951 MLK graduates from seminary. *(Chester, Pennsylvania)*
1953 MLK married Coretta Scott. *(Marion, Alabama)*
1954 MLK began in his first position as a minister. *(Montgomery, Alabama)*
1955 MLK earned his doctoral degree. *(Boston, Massachusetts)*
1963 Dr. King gave his famous "I Have A Dream" speech. *(Washington, DC)*
1964 Dr. King was awarded the Nobel Peace Prize. *(Norway)*
1968 Dr. King died. *(Memphis, Tennessee)*

Peace-Prize Awards

Dr. Martin Luther King, Jr., worked very hard and gave his life for a more peaceful nation. He was honored with one of the most important prizes in the world—the Nobel Peace Prize. Each year this award is given to the person (or persons) who has (have) done the most for peace. In December of 1964, Martin Luther King was awarded this distinguished prize. He was given a medal and $54,000. He gave the money to several black organizations because he said it belonged to all Black Americans.

After sharing this information with your students, help them recognize the positive strengths in their classmates by creating Peace-Prize Awards. Duplicate one of the patterns on page 127 for each of your students. Have them color and cut out the awards. Next have each child glue the award on cardstock or construction paper and trim it, leaving a border around the award. Each child then applies glue in a design around the border of the award and sprinkles the glue with gold glitter. After the glue has dried, shake the excess glitter into a container and punch a hole at the top of each award. Then help each student thread a 24-inch piece of yarn through the hole and tie it to make a necklace.

To prepare to give out these special awards, call out a student's name. His classmates will then take turns saying something nice about him. (For example, "Juan helps others by treating them kindly.") Write down at least one good statement that is said about that student. Repeat this activity for each student. Save these statements and awards to present at the upcoming Freedom Tea (see page 125). You will be amazed at how proud your students will be at receiving the awards!

Man Of The Year

In January 1964, *Time* magazine chose Martin Luther King, Jr., to be its Man Of The Year. His face was on the cover of the magazine. If possible show your students a copy of *Time* magazine and discuss why it is an honor to be on the cover.

Then let your students create two covers for a new *Time* magazine. Give each student one sheet of 9" x 12" white construction paper. On one side of the paper the student will draw a picture of Martin Luther King, Jr., and write a sentence stating why Dr. King was chosen. On the other side of the paper, the student will draw a picture of himself and then write a sentence about what he might do in the future to get on the cover of *Time* magazine. After everyone is finished, have your students share these new magazine covers. They're hot off the presses!

Martin Luther King by peacefully protes...

Korita Steverson, first black woman on the Supreme Court

Getting Some Big Words

From a very early age, Martin Luther King was fascinated with words. He once said, "When I grow up I'm going to get me some big words." Well he did. In one year alone, Dr. King gave more than 350 speeches about freedom for everyone.

Share the above statement with your students and then read the following excerpt from one of his famous speeches. He told Americans that it was his dream that...

"my four little children will one day live in a nation where they will not be judged by the color of their skin, but by the content of their character."

For vocabulary development, discuss with your students what is meant by "the content of their character." A good way to do this would be to connect the phrase to character traits such as *kindness, honesty, helpfulness,* and *respect.* Next make a copy of the reproducible titled "The Content Of Their Character" on page 128 for each student. Using the given word bank and a dictionary, if needed, have your students write the appropriate character trait in the sentence with its definition. Then have students think of character traits they have and list them, as well as traits of Martin Luther King.

We Shall Overcome

Get your students in tune as they learn the civil rights song "We Shall Overcome." Refer to *…If You Lived At The Time Of Martin Luther King* by Ellen Levine (Scholastic Inc., 1990) for the words of the song. Before the singing starts, share with your students the following information about Martin Luther King:

- Dr. King spent his life leading the movement for Black Americans to be treated equally and fairly.
- Dr. King used only peaceful, nonviolent types of actions.
- He led a bus boycott, freedom marches, and sit-ins.
- Dr. King and his followers marched to the song "We Shall Overcome." The song tells people not to give up.

To teach your students the words to this song, write the words on chart paper. After reading the words and then singing the song, discuss what Dr. King wanted to "overcome." Then ask students to brainstorm some hardships or changes that they have had to overcome in their lives, such as moving to a new school and making new friends or learning how to read. List what students have had to overcome on the board. Have each student choose one obstacle he has overcome and write a short story about it. Be sure to have students share their stories with the class so students can acknowledge each other for their accomplishments. Save these stories to share at the Freedom Tea (see page 125).

Memory Booklets

Here's a booklet to help your students remember facts about Martin Luther King. Reproduce the booklet cover and pages on pages 131 and 132 for each child. Have the students cut them out, sequence them, and staple them together on the left-hand side. After reading through the booklets with your students, ask them to write a response to the question on the last page. Be sure to keep these memory booklets to share with parents and friends at your upcoming Freedom Tea (see page 125).

> Would Martin Luther King think today's world was peaceful? Why or why not?
>
> I think Martin Luther King would not think the world is peaceful. There is a lot of crime in the cities. Also many people have guns and break the law.

7

Freedom Tea

At the end of your unit on Martin Luther King, invite parents to school for a Freedom Tea. Reproduce the invitation on page 127 for your students to fill in, cut out, decorate, and take home. Ask some parents to provide tea and cookies for refreshments.

Several days prior to the event, make one copy of "Facts For The Freedom Tea" on pages 129 and 130. Cut the strips apart and assign one fact to each student to memorize for a choral speaking at the tea.

Prior to your guests' arrival, have the memory booklets (see page 124) and the "We Shall Overcome" stories (see page 124) out on the tables. As your guests arrive, suggest that they enjoy these booklets and stories. When everyone has arrived, have your students line up around the room and say their memorized lines. Then have your students join hands and sing "We Shall Overcome." At the conclusion of your event, present the "Peace-Prize Awards" (see page 122) to each member of the class and serve the refreshments.

A "Dreamful" Of Good Reading

The Story Of Ruby Bridges
by Robert Coles
(Scholastic Inc., 1995)

This moving story portrays the hostility of segregation seen through the eyes of a six-year-old girl named Ruby Bridges. Ruby was the first African-American girl to integrate Frantz Elementary School in New Orleans in 1960. She found herself surrounded by prejudice and hatred.

After sharing this story about this important event in American history, discuss the following thought-provoking questions and statements:
- How do you think Ruby felt at first about moving to New Orleans?
- Why couldn't Ruby go to any school she wanted?
- How did Ruby's parents feel about her going to this new school?
- Describe Ruby's first day at her new school.
- Compare Ruby's first day of school to your first day of school.
- How did Ruby's teacher feel about her?
- Do you think Ruby was scared to go to school every day?
- Describe Ruby's character.

When your students are finished answering the questions and following the directions, read the afterword at the end of the story. It lets the reader know what became of Ruby Bridges.

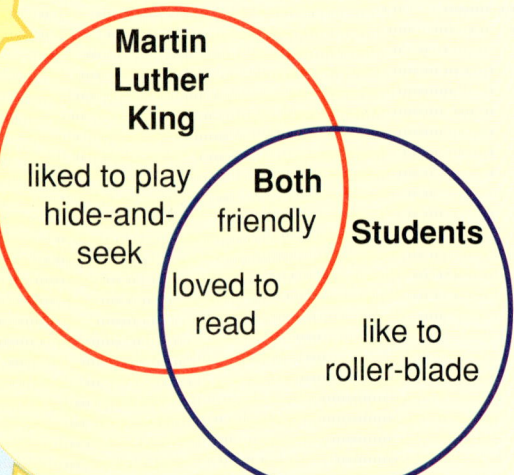

Martin Luther King, Jr.: A Biography For Young Children
by Carol Hilgartner Schlank and Barbara Metzger
(Gryphon House, Inc.; 1990)

This book is a biography of Dr. Martin Luther King, Jr., that was written especially for younger children. It gives a good account of what Martin's life was like as a child. It describes his crusade for equality for Black Americans as he got older.

After reading this story to your students, discuss Martin Luther King's childhood. Ask them to compare his childhood to their own childhoods. Draw a large Venn diagram, as shown, on the board to record their responses. Students will enjoy comparing themselves to the great Martin Luther King, Jr.

Martin Luther King, Jr.
by Kathie Billingslea Smith
(Simon & Schuster, Inc.; 1987)

This biography gives the details of Martin Luther King's interesting life—presenting them so students in the primary grades can understand. After reading it, refer back to the pages in the book that mention the *bus boycott, sit-ins,* and *marches.* Starting with the bus boycott, briefly explain each term. When the students have a good understanding of each term, ask them to pretend that their favorite fast-food restaurant has decided that children are not allowed to sit down while they are eating. Only adults can sit down. Most students will think that is not fair. Have your students work in groups of three to design signs that they could carry if they were going to hold a protest march. Be sure to display their signs around your room.

Pattern
Use with "Peace-Prize Awards" on page 122.

Invitation
Use with "Freedom Tea" on page 125.

Name _____   *Dictionary skills*

"The Content Of Their Character"

Use the word bank to write the correct word in each blank. Look up each word you don't know in a dictionary.

Word Bank

peaceful   helpful   polite   honest   risk taker   conscientious

1. A person who takes chances is a _____.
2. A person who helps others is _____.
3. Someone who is calm and doesn't like fighting is _____.
4. A _____ worker always does his best work.
5. A person who uses good manners is called _____.
6. Someone who tells the truth is called _____.

In the spaces below, write four character traits that describe Martin Luther King and four character traits that describe you. Draw a picture of yourself in the frame.

Martin Luther King, Jr.

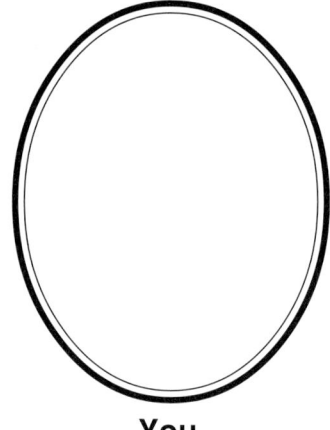

You

_____   _____

_____   _____

_____   _____

_____   _____

Bonus Box: On the back of this sheet, use a dictionary to help you write some other words that describe yourself.

©The Education Center, Inc. • *Big Book of Monthly Ideas* • TEC1487

Note To The Teacher: Use with "Getting Some Big Words" on page 123.

Facts For The Freedom Tea

1. Thank you for coming. We are going to tell you a little bit about Martin Luther King, Jr.

2. Martin Luther King, Jr., was born on January 15, 1929, in Atlanta, Georgia.

3. He studied hard in school and did very well.

4. He loved to read books.

5. He enjoyed listening to his father preach.

6. Martin Luther King, Jr., graduated from college in 1948.

7. Then he went to study in Pennsylvania to be a preacher.

8. In 1953 Martin married Coretta Scott.

9. For awhile they lived in Boston, where Martin was in graduate school.

10. Then they decided to go back to the South and help other blacks.

11. In May of 1954, Martin became a preacher at a church in Montgomery, Alabama.

12. He wanted to help people understand that a person's skin color is not important.

Note To The Teacher: Use these with "Freedom Tea" on page 125.

Facts For The Freedom Tea

13. In 1955 Martin received another degree. Then he was called Dr. King.

14. Dr. King had a dream that all people would be treated equally.

15. Dr. King chose nonviolent ways to try to make a difference.

16. He led a bus boycott, sit-ins, and protest marches.

17. He gave many speeches.

18. His most famous speech is the "I Have A Dream" speech that he gave in Washington, DC.

19. Dr. King and his followers marched and sang the civil rights song "We Shall Overcome."

20. In 1964 Dr. King won the Nobel Peace Prize.

21. Congress soon made new laws for everyone.

22. In 1968 Dr. King was shot and killed in Memphis, Tennessee.

23. Dr. King's birthday is now a federal holiday.

24. We celebrate his birthday every year on the third Monday of January.

25. We will always remember Martin Luther King, Jr., for working so hard to solve problems in peaceful ways.

©The Education Center, Inc. • Big Book of Monthly Ideas • TEC1487

Note To The Teacher: Use these with "Freedom Tea" on page 125.

Memory Booklet Cover and Pages

My Memory Book of Martin Luther King, Jr.

By _____

©The Education Center, Inc.

1

Martin Luther King, Jr., was born on January 15, 1929. He worked hard in school.

2

After graduating from college, he went to school to become a preacher. He married Coretta Scott.

3

King's first work as a preacher was in Alabama. He wanted to help people understand that all people are important, no matter what color they are.

Memory Booklet Pages

4

Dr. King gave speeches all around this country. He had a dream that one day all people would be treated equally.

5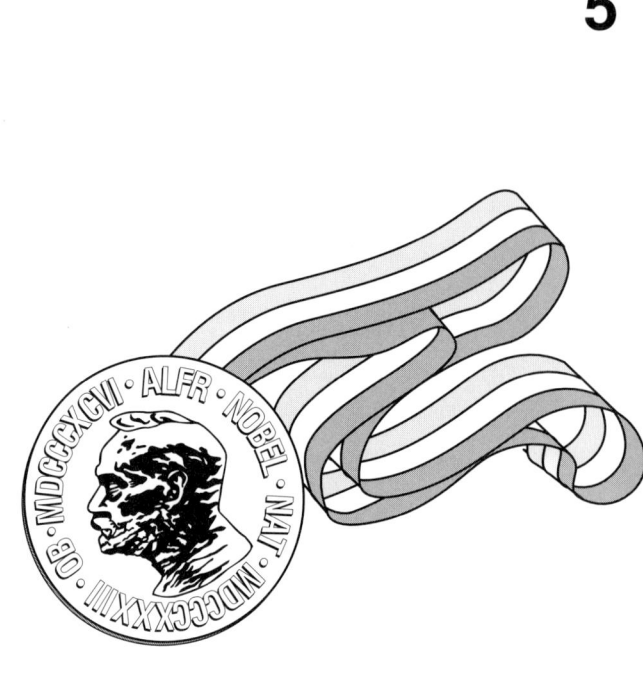

He taught people to use words and peaceful actions, not fists, to solve their problems. In 1964 Dr. King won the Nobel Peace Prize.

6

In 1968 Dr. King was shot and killed. We celebrate his birthday every year because he worked hard to make his dream of peace come true.

7 Would Martin Luther King think today's world was peaceful? Why or why not?

Black History Month

Celebrate the power of positive role models, awesome athletes, dynamic leaders, and inspirational authors. Spotlight African-American heroes to teach cultural awareness through music, literature, science, and map skills.

by Cynthia Holcomb

The ABCs Of Black History

Begin your study with a look at some famous African-Americans. Familiarize students with important figures in history with AFRO-BETS® *Book Of Black Heroes From A To Z* by Wade Hudson and Valerie Wilson Wesley (Just Us Books, 1993). This collection of past and contemporary heroes gives a picture and brief history of important leaders and their contributions. Assign a hero from the book to each student. Have the student research the person and present an oral report to the class. With 26 listings in the book, your class can share a wealth of knowledge.

Sports-Page Heroes

Students may be familiar with current sports figures—such as basketball players Michael Jordan, Magic Johnson, and Charles Barkley—but may not know some African-American athletes whose achievements stand out in history. Introduce some athletic heroes and their accomplishments by using the reproducible on page 139. Continue this lesson by having your students write sports articles about those famous athletes. Have your students choose from the list of athletes and then write their articles as though they were reporting on events that had just occurred (for example, when Hank Aaron hit his 715th home run). Post the articles on a bulletin board titled "African-American All-Stars."

Founding Father

Incorporate a geography lesson with this look at the man who founded Chicago, Illinois. Jean Baptiste Point Du Sable was a fur trader who established a successful business in Peoria, Illinois. Du Sable made many trips to Canada to get furs for his business and always passed by a place known as Eschikagov. In 1774 he decided to build a cabin and move his family there. Soon other pioneers decided to settle near his post. As more homes and stores were built, the settlement grew into the city now called Chicago.

Make a copy of the map on page 140 for each student. Have students label the state of Illinois, locate Chicago, and note that it was founded by Du Sable. Continue to use the map during your study of African-Americans. Have students label other states and cities that are important in history as they meet each famous person (see pages 142–144).

Peanut Power

Although his accomplishments are many, George Washington Carver is best remembered for his work with the peanut. After presenting background information on this famous scientist, lead your students in a discovery activity that focuses on the peanut.

Carver was born a slave around 1864 and orphaned shortly after his birth. He was raised by his owners, who taught him to read and write, and he was able to attend a school for black children. Although he showed promise as a painter, Carver had a keen interest in plants and decided to pursue his agricultural interests instead. He promoted ideas on soil conservation and crop rotation. His research on peanuts received national attention in 1921. Carver made more than 300 products from peanuts, including a milk substitute, face powder, printer's ink, and soap.

Give your students a chance to investigate the peanut. Each student will need three peanuts in the shell and a copy of the reproducible on page 141. Guide the students through the exploration's steps as they complete the open-ended activities. After students complete their work, give them peanuts to munch for a tasty finale.

Overcoming Obstacles

Introduce the subject of *racial discrimination* with the story of a woman who overcame racial obstacles. Marian Anderson was a famous African-American contralto once described as having a voice "that comes once in a hundred years." Even with a talent of that magnitude, Anderson's career was affected by the color of her skin. Duplicate the reproducible on page 142 for your children to read and discuss. Anderson set a wonderful example of someone who refused to let obstacles stand in the way of success.

Catalyst For Change

When you think of heroes in African-American history, Rosa Parks always comes to mind. Present the story of Parks's brave decision to keep her seat on the bus by reading *Rosa Parks* by Eloise Greenfield (HarperCollins Children's Books, 1996) or *A Picture Book Of Rosa Parks* by David A. Adler (Holiday House, Inc.; 1993). Then have each student create a timeline of important dates in Parks's life by using page 143.

Make a copy of the reproducible on page 143 for each student. Have students complete the reproducible by using information about Parks's life to fill in a timeline of special events. Follow up with a discussion of nonviolent forms of protest, such as the bus boycott, sit-ins, and marches. Ask students to discuss what might have happened if another form of protest had been used. Have students share situations in which they have wanted to react in anger, but took another approach to solve a problem instead.

The Real McCoy!

The expression "It's the real McCoy!" has become a part of everyday vocabulary. But how many students know that it is associated with the work of an African-American engineer, Elijah McCoy? Share the story of McCoy's work by reading *The Real McCoy: The Life Of An African-American Inventor* by Wendy Towle (Scholastic Inc., 1995).

After reading the book, put students' creativity to work to invent laborsaving devices, much like McCoy's oil cup, lawn sprinkler, and ironing table. Ask each student to first think of a household chore that could be made easier with a new invention. Then have the student draw a sketch of her invention and write a paragraph explaining how it works. Encourage students to share their creations with the class. Who knows—one of them might just turn out to be "the real McCoy"!

Take The Bull By The Horns!

When it came to taming the Wild West, the African-American cowboy did his part. Almost one in seven cowboys were African-American. Cowboy John Ware had the reputation for being the best bronco tamer in the West. Nat Love won many rodeo competitions for his abilities with the rope and the revolver. Some of the exploits of Bill Pickett are so wild that they may sound like they're straight out of a tall tale.

Share one of Pickett's adventures on the rodeo circuit. Duplicate the reproducible on page 144 for each student. After reading the story, have students honor the legend of this great African-American cowboy by creating posters of his rodeo career. Supply each student with a half-sheet of poster board and instruct him to illustrate Pickett bulldogging a steer. Have the student decorate the poster as if it were announcing the rodeo coming to town with Pickett as the feature act. Display these posters in the hallway for an "incredi-bull" exhibit.

Noteworthy Success

When it comes to musical contributions, Louis Armstrong is high on the list of famous African-Americans. He is recognized as one of the most influential performers in the history of jazz. He is known for his distinctive, gravelly voice as well as his brilliance as a trumpeter.

Set the stage for the jazz era by reading *Ben's Trumpet* by Rachel Isadora (Greenwillow Books, 1979). The story tells of Ben, who is so intrigued by the sounds coming from the Zig Zag Jazz Club that he plays an imaginary trumpet everywhere he goes. Then treat the students to some of Louis Armstrong's recordings, such as the jazz arrangement "Potato Head Blues" or his later recordings of "Hello, Dolly!" and "What A Wonderful World." Ask the students to share their opinions about his music.

Invite a musician to your classroom to show students the different types of instruments played in jazz, such as the trumpet, saxophone, trombone, and stand-up bass. Students can "play" the instruments as Ben did—using their imaginations to hold the instruments correctly and imitate their sounds. What a way to jazz up a lesson!

African-American Authors

Introduce your students to this collection of stories by African-American authors. The art, literature, and culture of the people will come alive with these books and activities.

Amazing Grace
by Mary Hoffman
(Dial Books For Young Readers, 1991)

Your students will love Grace's determination and spirit. More than anything, Grace wants the part of Peter Pan in the class play. Her classmates do not offer her encouragement. They tell Grace that she shouldn't get the part because she is a girl and she is black. In spite of their objections, Grace proves that no one can impose limitations on her dreams.

Use Grace as a model for a character cube. Duplicate the pattern on page 145 for each student. Direct students to fill in each section of the cube with information about Grace or another character in the story. Help students assemble their cubes; then create a display by placing an arrangement of cubes on a bookshelf.

Follow The Drinking Gourd
by Jeanette Winter
(Alfred A. Knopf, Inc.; 1988)

The concept of slavery and the desire for freedom are explained in this easy-to-understand story. Students will appreciate the importance of the Underground Railroad and the bravery of those who dared to travel it.

The music to "Follow The Drinking Gourd" is written in the back of the book. Enlist the help of your music teacher to teach your children the words and melody of the song. Then divide the song into sections and have students create illustrations to go with the lyrics. Have your students perform the song for another class in celebration of Black History Month. Let the illustrators share their pictures at the appropriate times in the performance.

Cornrows
by Camille Yarbrough
(G. P. Putnam's Sons, 1992)

The significance of braiding hair into cornrows is explained in this story-within-a-story. To prepare, display a map of Africa; then have students locate the countries mentioned as you read the story.

After the story, teach your children the art of braiding by making friendship bracelets. Give each student three 12-inch pieces of yarn. Show students how to overlap the pieces into a braided string. Each student can trade his braided-yarn bracelet with another student, and they can tie the braids around their wrists to signify friendship.

Name _____   *Investigating and drawing conclusions*

Investigation Situation: Peanuts

Use the peanuts your teacher gives you to answer these questions.

1. Draw a picture of how one of your peanuts looks from the side.

2. Draw a picture of how that peanut looks from the front.

3. Describe the way the peanut shell feels. _____
   _____

4. What does the smell of the peanut remind you of? _____
   _____

5. Why do some peanut shells have two bumps? _____
   _____

6. Open one of the peanut shells and list all the colors that you see. _____
   _____

7. What are some other foods that come in a shell? _____
   _____

8. Open all the peanut shells and line up the nuts on your desk. What are some

   differences you see in the nuts? _____
   _____

9. What are some of the similarities you see in the nuts? _____
   _____

10. What is your favorite food that has peanuts as an ingredient? _____

Note To The Teacher: Use with "Peanut Power" on page 135.

Name _____   *Critical thinking*

Marian Anderson—A Lesson In Overcoming Obstacles
Read the following and discuss the questions at the bottom of the page.

Marian was born in 1897 in Philadelphia, PA. Her family was very poor, but Marian was a hard worker. As a girl she scrubbed the neighbor's front steps to earn a few pennies. She often sang as she worked. She wanted to be a famous singer. She tried to go to music school, but was told she was not welcome because of her race.

At last Marian found a voice teacher. In 1924 she won a prize for her singing. She began to perform in Europe and all over the United States. Before each performance in the South, Marian would always bow to the segregated black people in the audience before bowing to the whites. It was her way of showing that she was proud of her race.

In 1939, Marian was asked to sing in Washington, DC. The people who owned the concert hall would not let her sing, because of her race. President and Mrs. Franklin D. Roosevelt were angry about what happened to Marian. They supported a concert for her on the steps of the Lincoln Memorial. Marian sang on Easter morning to a crowd of 75,000 people. Mrs. Roosevelt became one of Marian's good friends.

In 1955, Marian became the first African-American soloist to sing with the Metropolitan Opera in New York. She also sang at the March on Washington in 1963. Dr. Martin Luther King gave his "I Have A Dream" speech at the March. Marian died in 1993. She was never one to let obstacles stand in the way of her future.

Questions For Discussion
1. As a young girl, Marian Anderson wanted to be a famous singer. What could have kept her from doing this?
2. Marian tried to attend a singing school, but was turned away because of her race. How do you think that made Marian feel?
3. Marian bowed to the black section at her concerts in the South before she bowed to the white section. Why did she do this?
4. President Roosevelt and his wife became Marian's friends. They asked her to the White House. It made some people angry. What does this tell you about the Roosevelts?
5. Why do you think Marian reached her goal even though some people tried to stop her?

©The Education Center, Inc. • *Big Book of Monthly Ideas* • TEC1487

Note To The Teacher: Use with "Overcoming Obstacles" on page 135.

Name _____   Critical thinking

Rosa Parks: Changing The Course Of History

When Rosa Parks decided to keep her seat on the bus on December 1, 1955, she set into motion events that would change civil rights in this country. Read about some other important events in Rosa's life.

Rosa was born in Tuskegee, Alabama, in 1913. It was a time when the color of her skin affected every part of her life. African-Americans could not attend school with whites. They were also segregated in many restaurants and movie theaters. They could not even drink from the same water fountain as whites. Rosa said it made her feel as if she weren't a normal human being.

Rosa married Raymond Parks in 1932. She worked as a seamstress in a department store. One day when she finished work, she took a seat on the bus. At that time in 1955, African-Americans had to sit in the back of the bus. Only whites were allowed in the front. If all the white seats were filled, African-Americans had to give up their seats and stand. On this day, the bus driver told Rosa to give her seat to a white person. Rosa refused. She was arrested.

Rosa was taken to jail. Some people were very angry. They decided not to ride the buses again until the laws were changed. For over a year, many people walked or found other ways to get to work. Finally, on December 20, 1956, the laws were changed.

Rosa's refusal to give up her seat caused other changes. She was fired from her job because of it. In 1979 she won an award for her work in civil rights. She founded the Rosa and Raymond Parks Institute for Self-Development in 1987. Young people learn leadership skills there.

When Rosa decided to stay seated on the bus, she brought about many changes for civil rights.

List the important events that happened in each of these years of her life:

1913 _____

1932 _____

1955 _____

1956 _____

1979 _____

1987 _____

©The Education Center, Inc. • Big Book of Monthly Ideas • TEC1487

Note To The Teacher: Use with "Catalyst For Change" on page 136.

Name _____   *Reading for comprehension*

Cowboy Bill Pickett

Bill Pickett was born about 1860 and grew up in southern Texas. He learned how to handle a horse with great skill. He became known for his skill at *bulldogging.* He would jump off his horse, grab a steer's horns, and twist the steer's head around until the animal fell over.

When he was almost 40 years old, Bill moved to Oklahoma. He was asked to perform in a rodeo. After he threw a wild steer to the ground, he would often stare at it face-to-face. The bulls were almost always afraid to charge at Bill.

The rodeo moved to Madison Square Garden in New York City. Bill got ready to perform the bulldogging on opening night. When it was time for him to catch the steer, the animal jumped a gate and ran straight into the crowd! Bill followed close behind the steer and managed to grab it by the horns. Another cowboy roped the steer and pulled it back into the arena, with Bill still hanging onto the horns. It's no wonder that Bill Pickett was honored in the Cowboy Hall of Fame as the first bulldogger.

Now you know a true story about Bill Pickett. Write a make-believe story about a rodeo adventure for Bill. Give the story an interesting title.

_____
(title)

_____
_____
_____
_____
_____
_____
_____
_____
_____
_____

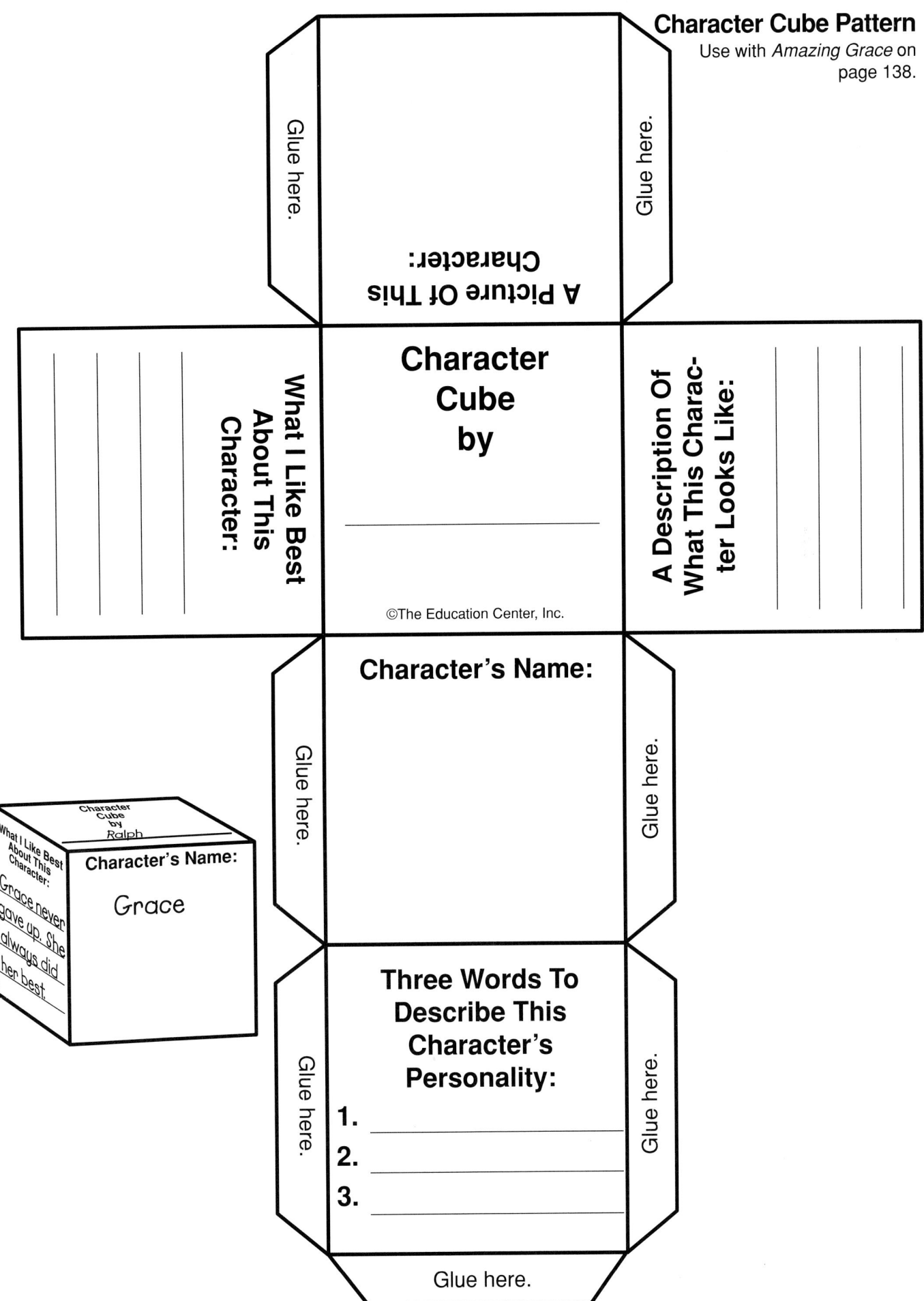

Character Cube Pattern
Use with *Amazing Grace* on page 138.

Valentine's Day Delights

These cross-curricular activities are bursting with love.

ideas by Amy Barsanti and Sharon Murphy

The Facts About Valentine's Day

Get to the heart of Valentine's Day with this literature-based activity. Valentine's Day began in Rome over 2,700 years ago. No one knows exactly how it started, but there are several stories behind it. One popular story traces Valentine's Day to Lupercus, the Roman god who watched over sheep and shepherds. The Romans held a holiday for him each year, asking him to keep them safe and drive the wolves away. As the years passed, the holiday changed. It became a holiday for Juno, the queen of the Roman gods. She ruled over marriage. It became a holiday of love. Many years later, Pope Gelasius tried to stop the holiday because he didn't want people to worship the Roman gods. People enjoyed the holiday too much, so he decided to make it a church holiday. He decided to honor a saint named Valentine. Pope Gelasius ended Juno's holiday and changed it to Saint Valentine's Day.

Brainstorm with your students a list of symbols, customs, facts, and questions about Valentine's Day. List their responses on chart paper. Then read aloud *Valentine's Day* by Joyce K. Kessel (Carolrhoda Books, Inc.; 1981). This easy-to-read book details the history of Valentine's Day with its customs and their origins. After sharing the book, reread the chart to the class. Call on students to place a heart sticker next to the items that were explained in the book. Add any additional facts from the book to the chart. As a follow-up to this activity, reproduce the fact-or-opinion sheet on page 150 for students to complete.

VALENTINE FACTS

- ♥ Valentine's Day is Feb. 14.
- ♥ People give valentine cards to their friends.
- ♥ red hearts
- ♥ People send flowers.
- ♥ holiday of love

Valentine's Day began over 2,700 years ago.
Cupid was the Roman god of love.

Love Makes The World Go Around

Your students will be speaking the language of love with this Valentine's Day bulletin board. To prepare, write these phrases that mean "I love you," on chart paper:

- French—Je t'aime.
- German—Ich liebe dich.
- Spanish—Te amo.
- Italian—Ti amo.
- Swedish—Jag älskar dig.
- Chinese—Wo ai ni.

Provide students with eight-inch, heart-shaped templates; scissors; and several old road maps. Have each student trace and cut out a heart from an old map. Next give each student a 1" x 8" strip of white construction paper. Instruct the student to write "I love you" in one of the languages on his strip. Have each student glue his strip across the heart as shown. When students have finished their messages of love, display the hearts on a bulletin board that has been covered with red paper. Add a white border and the caption "Love Makes The World Go Around."

Let Your Heart Do The Talking

Candy hearts make great story starters for a writing activity that's hot stuff! Cover your bulletin board with purple background paper. Add a white border and the title "Hearts Do The Talking" in white letters. Provide each student with a nine-inch square of pastel construction paper. Show students how to fold and cut the square into the shape of a heart (see the diagram). Pass out conversation hearts, and have students share some of the slogans and phrases with the class. Next have each student choose one candy heart and write its slogan on his paper heart. Have each student then write a story using that slogan as his story starter. Display the stories and paper hearts. Add smaller, paper conversation hearts to the board if desired.

Pinprick Valentines

These valentine cards for parents or loved ones will become keepsakes. Supply each student with a 9" x 12" piece of white construction paper. Instruct students to fold their papers in half and lightly draw or trace valentine designs on the front. Have each student place a piece of corrugated cardboard or a Styrofoam® meat tray behind the front cover. Using a pushpin, show students how to poke holes to outline their designs. When the pinprick designs are complete, have students erase any remaining pencil marks. Then have each student glue a 6" x 9" piece of bright-colored construction paper to the inside front cover. To complete the card, have each student write a message for a loved one on lined paper and glue it inside the card.

Broken Hearts

Have students mend broken hearts and present them as tokens of affection. Before beginning this activity, purchase a class supply of air-drying clay or make homemade craft dough. To make the craft dough, mix 1 1/2 cups of salt, 1 1/2 cups of flour, 3/4 cup of water, and a few drops of red food coloring or powdered tempera paint. Give each student a ball of clay. Have students roll the clay or dough on waxed paper to about 1/8-inch thickness. Provide heart-shaped cookie cutters (or stencils and plastic knives) to cut out the heart shapes. Demonstrate how to cut each heart into five or less large pieces. Allow these heart pieces to air-dry overnight; then flip them over and dry them for one additional night. When the clay is hard, have students assemble their heart puzzles and add valentine messages and designs with poster, puffy, or tempera paints. Let the paint dry. Encourage students to bring in old gift boxes from home and decorate them for their broken hearts. Have students give these hearts to loved ones for one-of-a-kind valentine presents.

Heartwarming Reading

The Valentine Bears
by Eve Bunting
(Clarion Books, 1985)

This delightful book tells the story of Mr. and Mrs. Bear and their efforts to show their love for each other on Valentine's Day. The problem is that they have never celebrated this holiday before because they hibernate in winter.

After sharing *The Valentine Bears,* ask students to recall the food gifts Mr. and Mrs. Bear gave each other for Valentine's Day, such as chocolate-covered ants and Crispy Critters. Challenge your students to think of other food gifts that these bears might have enjoyed. Record students' responses on the board. Then have each student write a recipe for one of these foods. Compile these recipes in a book titled " 'Beary' Good Valentine Recipes."

Roses Are Pink, Your Feet Really Stink
by Diane de Groat
(Morrow Junior Books, 1996)

This warm and funny story sends a subtle message about forgiveness and friendship. In this story Gilbert is having trouble deciding whether to send nice or mean valentine poems to the boy and girl who have been unkind to him.

After reading the story, have your students cut out red and pink hearts from construction paper. Challenge your students to write their own positive, rhyming valentine poems to other classmates. When students have finished writing, collect the poems to deliver on Valentine's Day.

Guess How Much I Love You
by Sam McBratney
(Candlewick Press, 1995)

The warm and touching illustrations in this book capture perfectly the bond between parent and child. Throughout the story, Little Nutbrown Hare tries to show how much he loves his father. In turn, the father demonstrates an even greater love for him.

After sharing this story, introduce the concept of *simile*. (A simile is a descriptive comparison using the word *like* or *as*.) Give students examples of similes from the story, such as "I love you as high as I can hop!" Then have students create their own similes of love for their parents. To create a three-part simile, give each student three 10-inch hearts cut from pink construction paper. Next have each student write the parts of his simile on the hearts as shown. Have each student assemble his three hearts with a brad. When students are finished writing, let them decorate their hearts with valentine designs and take them home to their parents.

Name _____ *Fact or opinion*

A Fact-Filled Valentine

Read the sentences below. Sort the facts from the opinions. Glue the facts inside the heart. Glue the opinions outside the heart.

©The Education Center, Inc. • *Big Book of Monthly Ideas* • TEC1487

Everyone should send at least one valentine.	Cupid was the Roman god of love.	All valentines should have lace on them.
Red is the best color for valentines.	Girls like valentines better than boys do.	Roses are often seen on valentine cards.
Snowdrops are flowers.	Valentine's Day is celebrated on Feb. 14.	No one knows who sent the first valentine.

Note To The Teacher: Use with "The Facts About Valentine's Day" on page 146.

By George, It's Honest Abe!

Salute two favorite American presidents with this collection of patriotic projects.
ideas by Susie Kapaun and Cynthia Holcomb

Cherry Tree Math

No lie—this fun, hands-on center is a "tree-mendous" way for students to brush up on their subtraction skills. Before setting up your center, make a cherry tree using 9" x 12" green construction paper for the treetop and brown paper for the trunk. Laminate the tree for durability. Place a pair of dice, a bottle of rubber cement, and a box of red-hot candies (cherries) at the center.

Allow two students at a time at the center. One student rolls both dice, announces the number to his partner, and places that amount of cherries on the tree. The student rolls again, using only one die this time. He announces the number and takes that amount of cherries from the tree. The partner writes down the problem and solves it. The student checks the answer and tells how many cherries were left on the tree. Help students affix their cherries to the tree with rubber cement. Continue in this manner until everyone has had a turn at the center. Display the finished tree as a decoration for Presidents' Day.

Presidential Punctuation

Put your patriotic students on punctuation patrol! Give each student a copy of page 157 and some red and blue star stickers. The students read each sentence on the reproducible and decide whether it is a statement or a question. If the sentence needs a period, students place a red star at the end of the sentence. A blue star is used if a question mark is needed. Add a gold star to the top of each paper with all sentences correctly punctuated.

Barry Slate

If I Were President

You'll get the Presidential Seal of Approval with these student-made books. Discuss with students the importance of the president's job. Have students research the accomplishments of Presidents Lincoln and Washington. Ask each student to think about what he would accomplish if he were in office, then create a booklet with this theme.

To prepare, cut a supply of handwriting paper into six-inch squares. Give each student five pieces of paper to complete this sentence starter: "If I were president, I would…." To make a cover, provide each student with a pattern of the presidential seal on page 158. Have each student cut a 6" x 12" piece of construction paper, fold it in half, and then cut out and glue the seal to the front. Then staple his pages between the covers. Provide time for everyone to share their booklets. Who knows—you may have some presidential hopefuls in your class!

The Original Thirteen

While George Washington was president, the last two of the original 13 colonies became states. Help your youngsters become more familiar with the "original 13" with this geography lesson. Have each student work with a partner to create a giant postcard highlighting one state.

To create these impressive postcards, give each pair of students a piece of tagboard with the name of one of the original 13 states written on it. Each pair finds its state on a map and draws a picture of it on the card. Tell them to research the state's capital, tree, bird, motto, and the date it became a state, and write the information on the card.

Once all of the cards have been completed, have the partners share their research with the class. Record the date of statehood on the board after each presentation. At the conclusion of the presentations, have students number papers from 1 to 13 and then list the states in the order that they became part of the union. Display the postcards in the hallway for an eye-catching review of our first 13 states.

Monumental Measurement

To see how the faces of Washington and Lincoln measure up, have students re-create the dimensions of the monumental faces on Mount Rushmore.

Show a picture of Mount Rushmore to your class and discuss its location and history. Tell students that if the 60-foot heads carved in the mountain had bodies, each man would have been 465 feet tall! Find an area large enough for students to measure the gigantic features using the following dimensions:

- Each man's face is 60 feet from the top of his head to his chin.
- Each nose is 20 feet in length.
- Each eye is 11 feet across.
- Each mouth is 18 feet wide.

After students have finished the activity, explain that the actual completion of Mount Rushmore took more than 14 years. That's longer than your students are old!

Handwritten Rules

For handwriting practice, George Washington would copy rules of behavior. Share some of the rules of Washington's time; then have students rephrase them. Finally have students copy the rules in their best handwriting.

- Turn not your back to others, especially in speaking.
- Jog not the table or desk on which another reads or writes.
- Lean not upon anyone.
- While you are talking, point not with your finger at whom you discourse, nor approach too near him to whom you talk, especially to his face.
- Be not curious to know the affairs of others, neither approach those that speak in private.
- It's unbecoming to stoop much to one's meat.
- Keep your fingers clean, and when foul wipe them on a corner of your table napkin.

Descriptive Leaders

Give your class descriptions of the two famous presidents as recorded in history. Washington was described as tall, with pale skin, reddish hair, and blue eyes. Lincoln was known for his 6-foot 4-inch height, thin frame, homely face, and coarse black hair.

Motivate your students to write a description of one of the presidents. Photocopy several presidential portraits from a resource book. Distribute one picture to each student and have him write a description of the president. Display the descriptions on a bulletin board. Post the presidential portraits at the top of the bulletin board so students can match the pictures to the descriptions.

Making "Cents"

Cash in on these presidential ideas by using coins that depict Presidents Lincoln and Washington.

Heads Or Tails?

This probability activity will turn some heads. Give each pair of students a penny. Have them toss the coin ten times each, tallying the number of heads and tails in their turns. Discuss the outcome of the tosses, and make a tally of class results on the board.

Give each pair another penny. Point out that one penny has two possible outcomes in a toss: heads or tails. Ask students how many combinations are possible with two coins. Have partners toss the coins ten times each and tally their results. Discuss the class findings and write them on the board.

Extend the lesson by adding a third coin and posting the results of the tosses. Discuss the class findings and compare them to the previous results. Students are using their heads—and President Lincoln's!

Memorable Mobiles

Honor the presidents with a coin display to hang from the ceiling. Each student needs a copy of the president patterns on page 159, a piece of 9" x 12" silver tooling foil (found at craft stores), and a dull pencil. Tell students to place the patterns on top of the foil and trace the outline, pressing hard to imprint the pattern designs onto the foil. (Place a layer of newspaper under the foil to protect the surface of the table.) To create a copper look for the penny, students color the foil with brown permanent marker using vertical strokes. Instruct students to cut out the circles and glue the two coins back-to-back with a 15-inch piece of string between them. Suspend the projects from the ceiling for a democratic decor.

A Pretty Penny

This science experiment is right on the money for demonstrating chemical reactions. Have students make old pennies look like new with water, salt, and vinegar. Distribute two tarnished pennies and a copy of page 160 to each student pair. Provide paper towels, a magnifying glass, and two plastic cups labeled "A" and "B" at each pairs work area. Before distributing, add 1/4 cup of vinegar to cup A and 1/4 cup of water to cup B.

Ask students to observe the liquids in the cups using their magnifying glasses and senses of sight, smell, and touch. Tell students to identify each liquid and record it on their sheet. Direct each student to drop a penny into each cup. After a few minutes have passed, ask students to examine the pennies for any changes. Have students record their observations.

Have each pair of students add two teaspoons of salt to each cup and watch for further changes. (The pennies in the salt and vinegar look cleaner. The pennies in the saltwater show no change.) Have students record their observations and discuss the changes that occurred. Explain that when pennies are exposed to air, the copper in the pennies oxidizes, turning them dark in color. The combination of the chloride in the salt and the acid in the vinegar breaks down the oxide film, making the pennies look new again.

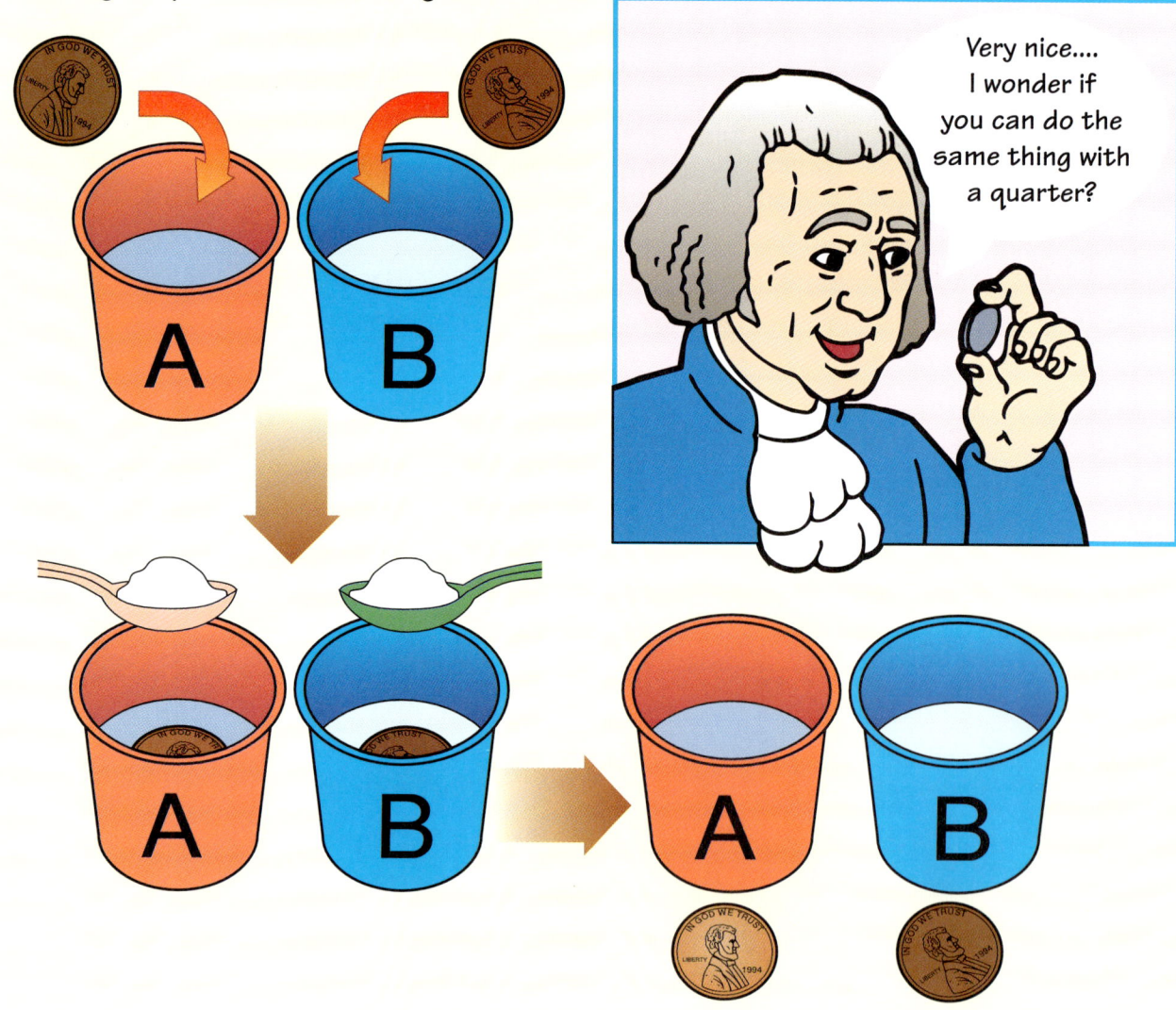

Name_____   *Ending punctuation*

Presidential Punctuation

Read each sentence and decide if it is a statement or question.
Stick a red star at the end of each statement.
Stick a blue star at the end of each question.

1. Abraham Lincoln was our sixteenth president

2. Was George Washington our first president

3. General Washington was a great leader

4. Why did Abraham Lincoln love to read books

5. George Washington's home was called Mt. Vernon

6. Was Abe Lincoln a lawyer

7. Did George Washington really chop down a cherry tree

8. President Lincoln freed the slaves

Bonus Box: Write four more sentences about these two presidents on the back of this sheet. Have a friend fill in the correct punctuation marks.

©The Education Center, Inc. • *Big Book of Monthly Ideas* • TEC1487

Note To The Teacher: Use with "Presidential Punctuation" on page 151.

Patterns
Use with "If I Were President" on page 152.

Patterns
Use with "Memorable Mobiles" on page 155.

Name _____   *Recording observations*

A Pretty Penny

1. What do you think is in each of the cups?

   Cup A _____

   Cup B _____

2. Which observation helped you decide what was in each cup?

   Cup A: Sight_____   Smell_____   Touch_____

   Cup B: Sight_____   Smell_____   Touch_____

3. What happened when you dropped the penny in:

   Cup A
   _____
   _____

   Cup B
   _____
   _____

4. What happened to the penny when you added salt to:

   Cup A
   _____
   _____

   Cup B
   _____
   _____

Bonus Box: On the back of this page, draw and color what each of your pennies looked like before and after the experiment.

©The Education Center, Inc. • *Big Book of Monthly Ideas* • TEC1487

Note To The Teacher: Use with "A Pretty Penny" on page 156.

Look Out For Leprechauns!

Across-the-curriculum activities for St. Patrick's Day

A Leprechaun Visit

Faith and b'gorra! Leprechauns at school? A mysterious visit from one of the little people will put your students in the mood for the St. Patrick's Day holiday. Begin by purchasing a pair of doll shoes at a craft store or bringing in an old pair of children's shoes. Spray-paint the shoes green and sprinkle gold glitter on the wet paint. When the shoes are dry, leave them in the classroom one afternoon, along with some other signs of a visit from a mischievous leprechaun, such as green glitter sprinkled about, a slip of green fabric caught in a window, green paint footprints on top of desks or along the chalkboard, shamrock cutouts dropped on the floor, and a general messing-up of the room (chairs overturned or items out of place). Write a note in green chalk on the board.

Of course, your surprised students will want to return the leprechaun shoes. Help students write a note back to the leprechaun and choose a prominent place to display the shoes. Have older students write individual notes for some creative writing practices. After school, remove the shoes and leave a trail of green glitter from a windowsill to a closet. Inside the closet, leave a black pot filled with gold, foil-wrapped candy coins, and another note from the leprechaun:

Thanks, boys and girls! I got the shoes. Here's a little treat to say thanks for helping me!
Your friend,
Liam Leprechaun

Hi, boys and girls!
I had a wonderful, wee time dancing and playing in your classroom last night! But I misplaced my shoes. If you find them, could you leave them for me? I'll be back to get them tonight!

Your friend,
Liam Leprechaun

Green Riddles

Duplicate the shamrock pattern on page 173 for each student to cut out. Then have students brainstorm a list of green objects. Have each student make up a riddle about something green, then write the riddle on one side of the shamrock cutout and the answer on the opposite side. Let students exchange shamrocks and try to answer each other's riddles.

It grows in your yard. You have to mow it. What is it?

Creative Writing At The End Of The Rainbow

Legend has it that if you catch a leprechaun, stare him straight in the eye, and ask him for his pot of gold, he must give it to you. To encourage creative writing with a twist, enlarge, color, and cut out the leprechaun on page 170. Ask students to imagine that they have caught the leprechaun with his pot of treasure. But—surprise!—the pot is not filled with gold. What might they find instead?

Provide the pot pattern on page 169 for each student. Have the student trace and cut around his pot on black paper. Then, on a piece of 6" x 6" lined paper, have him write and illustrate what kind of treasure he'd like to find. Mount the finished stories on the pot cutouts and display them with the leprechaun cutout on a bulletin board titled "Leprechaun Treasures."

Do You Believe In Leprechauns?

Have your students conduct a survey to see how your school population feels about leprechauns. Divide your class into groups of four and have students assign roles in each group: communicator, counter, recorder, and reporter. Have each group visit another classroom, taking along a copy of the survey form on page 174. The *communicator* explains the visit and asks the students if they believe in leprechauns. The *counter* counts hands raised for the responses "yes," "no," and "maybe." The *recorder* fills out the sheet, and the *reporter* reads the group's findings upon return. Tally the responses by grade or for your whole school on a chart or graph in your classroom. You'll want to report your findings during the morning announcements on St. Patrick's Day.

Pot O' Gold Math

A leprechaun's pot of gold will help your students practice math skills with money. Fill a small black bucket with real coins. Depending on your students' level, try one of these games:

—Have two students take turns drawing out one coin each; the highest value wins the round.

—Have two students take turns drawing out two or three coins each; the students add the coin values and the highest value wins the round.

—Cover the top of the bucket with a cloth. Have students take turns reaching under the cloth and attempting to draw out a certain coin by feeling its size.

Lucky Charms® Graphing

Your students will eat up this math activity! Purchase a box of Lucky Charms cereal and fill a zippered plastic bag half-full for each student. Have each student sort out the marshmallow shapes from the cereal pieces in his bag and group them by type. Give each student a copy of page 171. Have students graph the results of their sorting and answer the math questions at the bottom of the page. Students may nibble on the cereal pieces as they work and eat the marshmallow shapes when they finish.

Leprechaun Finders

Your students will have fun hunting for leprechauns and writing directions for using these special leprechaun finders. Reproduce two copies of the pattern on page 172 on tagboard for each student to color and cut out. Provide each student with a circle of green plastic wrap. Have him assemble the leprechaun finder by gluing the two cutouts together with the plastic wrap between them to form a magnifying glass look-alike. Have him decorate the frame of the finder with shamrock-shaped stickers. Then have each student write out directions on an index card on how to use the finder to hunt for leprechauns. Have each student attach the directions to his finder by punching a hole in the handle and another in the card, then tying the card on with a length of string. Students may want to present the finders as gifts to younger buddies or siblings. Allow volunteers to read their directions to the entire class.

Crafty Leprechauns

Have students create these lively leprechauns from simple craft materials. Provide each student with a paper plate and have him glue on two wiggle eyes. Students can add facial features, hats, and pipes to their leprechaun faces using crayons or construction-paper scraps. Have each student glue on several strips of green crepe paper for a beard to finish the leprechaun.

Potato-Print Project

For potato fun, try potato-printing a souvenir of St. Patrick's Day! Carve shamrock shapes into several potatoes and let students print the shapes with green tempera paint onto 1 1/2" x 5" strips of white poster board to make festive bookmarks. As a variation, have students potato-print on folded white drawing paper to create greeting cards for St. Patrick's Day.

St. Patrick's Day Shenanigans
Ideas for a classroom celebration

Irish I.D.
Since everyone is allowed to be a little Irish on St. Patrick's Day, start your celebration by duplicating the Irish nametags on page 172 for students to decorate and cut out. Label each nametag with an Irish version of a child's name by adding "O" or "Mac" to each surname, such as "Jenny O'Lewis" or "Eduardo MacPerez."

Festive Fare
Let students assist you in preparing a snack of Leprechaun Pies and Pot O' Green Punch. You might also provide shamrock-shaped gelatin snacks or sugar cookies with green icing.

Leprechaun Pie
Vanilla wafer cookie
Pistachio pudding
Whipped topping, tinted with green food coloring
Gold-foil-wrapped candy coin

Have each child place the vanilla wafer in the bottom of a paper cupcake liner. He adds a dollop of pistachio pudding and a dollop of green whipped topping. Stick the candy coin into the whipped cream to finish the pie.

Pot O' Green Punch
Clear soda, such as 7-Up®
Green food coloring
Lime sherbet

Pour one or two, two-liter bottles of clear soda into a large bowl and add just a few drops of green food coloring. Spoon in one quart of lime sherbet. Serve in individual cups.

Leprechaun Games
Try this relay race to add new meaning to the phrase, "the wearin' o' the green"! Gather a collection of green clothing—green hat, socks, shoes, scarf, mittens, etc. Divide the class into two teams. Have each team line up in front of a pile of clothing. At the starting signal, the first team member puts on all the green clothes and turns to face the second team member, who must remove all of the green clothing and put it on herself. Play continues until the last team member has removed all the green clothing and placed it back in a pile at the front of the line.

How about a Shamrock Hunt? To prepare, cut out a large number of shamrock shapes from green construction paper and hide them all around the classroom. Distribute paper cups to the children and let them hunt for shamrocks as you play a recording of Irish music. Set a time limit and award a prize to the student who finds the largest number of shamrocks. You might also hide a four-leaf clover cutout redeemable for a special prize.

Quiet things down with a word game. Duplicate a pencil topper pattern on page 173 for each student to cut out and slip onto her pencil for good luck. Then have students make as many words as possible from the letters in the word *leprechaun*.

St. Patrick's Day Science

Spring into March science with Irish potatoes.

Super Spuds

Let your budding scientists grow potatoes for St. Patrick's Day. Supply each student with a small potato, four toothpicks, and a plastic cup large enough to hold the potato. Begin by having students observe their potatoes, calling attention to the buds (eyes) that may turn into sprouts. Have students count the number of eyes on their potatoes, then estimate how many they think might sprout. Place the four toothpicks around the middle of the potato as shown, and place the potato in the cup (the end with the most eyes facing upward). Place the cups near a sunny window and fill with water to cover the bottom halves of the potatoes. Assign a student to check the water levels in the cups each day and add water if necessary. Take a few minutes every day to observe the potatoes and have students use copies of the chart on page 174 to record any growth. Challenge older students to measure the daily growth in inches or centimeters, then fill in their charts.

Sniff A Slice

Have some potato fun on St. Patrick's Day with the senses of taste and smell. Cut several slices of raw potato and raw apple. Place the slices in ice water to stay fresh. Ask your students if they think smelling or tasting is more important when they are eating food. Choose a volunteer to participate in a small experiment to help answer that question. Have the student close his eyes, and then place a slice of apple under his nose close enough to smell the aroma. Have him open his mouth and take a small bite of a potato slice while smelling the apple. With his eyes still closed, have him tell you what he just tasted. Many students will tell you that they have eaten a bite of apple. Allow several children to try the experiment, sometimes giving a bite of apple and sometimes giving a bite of potato. Record the results of each volunteer; then have the students make a conclusion about tasting and smelling.

The Great Potato Race

Use potatoes to give your students practice in making hypotheses. Select two potatoes of different sizes such as a baking potato and a new (red) potato. Set up a ramp that will allow the potatoes to roll down without bumping into each other or fall off the edges. Show both potatoes to your students and ask them to decide which potato they think will reach the bottom of the ramp first. Remind them to think about the size, weight, and shape of the potatoes before making a hypothesis; then record the number of students for each potato on the board. Before the race, have students think about the parts of the experiment that must remain constant: both potatoes use the same ramp and both potatoes are let go at the same time. Choose students to release the potatoes at a given signal. Conduct the experiment at least ten times. Students record the results on copies of the graph below and then discuss the findings.

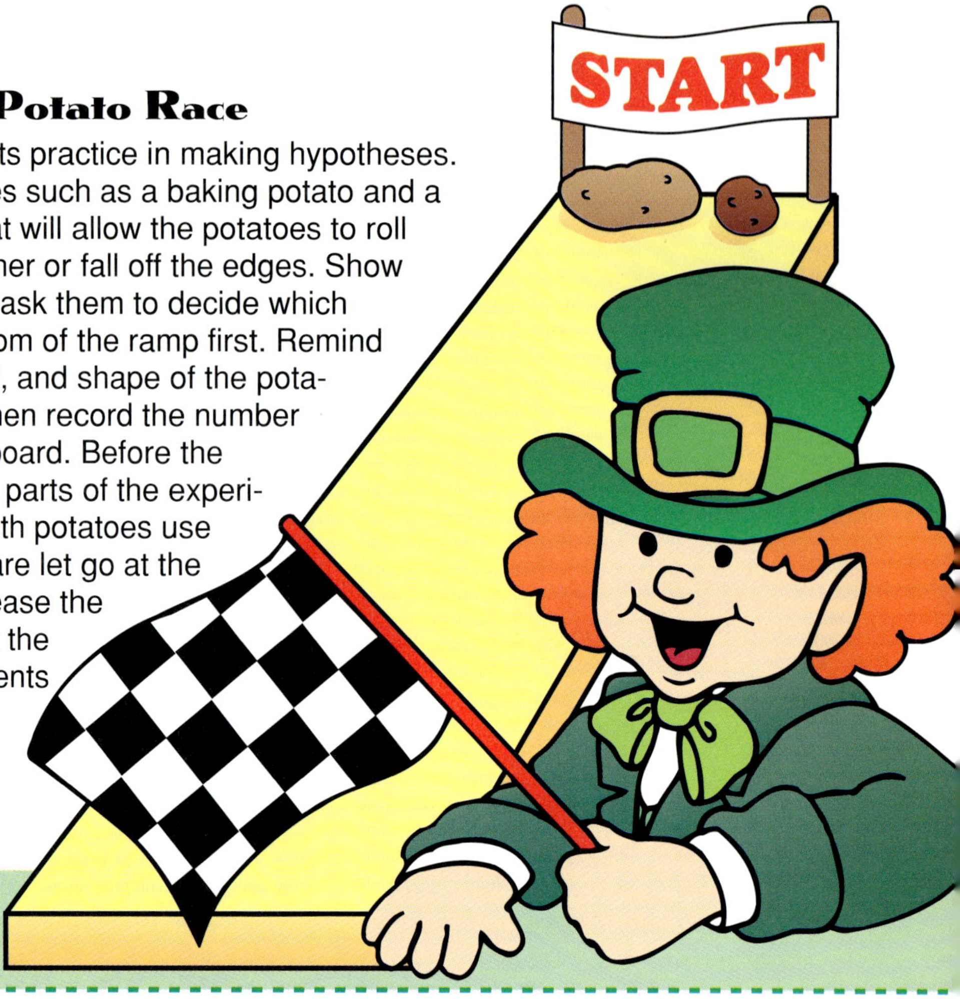

Use with "The Great Potato Race" above.

Name _____
Hypothesis: _____

Potato #1 _____ (type)
Potato #2 _____ (type)

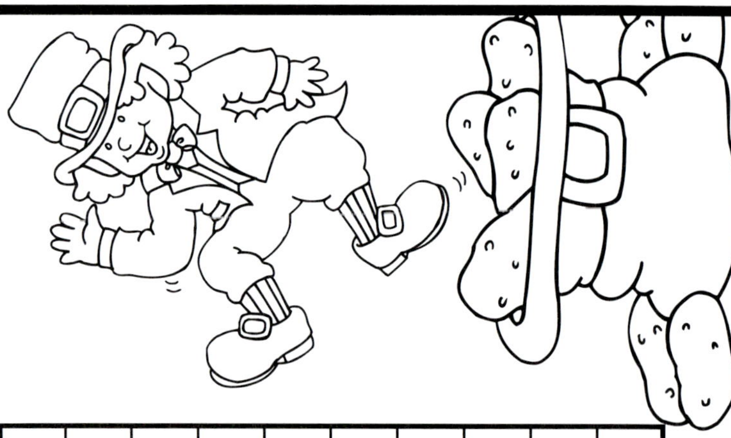

# of students

Make a graph to record the results.

Pattern
Use with "Creative Writing At The End Of The Rainbow" on page 163.

Pattern
Use with "Creative Writing At The End Of The Rainbow" on page 163.

Name _____   Creating a graph

A Charming Graph

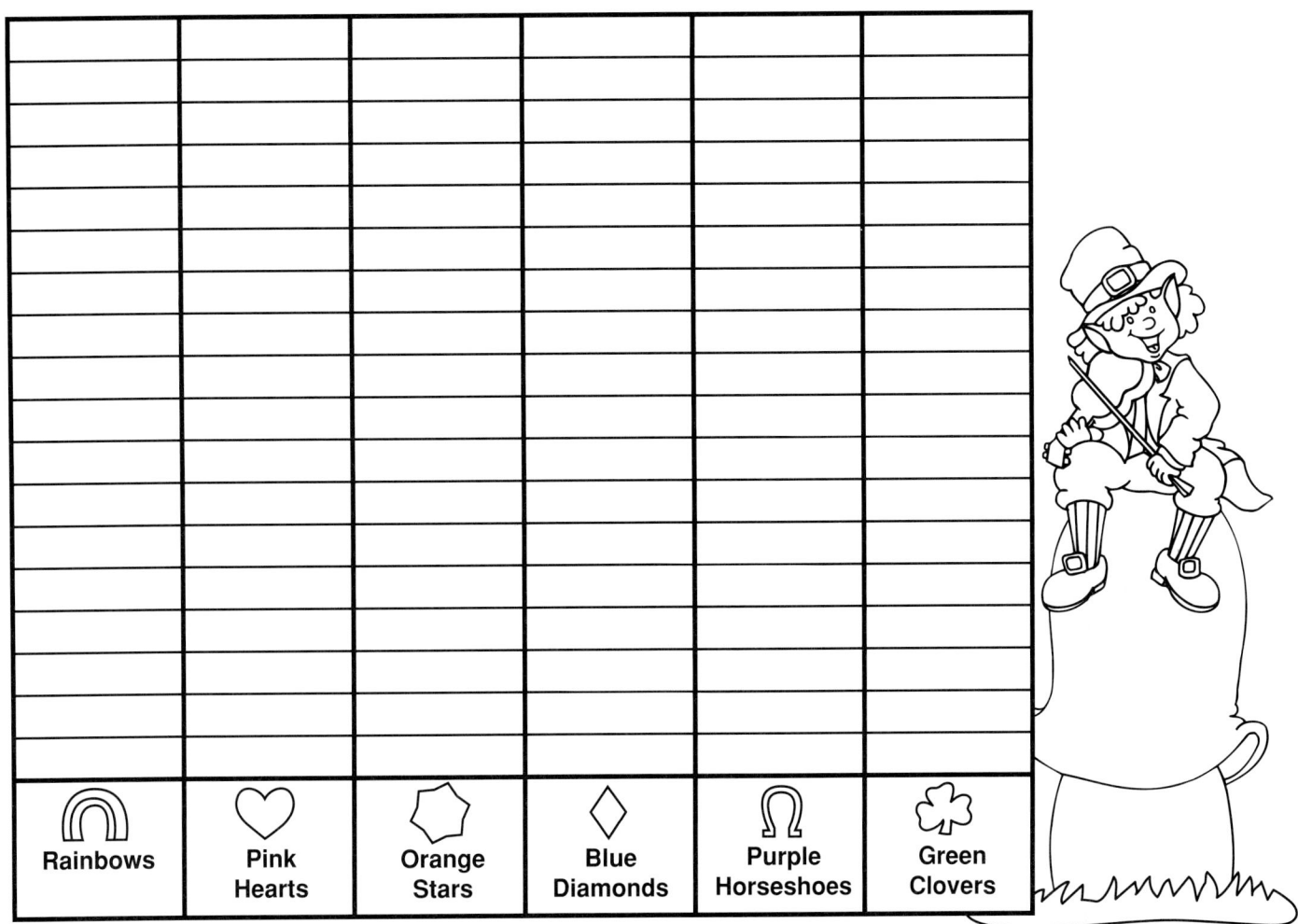

1. Which shape(s) do you have the most of? _____

2. Which shape(s) do you have the least of? _____

3. Add together your rainbows and orange stars. _____

4. Add together your blue diamonds and purple horseshoes. _____

5. Do you have more green clovers or pink hearts? _____

6. Subtract the smallest total from the largest. _____

7. Do you have the same number of any shapes?   yes   no

    If so, which ones? _____

©The Education Center, Inc. • Big Book of Monthly Ideas • TEC1487

Note To The Teacher: Use this reproducible with "Lucky Charms® Graphing" on page 164.

Pattern
Use with "Leprechaun Finders" on page 165.

Nametag Patterns
Use with "Irish I.D." on page 166.

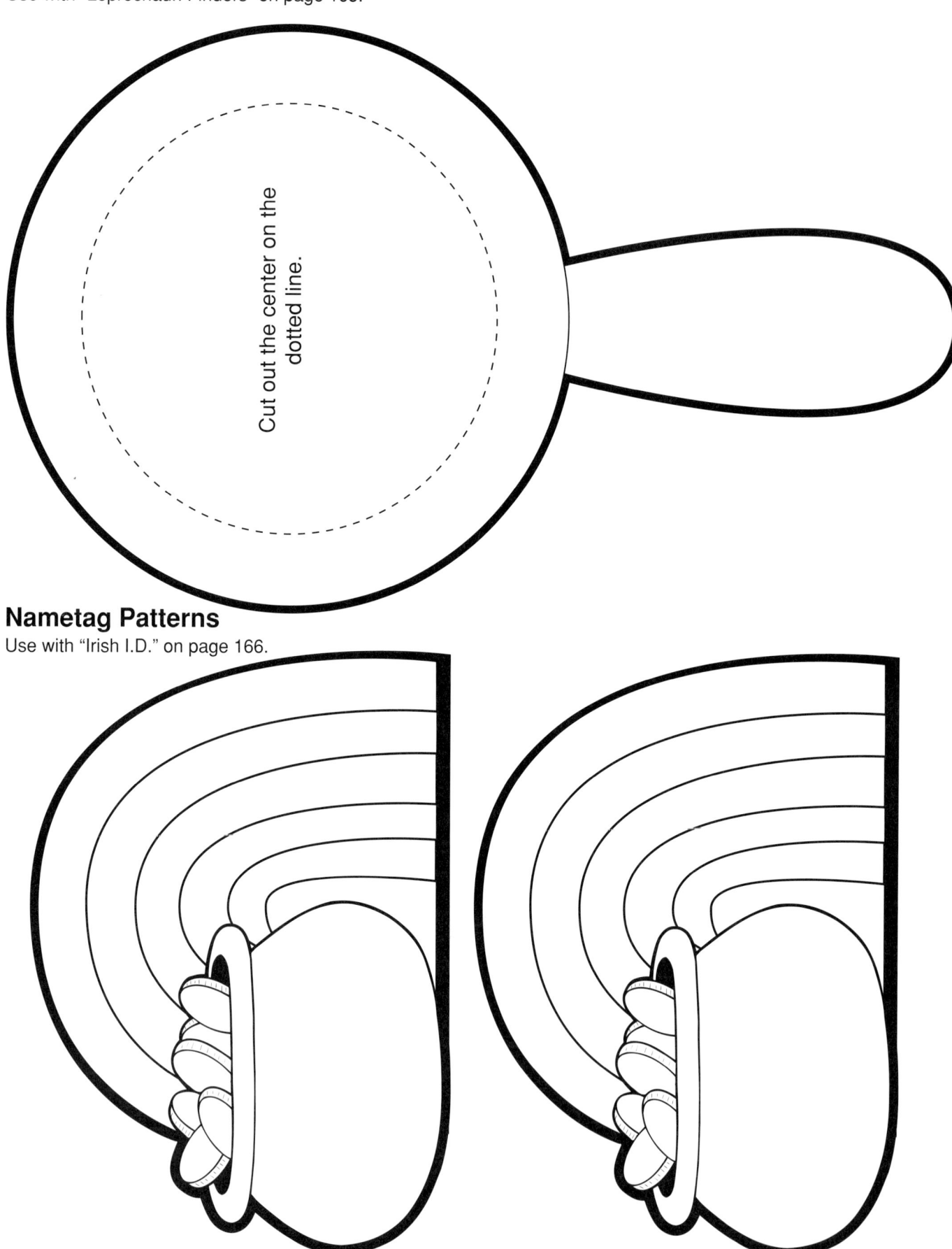

Pattern
Use with "Green Riddles" on page 163.

Pencil Toppers
Use with "Leprechaun Games" on page 166.

Cut on dotted lines.

Cut on dotted lines.

Potato Growth Chart
Use with "Super Spuds" on page 167.

Name _____

How many eyes did you find on your potato? _____

How many eyes do you think will sprout? _____

Draw a picture or record a measurement in each box.

Daily Growth

	Monday	Tuesday	Wednesday	Thursday	Friday
Week 1					
Week 2					
Week 3					
Week 4					

©The Education Center, Inc. • Big Book of Monthly Ideas • TEC1487

Survey Form
Use with "Do You Believe In Leprechauns?" on page 164.

LEPRECHAUN SURVEY

Group members: _____

Date of survey: _____
Class surveyed: _____
Grade: _____

Responses
Yes _____
No _____
Maybe _____

©The Education Center, Inc.

Up, Up, And Away!

Explore March weather with these thematic ideas on kites and wind.

What Is The Wind?

Have students list what they already know and what they'd like to find out about the wind. Make a class chart outlining the information and questions to use as a reference throughout your unit. Then read *Feel The Wind* by Arthur Dorros (Trophy, 1990) to introduce your students to some basic concepts about wind. (You can review the following facts at the conclusion of the unit by having students complete the " 'What Is The Wind?' Booklet" idea on page 176.)

—Wind is moving air.
—The air moves when hot air and cold air change places. A good example is a sea breeze, caused by the warmer air over the land rising and the cooler air over the water moving in to take its place.
—Winds can be gentle or strong. Very strong winds can occur during thunderstorms, tornadoes, and hurricanes.
—People can use the wind's power to move objects (like kites and sailboats) and to provide power (as with a windmill).
—Winds are named according to the direction they come from (for example, a west wind blows from the west). Weather vanes help people figure out the direction of the wind.
—Wind affects the weather by blowing storms and clouds from one place to another.
—Wind affects the earth by shaping rocks, trees, and beaches; eroding soil; and moving seeds from place to place.

The Weatherman Says...

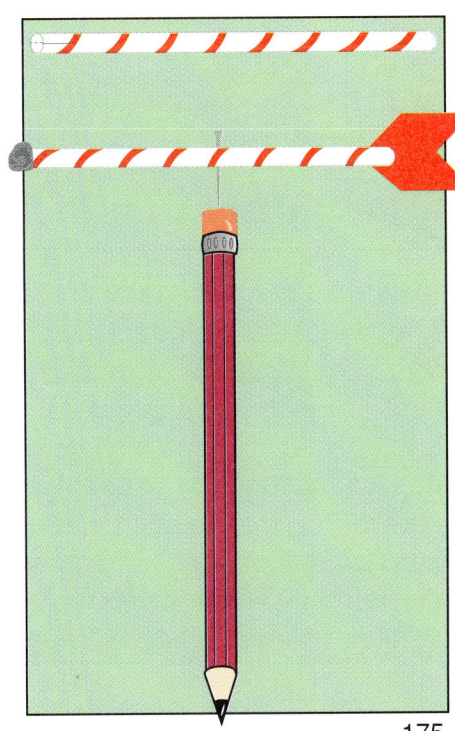

A *meteorologist* uses several different tools to help forecast the weather. To investigate weather instruments, divide your class into groups. Assign each group a weather instrument to research (such as *anemometer, wind direction indicator, barometer, rain gauge,* or *thermometer*), and then have students share their report information with the rest of the class. You may want to invite the meteorologist from your local TV station to make a presentation about his job and the instruments he uses. Then make simple weather vanes following these directions:

—Have each child use scissors to cut a "tail" from tagboard and make two small slits in one end of a straw as shown. Slip the tail into the slits.
—Place a small bit of clay on the other end of the straw.
—Find the balancing point on the straw; then poke a straight pin through it and into the top of a pencil eraser.
—To use the weather vane, go outside and determine north, south, east, and west by using a compass. Read the weather vane by looking at the direction in which the clay end of the straw is pointing—that is the direction from which the wind is blowing.

Hurricane

For a look at stormy weather, read the book *Hurricane* by David Wiesner (Houghton Mifflin Co., 1992). Ask students if they know an adult who has been through a tornado or hurricane. If possible, arrange for the person to visit your class to tell about her experiences. Guide students in formulating a list of questions for your visitor beforehand, such as:

—How much notice did you have that the storm was coming?
—What did you do to prepare?
—What did the storm sound like?
—Did the storm damage your house? Your car? How?

When The Wind Blows...

Power up some pinwheels to further illustrate the wind's ability to move things. Duplicate the pinwheel pattern on page 179 for each student. Have each child color her pinwheel and then cut it out and fold the marked corners to the center. Have her secure the overlapping corners in the center with a pushpin and then push the pin into the side of a pencil eraser. Hold the pinwheels by their pencil handles and take them outside to check out air movement firsthand! If desired, stick the tip of each pencil into the ground outside your classroom or building to create a "pinwheel garden." Each time you leave or return to your classroom or main building, students can check the strength of the wind. And the pinwheels will present a colorful greeting to visitors!

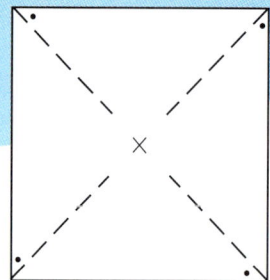 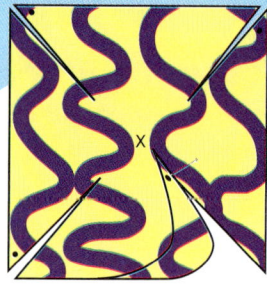

"What Is The Wind?" Booklet

To review important facts about wind, duplicate the student booklet and patterns on pages 180–184 for each student. To create a cover for the booklet, provide each child with a half-sheet of light blue construction paper. Have her place a small blob of watered-down white tempera paint on the paper and blow through a straw to move the paint around for a "picture" of the wind. If desired, glue on small bits of leaves for a windblown effect. Staple the booklet together, using another half-sheet of construction paper for a back cover.

A Whale Of A Tail

Bring in a kite to get this language arts activity off the ground! Mount the kite on a bulletin board and add a long string tail across the board. As a reading incentive, add a bow to the kite tail for each book read by your students. Duplicate a few copies of the bow pattern on page 180 for each child. As a student reads a book, he fills in the blanks on the bow with the appropriate information about the story, then adds it to the kite tail. Your kite tail may stretch out the door and down the hallway as reading takes off in your classroom!

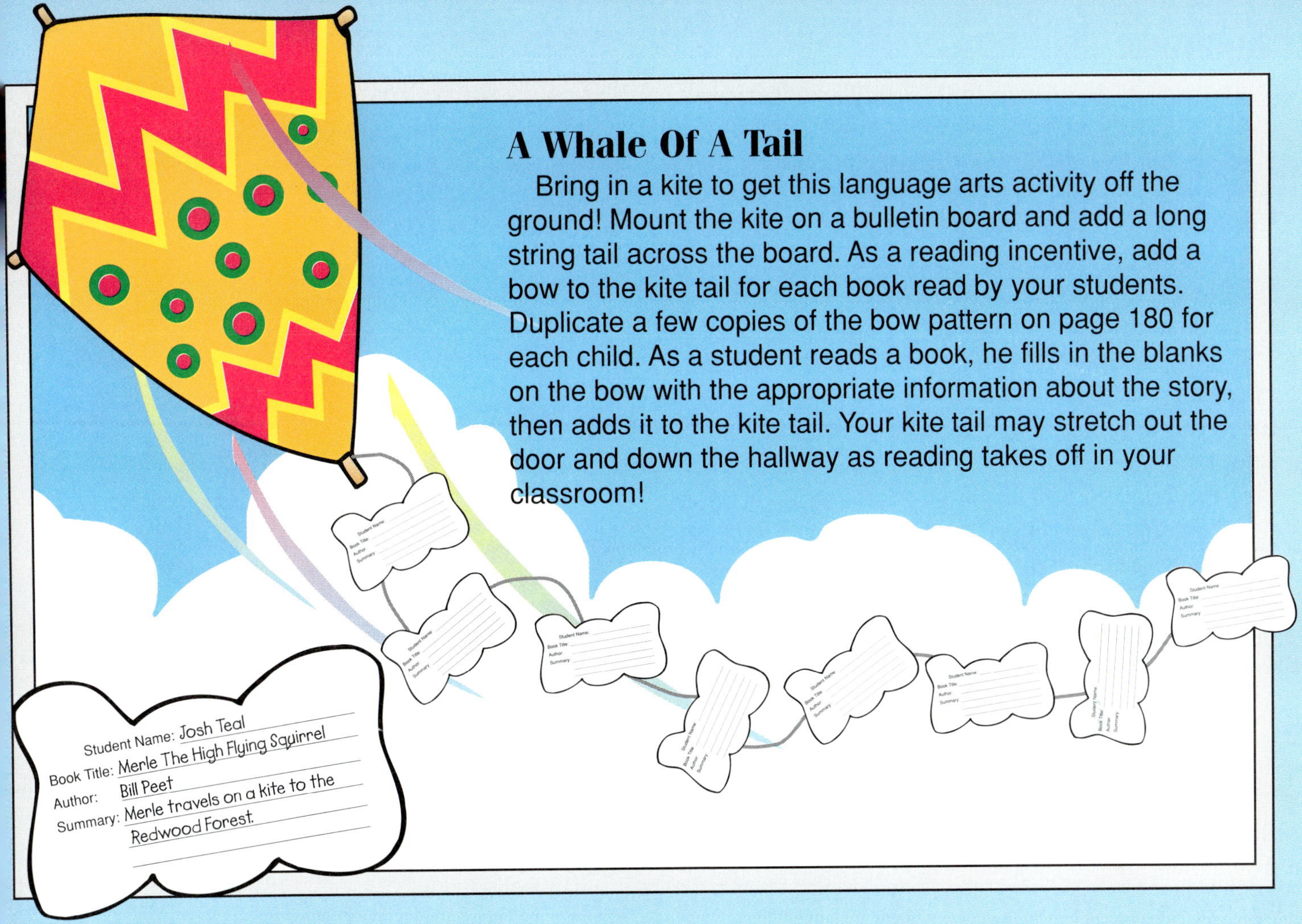

Windy Poetry

Teach students the following poem:
> I can't see you, Wind,
> But I know you are there—
> Blowing the trees,
> And blowing my hair.
> Snatching up leaves,
> And whistling at night—
> You might make me cold,
> But you're good for a kite!

Let students write their own poems about the wind. Mount the poems on kite-shaped construction paper. Construct a bulletin-board display by having students create a cloudy sky on light blue background paper, using various art media. Glue on cotton balls or foam packing pieces, or sponge-paint with white tempera. Mount the poems on the kite-shaped papers. Attach a colorful yarn string to each kite to complete the display.

Japanese Fish Kites

Teach your students about the Japanese tradition of families flying kites in the shape of fish (carp kites) on Children's Day (which occurs in May). The kites are flown to represent the sons in the family, with the biggest kite for the oldest son measuring up to 15 feet long!

Let students create their own fish kites. For each child, fold a sheet of tissue paper in half. Cut a fish shape from both thicknesses of tissue. Have each student draw on scales, a gill, and a face with markers. Cut a 3" x 12" strip of construction paper. Roll the strip into a cylinder and staple. Glue the fish together on the sides, but not at the head or tail. Glue the head to each side of the construction-paper cylinder, forming a mouth opening. Cut slits in the tail. Punch a hole on opposite sides of the construction-paper cylinder and tie on a loop of string. Suspend the kites from the ceiling for a beautiful classroom display.

Kite-Tail Match-Ups

Create a "High-Flying Facts" file folder game to help students practice math facts for addition, subtraction, or multiplication. Use markers to decorate and label the outside of a file folder. Cut several kite shapes from colored construction paper and glue them along the inside top edge of the open file folder. Draw strings reaching from the bottoms of the kites to near the bottom edge of the folder as shown. Mask out the copy and lines from the bow pattern on page 180; then reduce the pattern and duplicate it several times on colored construction paper. Program each bow with a math fact and each kite with a corresponding answer. (You may want one bow per kite or multiple facts for each answer.) Store the bows in an envelope clipped to the folder. To play, a student matches each bow to the correct kite's string. If desired, provide an answer key on the back of the file folder.

Pinwheel Pattern
Use with "When The Wind Blows…" on page 176.

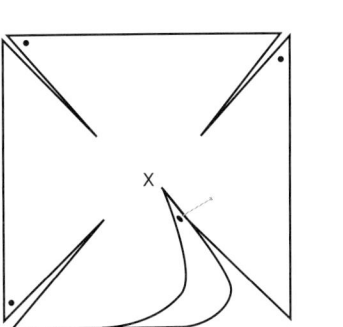

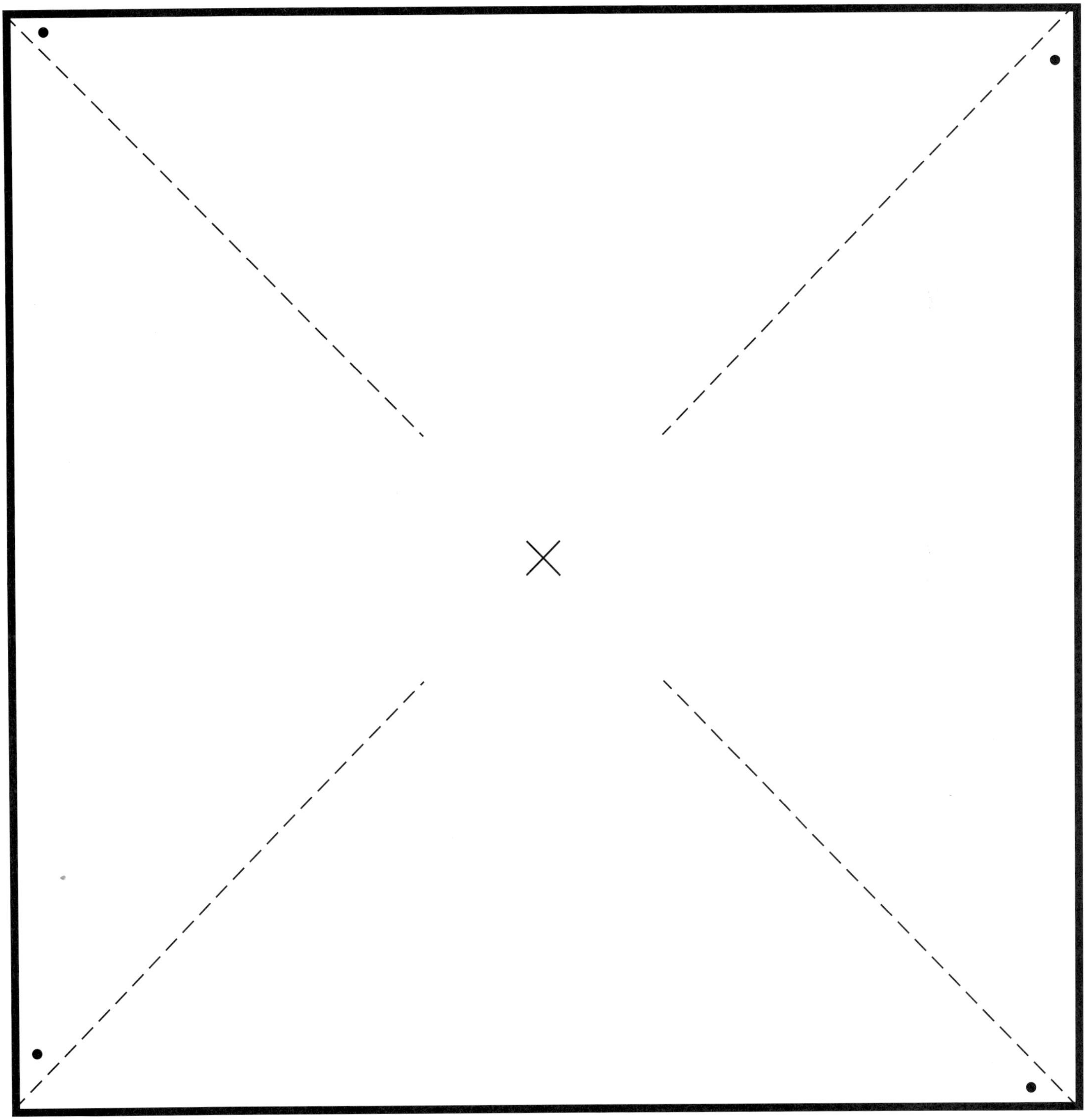

Kite Bow Pattern
Use with "A Whale Of A Tail" on page 177 and "Kite-Tail Match-Ups" on page 178.

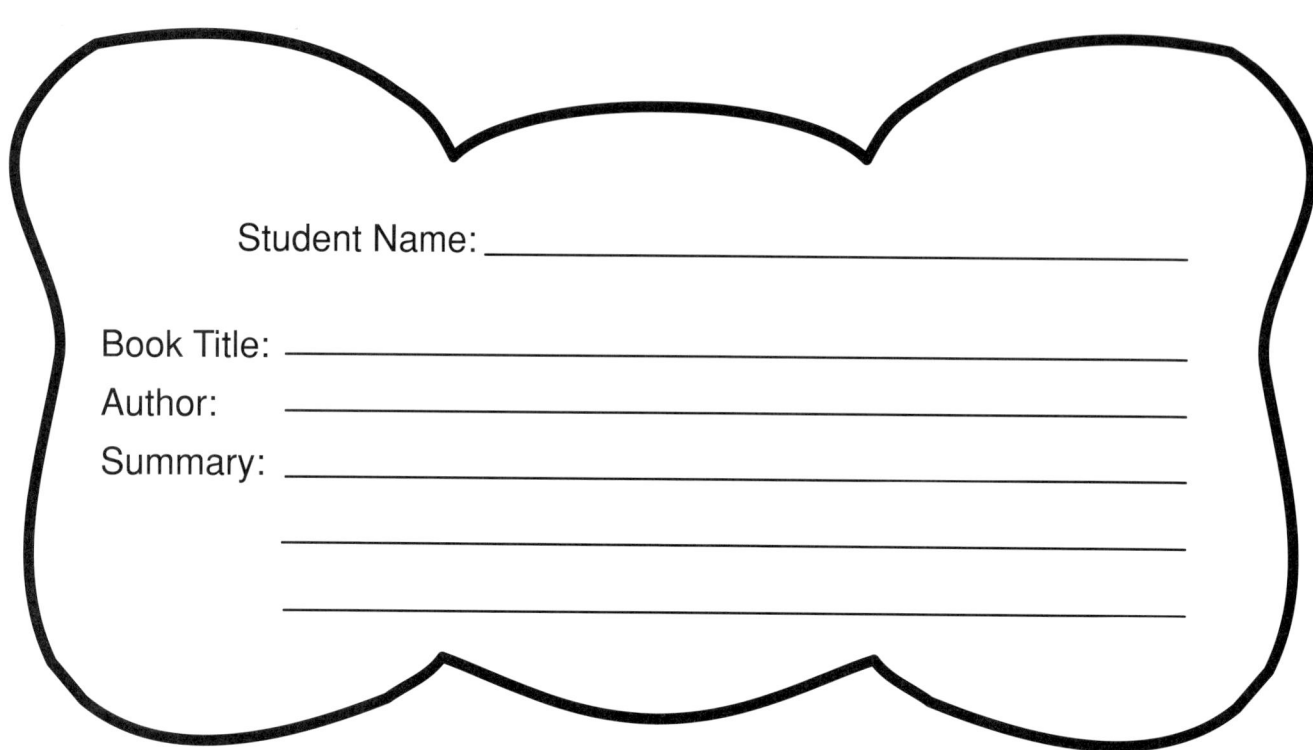

Student Name: _____

Book Title: _____
Author: _____
Summary: _____
_____
_____
_____

Booklet Patterns
Use with "What Is The Wind?" booklet on pages 180–184.
(See page 176 for instructions on assembling the booklet.)

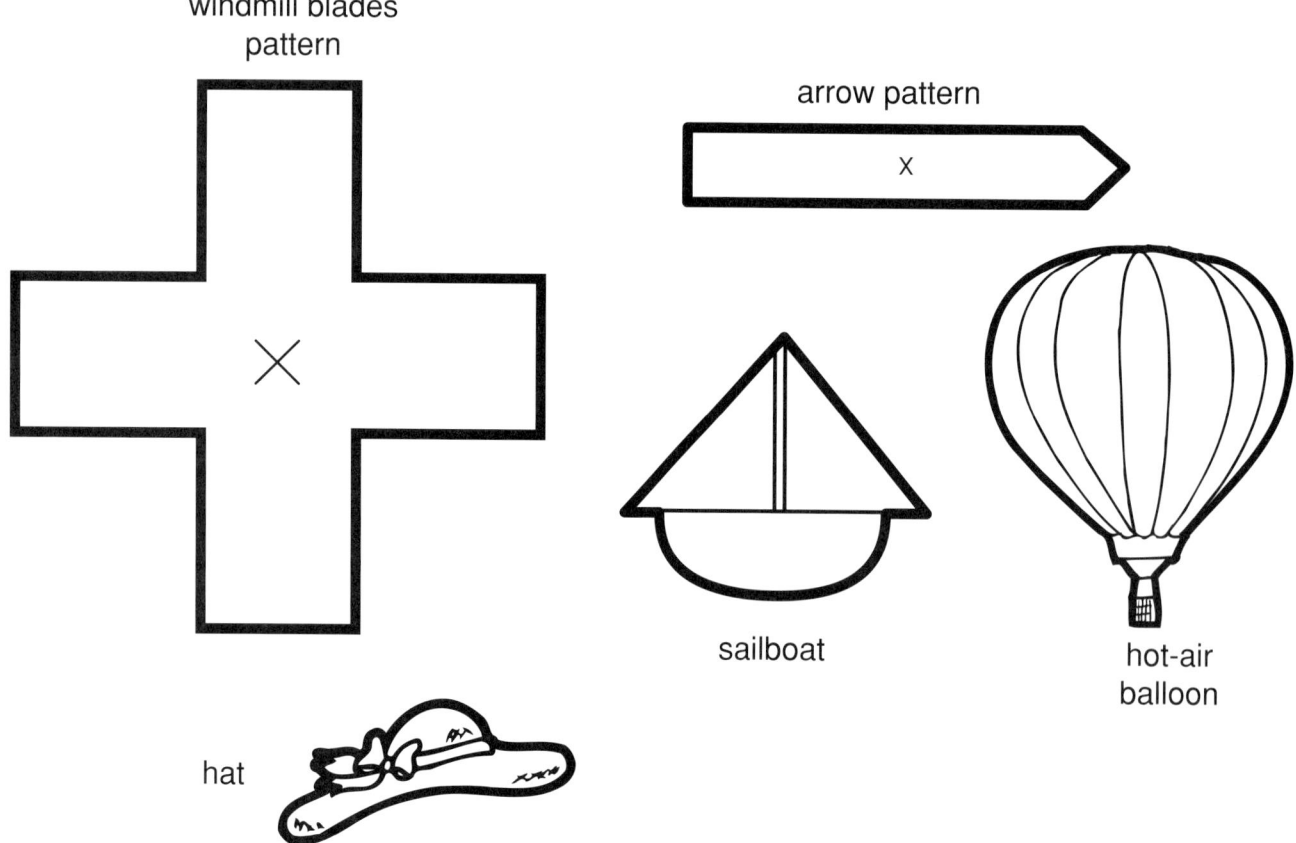

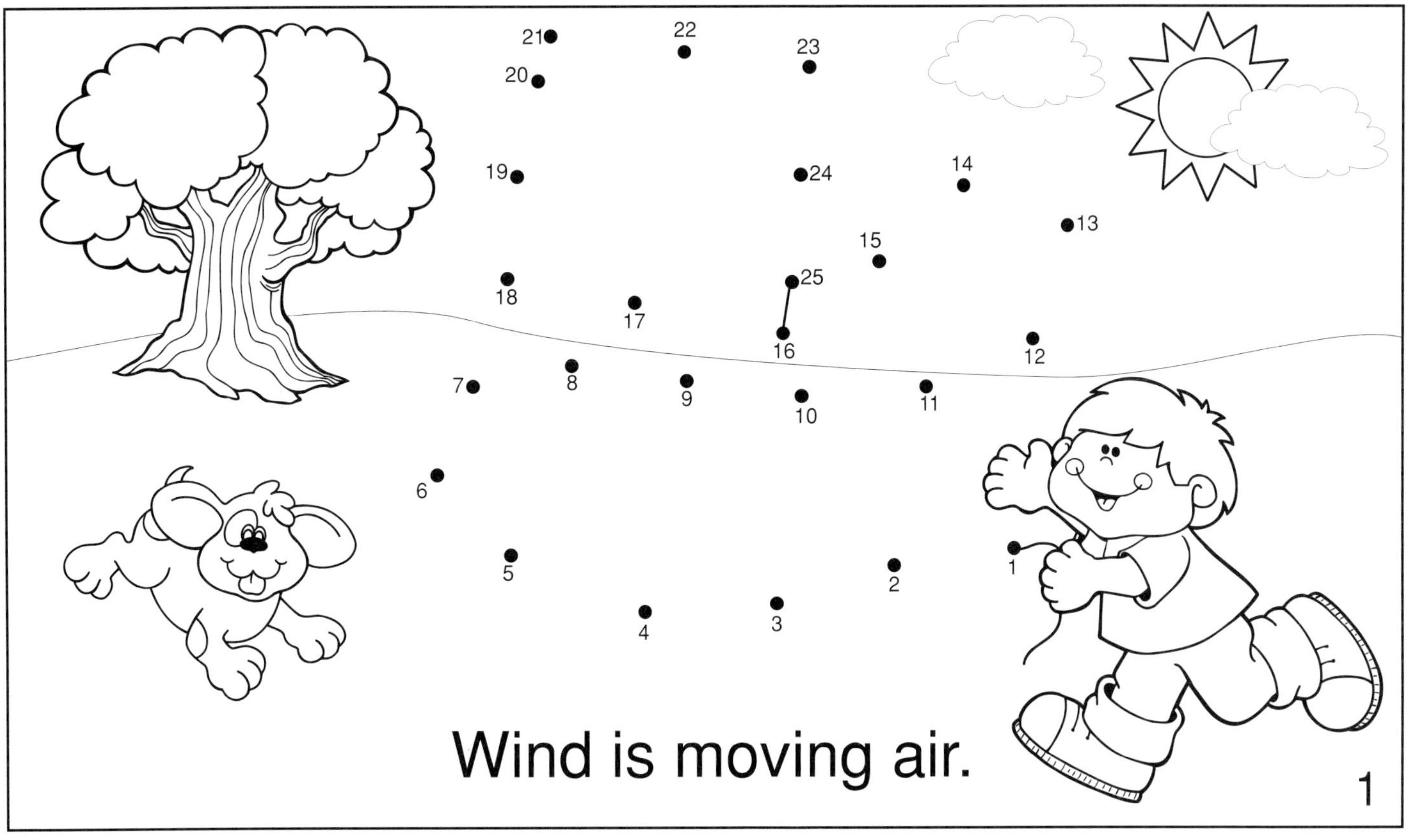

Wind is moving air.

1

Wind moves things.

2

Instructions:
Page 1: Connect the dots.
Page 2: Color and cut out the sailboat, hat, and balloon patterns on page 180. Glue them on the picture.

Wind provides power.

3

Winds can be gentle...

4

Instructions:
Page 3: Cut out the windmill blades on page 180. Attach at the X using a brad.
Page 4: Color the scene.

...or dangerous.

5

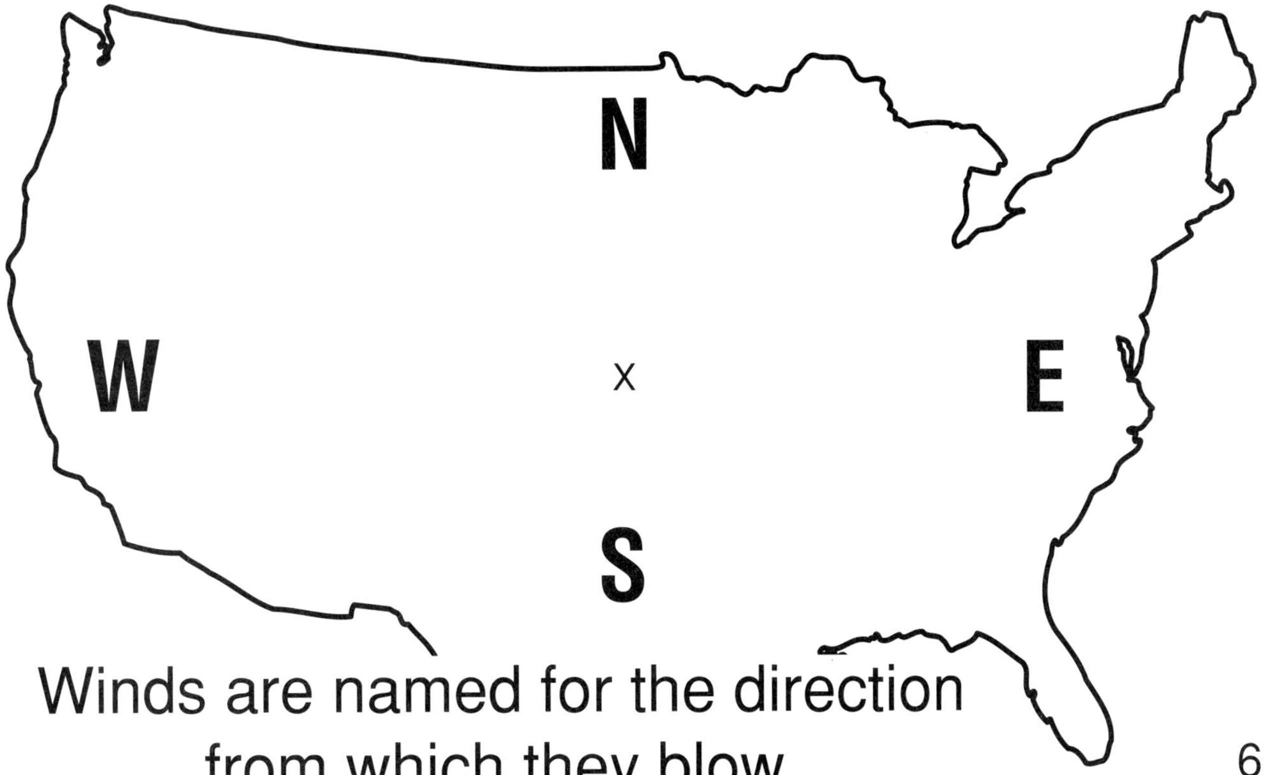

Winds are named for the direction from which they blow.

6

Instructions:
Page 5: Draw a tornado in the scene.
Page 6: Cut out the arrow on page 180. Attach at the X using a brad.

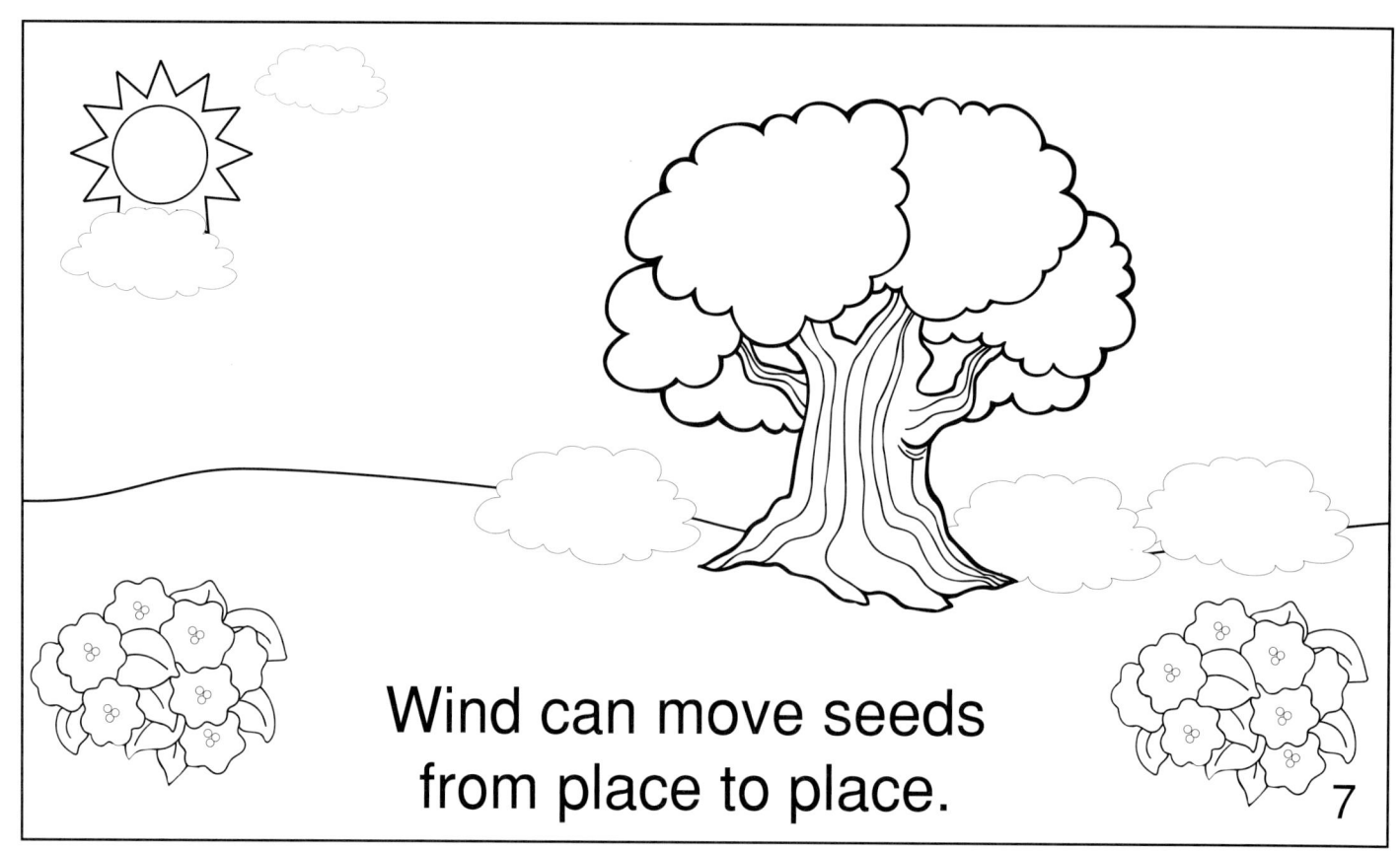

Wind can move seeds from place to place.

7

My favorite thing about the wind is

_____.

8

©The Education Center, Inc.

Instructions:
Page 7: Glue on real seeds (such as marigold or dandelion seeds).
Page 8: Complete the sentence and draw an illustration to match.

Raindrops Are JUST DUCKY!

Chase away the rainy-day blues with a shower of activities!

A Great Day For Ducks!
Welcome students to rainy-day fun with Dilbert Duck! To create Dilbert, enlarge the pattern on page 190. Color and cut out Dilbert, and attach him to a ruler to make a stick puppet. After introducing the duck to students, explain that he will be helping them learn about rain. Ask students if they, like Dilbert, think rain is just ducky! Challenge students to tell why rain is helpful to humans—and ducks! List all the students' responses on the board. Then provide each student with a raindrop cutout. Instruct students to write on their cutouts the ways that rain is helpful to all living things. When they finish, add the cutouts to the bulletin board described below.

Just Ducky!
Decorate your bulletin board with these delightful ducks! Cover your board with light blue or navy blue background paper. Provide each student with a copy of the duck patterns on page 191, glue, scissors, yellow and black construction paper, yellow and orange crayons, two wiggly eyes, wallpaper scraps and an umbrella pattern. Instruct each student to color the duck's body yellow, and its feet and bill orange. Cut out all the pieces; then glue the bill and the feet to the body. To make the duck's wings, each student traces her hands on yellow construction paper and cuts them out. Glue the wings to the back of the duck's body. To complete the duck, glue on two wiggly eyes.

Next have students trace and cut umbrellas from wallpaper scraps. Cut handles from black construction paper and attach them to the bottoms of the umbrellas. Glue each umbrella to a duck's wing as shown. Mount the ducks on the bulletin board along with the raindrop cutouts and the title "Rain Is Just Ducky!"

Drip, Drop, Don't Stop...Reading, That Is!

Encourage students to read different books from literature genres with the help of this bulletin board. Begin by covering your bulletin board with blue background paper. Enlarge and color the cat-and-dog pattern on page 190, and mount it on the board. Then trace and cut out several large umbrellas from different colors of construction paper. Program each umbrella with a different literature genre. Construct handles from construction paper and attach them to the umbrellas. Mount the umbrellas on the bulletin board and add the title "It's Raining Books!" As each student finishes reading a book, he writes a summary on a raindrop cutout. Mount the cutouts under the appropriate umbrellas.

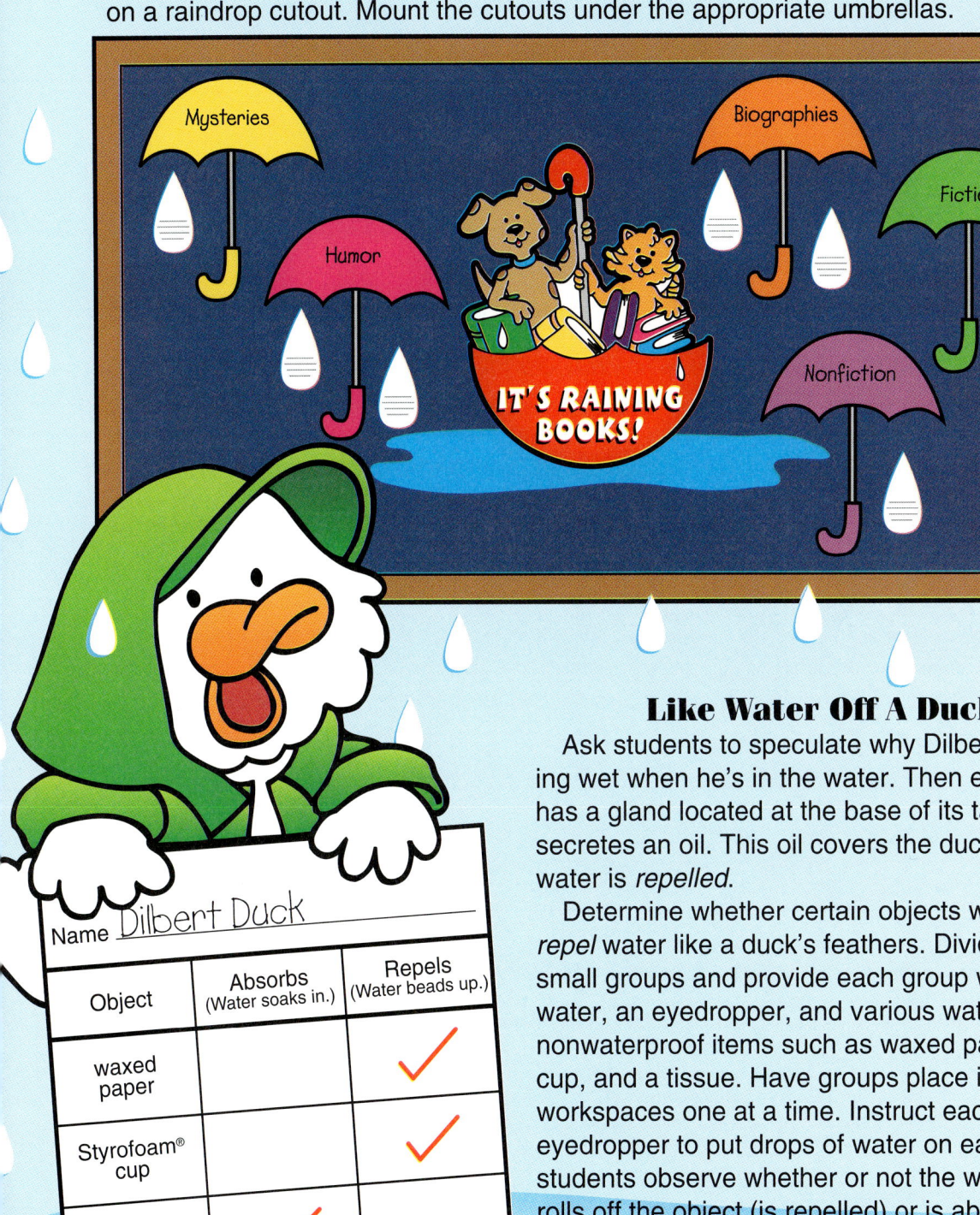

Like Water Off A Duck's Back

Ask students to speculate why Dilbert doesn't get soaking wet when he's in the water. Then explain that a duck has a gland located at the base of its tail feathers that secretes an oil. This oil covers the duck's feathers so that water is *repelled*.

Determine whether certain objects will *absorb* water or *repel* water like a duck's feathers. Divide students into small groups and provide each group with a container of water, an eyedropper, and various waterproof and nonwaterproof items such as waxed paper, a Styrofoam® cup, and a tissue. Have groups place items on their workspaces one at a time. Instruct each group to use the eyedropper to put drops of water on each item. Have students observe whether or not the water beads up and rolls off the object (is repelled) or is absorbed. Encourage each student to record his findings on a chart similar to the one shown. Conclude the lesson by discussing items that are *waterproof* and those that aren't.

Raindrops Keep Falling On My Head!

Pique students' interest in the *water cycle* when you explain that the water on earth today is the same water that was on earth millions of years ago. In fact, students could be drinking the same water that dinosaurs once drank!

Help students better understand the natural phenomena of the water cycle by sharing the story *Water's Way* by Lisa Westberg Peters (Scholastic Inc., 1991). Referring to the photos in the story, discuss the words *evaporation, condensation,* and *precipitation.* List them on the board and briefly explain each one. Then provide students with copies of the water cycle reproducible on page 192. Instruct students to cut out the words, glue them into the appropriate boxes and draw arrows. Then engage students in the three experiments that follow to help them better understand the water cycle.

Evaluating Evaporation

Investigate *evaporation!* Explain that evaporation occurs when the heat of the sun causes water to turn into tiny droplets—called *water vapor*—that rise into the air. Then have each student pick a partner, and provide each pair with two, four-ounce clear plastic cups; masking tape; a small piece of foil; and two sheets of paper. Instruct student pairs to fill both cups half full of water. Have students use pieces of masking tape to mark the water levels on the outsides of the cups. Instruct students to use the foil to cover *one* cup. Set all of the cups in the sun. Next instruct students to fold their papers in fourths and then unfold them to create four boxes. Have each student draw and label pictures of the cups as they appear on Day 1 of the experiment in the top two boxes.

Leave the cups in the sun for four days. Then have students work with their partners to compare the water levels on Day 4 of the experiment to the water levels on Day 1 of the experiment (on their pictures). Encourage students to hypothesize why the water level in one cup is lower than the water level in the other cup. Then instruct students to draw and label pictures of the cups as they appear on Day 4 of the experiment in the bottom two boxes on their papers. Conclude the lesson with a discussion of students' observations. Guide students to the discoveries that the water in the uncovered cup evaporated and the foil covering the other cup prevented the water from evaporating.

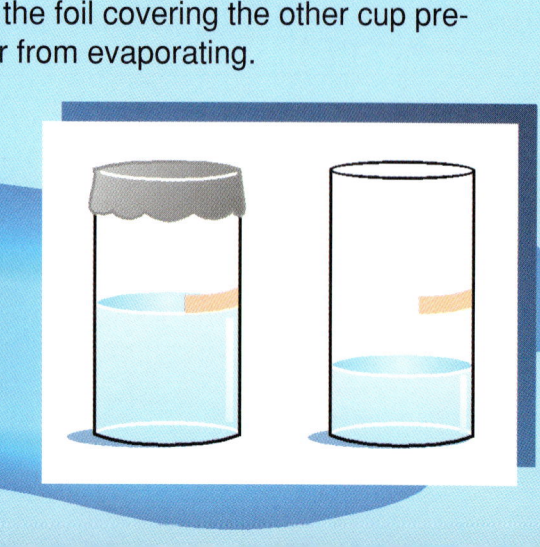

Condensation Is Cool!

Get a close-up look at *condensation!* Explain that water vapor does not always stay in the air. When water vapor cools, it changes from an invisible gas to droplets of water—this is called *condensation*.

Expand your discussion on condensation with this experiment. Divide students into pairs and provide each pair with two glasses, three ice cubes, and two sheets of paper. Instruct students to fill one of their glasses with warm water and the other with cold water. Have students place their ice cubes into the glass of cold water. Set the glasses aside for a few minutes.

While students are waiting, have them divide their papers into sections by folding them in fourths, and then unfolding them. Instruct students to draw and label pictures of the glasses as they initially appeared in the top two boxes. After a few minutes, have students observe their glasses. In the bottom two boxes on their papers, students draw and label pictures of the glasses as they now appear.

Encourage each student pair to make a hypothesis about why water droplets appeared on the outside of the cold glass but not on the warm glass. Guide students to the discovery that condensation occurred when the water vapor in the air touched the cold glass and was cooled. This caused the water vapor to turn into tiny water droplets. When the water vapor in the air touched the warm glass, it was not cooled so it did not condense. Students will agree that condensation is cool!

Pondering Precipitation

Demonstrate how *precipitation* occurs with a little help from a hot plate, a tray of ice cubes, two oven mitts, and a teakettle full of water. But first explain that as water vapor cools and condenses, it turns into tiny water droplets that form *clouds*. As each droplet falls through a cloud, it combines with many other droplets, resulting in precipitation. Precipitation is any moisture that falls from clouds—*rain, snow, hail,* or *sleet*.

To begin the experiment, place the teakettle on the hot plate. When steam begins to escape from the teakettle, use oven mitts to hold a tray of ice cubes about five inches above the steam. Explain that as water from the kettle evaporates, it collects where the air is cool. When several water droplets combine beneath the ice-cube tray, a raindrop is formed and it falls downward. Distribute sheets of white paper to students and have the papers fold them in half. Instruct students to draw and label pictures showing the beginning and the end of the experiment.

Patterns
Use with "A Great Day For Ducks!" on page 186.

Use with "Drip, Drop, Don't Stop…Reading That Is!" on page 187.

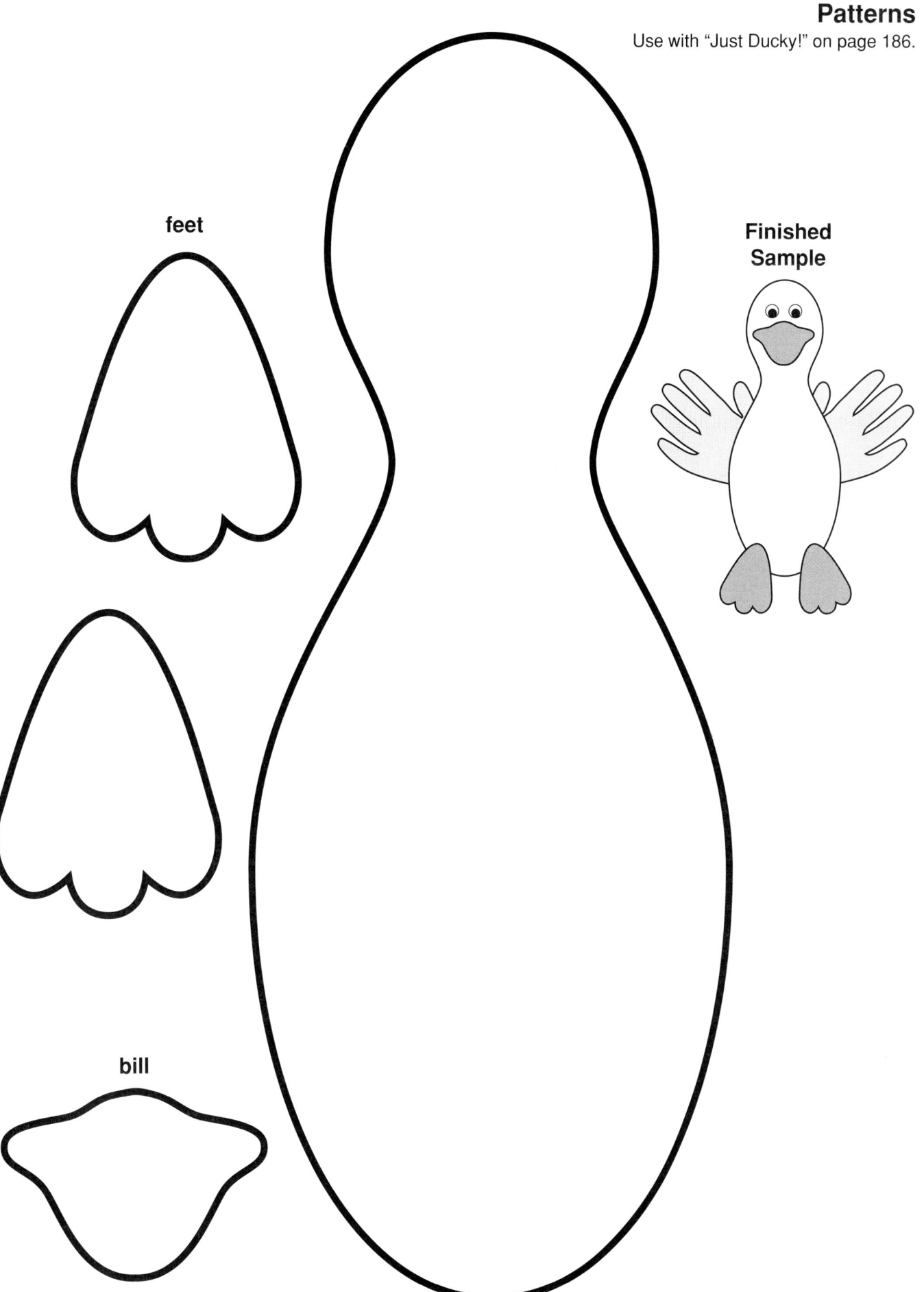

Name _____ The water cycle

Our Wonderful Water Cycle

Cut and paste the words in the correct boxes.
Draw arrows to show the water cycle.

| Precipitation | Condensation | Evaporation |

192 **Note To The Teacher:** Use this reproducible with "Raindrops Keep Falling On My Head!" on page 188.

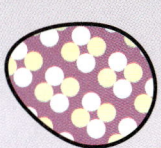

It's An Easter "Eggs-travaganza"!

Bunnies and baskets and beautiful eggs—find them all in this collection of fun ideas to celebrate the Easter season!

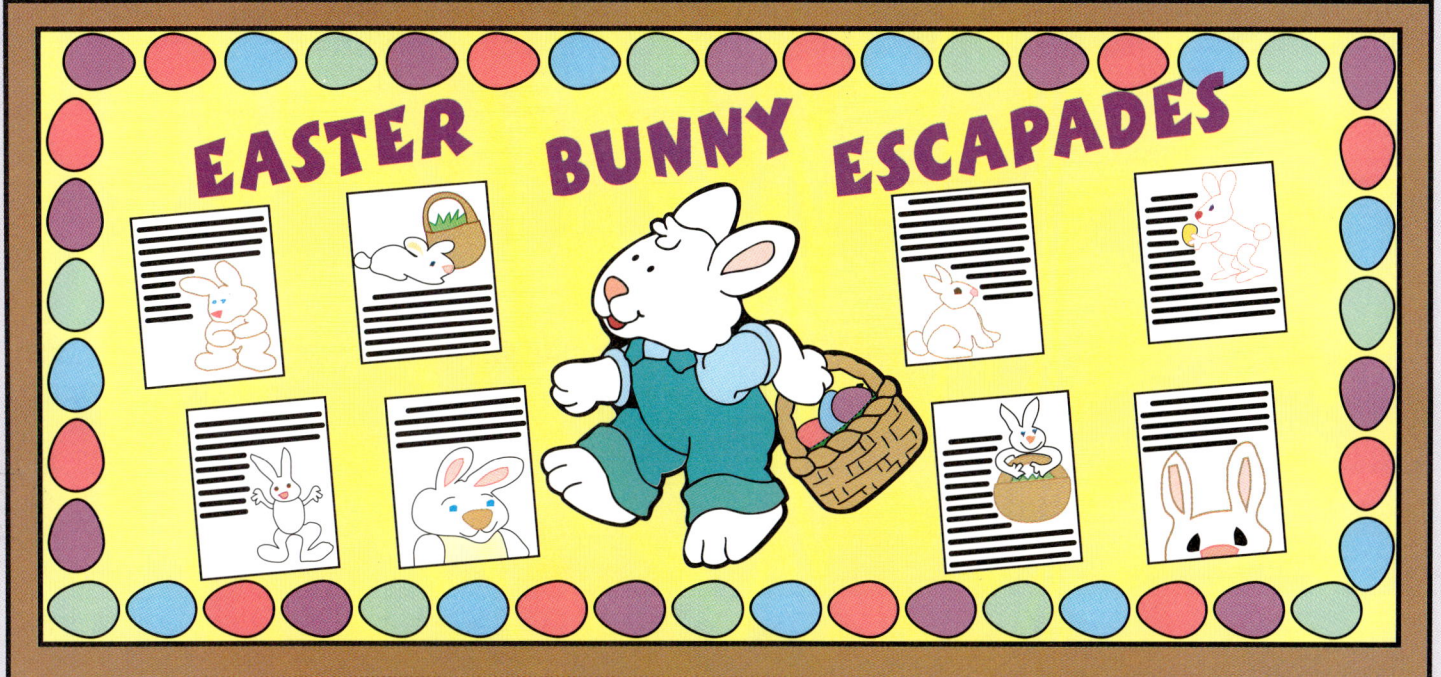

Bunny Tales

No doubt all of your students are familiar with the Easter Bunny. But each child probably has a different idea about this famous character's looks and behavior. Share several Easter Bunny–based stories, such as *The Big Bunny And The Easter Eggs* by Steven Kroll (Scholastic Inc., 1982), *The Country Bunny And The Little Gold Shoes* by Du Bose Heyward (Houghton Mifflin Company, 1967), and *Bunny Trouble* by Hans Wilhelm (Scholastic Inc., 1985). Have students compare and contrast these various depictions of the Easter Bunny. Discuss how Easter baskets were delivered in each story.

Then have your students write their own stories about the Easter Bunny, including descriptions of how the bunny completes his egg-delivery duties. Provide a variety of art materials so students can create their own illustrated versions of the famous rabbit. Display the students' completed stories on a bulletin board titled "Easter Bunny Escapades." Enlarge the Easter Bunny pattern on page 199 on poster board. Color and cut out the bunny; then use it as a centerpiece for the board. Duplicate copies of the egg pattern on page 199 on colored construction paper. Cut them out and use them as a border. Cut along the dotted line on the Easter Bunny's basket; then insert a few cutouts to finish the display.

Easter Around The World

Americans celebrate Easter with church services, Easter egg hunts, and the traditional baskets of goodies delivered by the Easter Bunny. But people in other countries have their own unique Easter traditions. Share these facts with your students and locate the countries where they take place on a map or globe.

—In Greece, people carry candles that are lighted at midnight services on Easter Eve. Many believe it is good luck to keep the candles burning until they reach home.

—In France, the church bells are silent from Good Friday until Easter morning. Legend has it that the bells are silent because they travel to Rome and then bring back gifts. On Easter morning, children rush outside to collect the candy and Easter eggs that have fallen from the sky.

—In Germany, many people believe it is good luck to eat a green food on the Thursday before Easter. Many Germans eat green salads on this day.

—In Australia, the seasons are the opposite of those in the Northern Hemisphere. While we are experiencing spring in America, Australians are greeting fall weather. Many Australians go camping during the Easter holidays.

—In Norway, people enjoy a five-day national holiday at Easter time. Many people go skiing at this time, and some ski trails have open-air chapels for worshipers.

Ask students which of these countries they might like to visit during the Easter season. Have them write about why they'd like to go there and what they would tell foreigners about American Easter traditions.

A-Hunting We Will Go

Your students will practice following directions when they participate in an Easter basket hunt. Divide your class into four or five groups. In advance, ask parent volunteers to help you prepare several large Easter baskets with treats such as candy, colored eggs, pencils, or other favors—one basket for each group. Hide the baskets in various locations around your school (with the informed help of school personnel such as a secretary, a media specialist, or other teachers). Then create a set of directions for each group to follow to locate its basket. If desired, make the hunt progressive by providing only one clue at a time, with a clue given at each new location. When all the groups have located their baskets, let them return to the classroom to enjoy the treats.

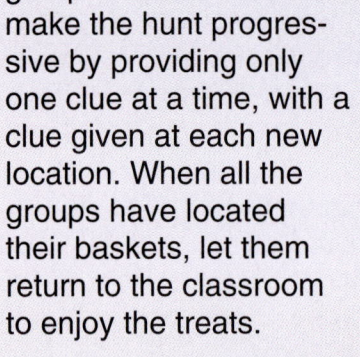

A Tisket, A Tasket

Your students will take to the task of creating these beautiful baskets. Provide each child with a small, inflated balloon and a supply of fabric squares cut with pinking shears. Mix up a batch of wheat paste (available at your local craft store). Have each student dip fabric squares into the paste to cover the bottom half of her balloon, being careful to layer and overlap the fabric squares so that no balloon shows through. Allow the paste to dry for one or two days; then deflate the balloons by carefully cutting off the knotted ends. Remove the balloons, leaving hardened fabric shells. To make a handle, have each child staple on a strip of colored construction paper.

Then plan a surprise visit from the Easter Bunny! While students are out of the room, fill each child's basket with commercial grass, jelly beans, and chocolate-candy eggs for a holiday surprise. Leave a note on the chalkboard that reads:

Hi, boys and girls!
I made an early visit to your classroom today! Have a "hoppy" Easter!
Love, the Easter Bunny

An "Eggs-tra" Special Tree

Add a beautiful dimension to your traditional egg-dyeing activities! Read aloud *The Egg Tree* by Katherine Milhous (Atheneum, 1981); then gather the necessary materials to create an egg tree for your classroom. Obtain a large branch and paint it white if desired. Anchor the branch securely in a large pot of sand or pebbles. Then have adult volunteers assist students in blowing out raw eggs. Each child should use a needle to poke a small hole in the narrow end of a raw egg and a slightly larger hole in the opposite end. Have him carefully blow air through the smaller hole, emptying the inside of the egg into a bowl. Rinse the eggs and allow them to dry overnight.

The following day, students can use egg dyes, watercolor paints, glitter pens, or tempera paints to decorate their hollow eggs. Have an adult use a hot glue gun to attach a loop of ribbon to the top of each egg. Hang your students' beautiful creations on your class egg tree for a delightful holiday decoration!

A Great Big Egg

Try some cooperative cooking to create an Easter treat. Provide your class with a roll of refrigerator sugar-cookie dough. Have student volunteers flatten the dough out on a pizza pan and pat it into the shape of a large Easter egg. Bake the giant cookie at the recommended temperature until golden brown. Then let students help to decorate the cooled cookie with various colors of icing, jelly beans, and colored sprinkles. Have students share their culinary creation while you read aloud the story *The Great Big Especially Beautiful Easter Egg* by James Stevenson (Scholastic Inc., 1983).

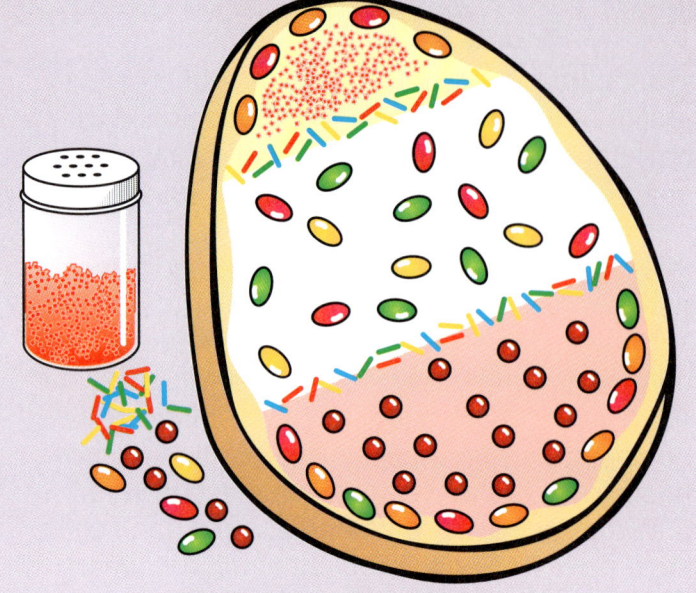

Funny Bunny

Make a bunny cake to celebrate the Easter season. Bake two round cake layers following the directions on the package. Let the cake cool; then use a sharp knife to cut one of the layers and assemble as shown. Frost the cake with vanilla icing; then sprinkle with coconut. Add jelly beans to resemble the nose and eyes. Use licorice strings to resemble the whiskers, and add other features such as the mouth and the ear outlines with pink tube frosting. Allow students to enjoy their cake while sharing the story *Rabbit Finds A Way* by Judy Delton (Crown Publishers, Inc.; 1975).

The Joys Of Jelly Beans

Jelly beans make memorable math manipulatives for these appetizing arithmetic activities! Don't forget to snack along the way!

Sorting And Graphing

Give each child a paper cup filled with jelly beans. Have her sort the jelly beans by color and fill in a copy of the graph on page 198. For more graphing fun, ask each child to choose her favorite color of jelly bean. Have her cut a jelly bean shape from a corresponding color of construction paper and label it with her name. Create a class graph on a large sheet of bulletin-board paper, and have students place their bean cutouts in the appropriate columns. Title the graph "On Which Bean Are You Keen?"

Addition And Subtraction

Make this jelly bean activity jump with compartmentalized plates from frozen dinners. To practice addition, provide each student with a plate, a supply of jelly beans, and some self-checking flash cards with addition problems. The child can place the number of jelly beans equal to each addend in one of the two smaller compartments, then transfer them to the larger compartment as he counts out the sum. He can check his work by turning over the flash card. To practice subtraction, use subtraction flash cards and follow the process in reverse.

Fractions

Give students practice with determining the fractional part of a set with this simple center. Obtain several film canisters and place a few jelly beans into each canister, taking care to put a varying number of pink jelly beans into each one. Have a student empty each canister in turn and determine what fractional part of the set is pink. To make the center self-checking, label the bottom of each canister with the correct answer.

Multiplication

Use jelly beans and cupcake liners to help students visualize multiplication facts. Tell students the cupcake liners are Easter baskets. Pose a sample problem such as "The Easter Bunny must deliver three baskets with four jelly beans in each one. How many jelly beans does he need?" Students should arrange three cupcake liners on their desks and fill each with four jelly beans. Have students count to figure out the total number of jelly beans. Write the multiplication problem on the board as a number sentence. Continue with other word problems or number sentences.

Estimation

Fill a medium-sized jar with jelly beans. Ask students to estimate the number of jelly beans in the jar. Place the jar where each child can observe it up close. Draw a number line on your chalkboard and record each child's estimate on the line. To check the answer, empty the jar and have groups of students count and add to find the total number of jelly beans. Find the closest estimate. Explore a multitude of math concepts by asking questions such as "Which estimate was the farthest from the actual number? Was it too high or too low? How many students gave estimates that were too high? Too low? What was the difference between the highest estimate and the lowest estimate?" Then divide the jelly beans equally and allow students to eat them.

Red, Pink, Purple, Green...
How Many Of Each Jelly Bean?

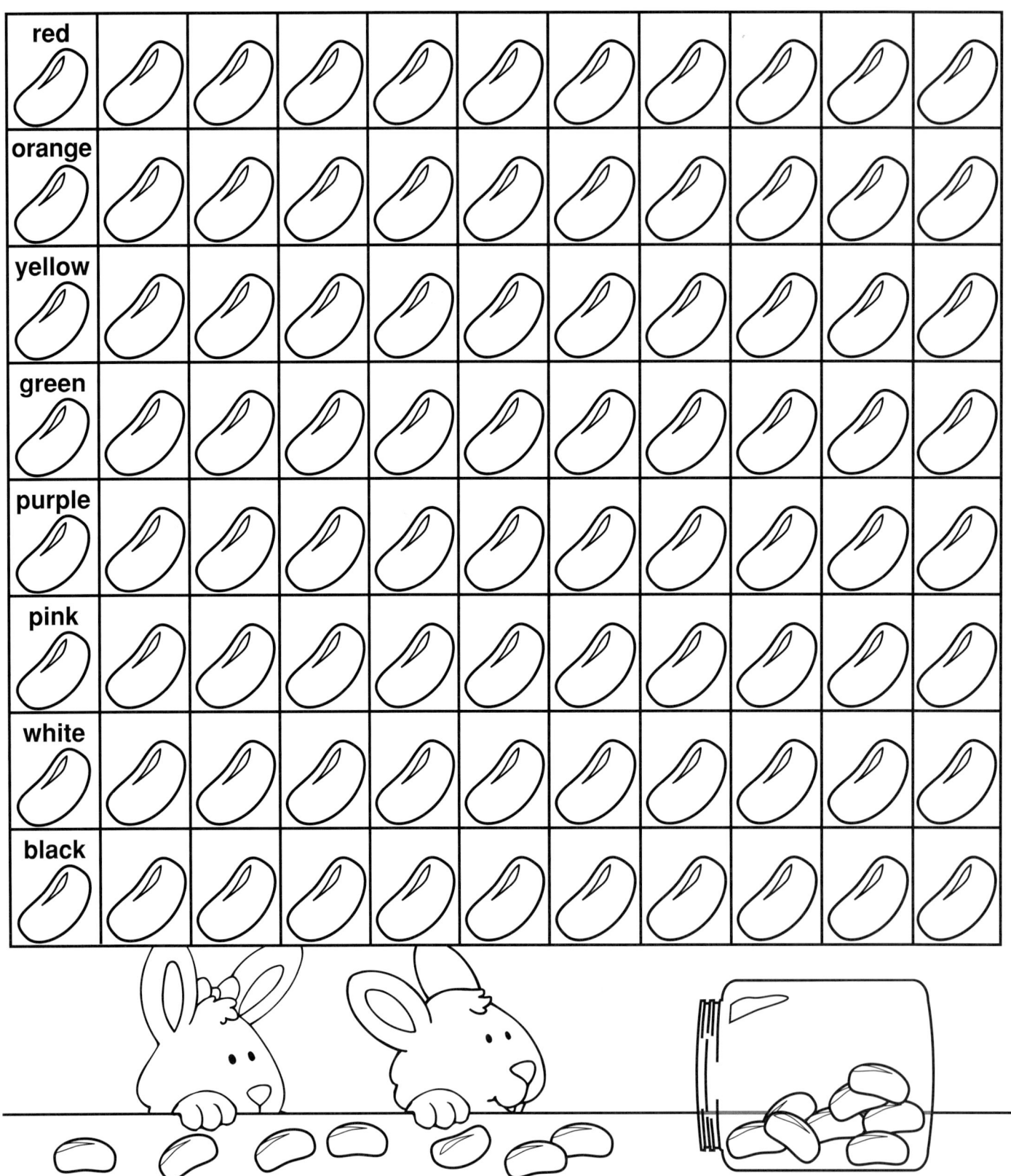

Patterns
Use with "Bunny Tales" on page 193.

The Endangered Earth

Earth Day has been observed on April 22 of each year since 1970. Plan a unit to inform students about environmental issues such as endangered species and resource conservation. From recycling to rain forests, your students are sure to get involved with these planetary projects!

There's No Place On Earth I'd Rather Be

Let music set the mood by teaching your students the traditional song "I Love The Mountains." (If your students are up to it, have them try singing this song in a round.) Then ask students to think of a place on Earth where they love to be, such as on the beach, in the mountains, under a favorite tree in the park, or in their backyard. Have students draw or paint pictures of their chosen spots. Mount the finished illustrations on colored construction-paper backgrounds, label each with the location depicted, and display them on a bulletin board titled "The Best Places On Earth."

I Love The Mountains
Traditional

I love the mountains, I love the rolling hills,
I love the fountains, I love the daffodils,
I love the fireside when all the lights are low;
Boom-ti-a-da, boom-ti-a-da,
Boom-ti-a-da, boom-ti-ay!

The Big Blue Marble

Help students develop a better understanding of planet Earth with this model art project. Begin by showing students some photographs of Earth from space, observing the colors. Ask students to speculate why Earth has nicknames such as The Blue Planet and The Big Blue Marble. Explain that oceans cover about 70 percent of Earth's surface, which accounts for all the blue they see. Help students determine that the patches of white are clouds, wrapping around the planet like a blanket. Explain that Earth is surrounded by an *atmosphere* of air, which allows our planet to sustain life. Finally, observe the shape of Earth. Although it appears round in photos, Earth is actually flattened out at the two poles and it bulges slightly at the equator. (The shape of the balloon in the art project that follows approximates this shape.)

After your discussion, have students create papier-mâché models of Earth. For each student, inflate a small balloon and tie it closed. Prepare a thin paste of flour and water, and provide a large supply of newspaper strips. Have each child dip newspaper strips in the paste, then cover the balloon completely. Be sure to have students overlap the layers, so that none of the balloon is showing. Allow the papier-mâché to dry for about two days, until it is hard. After drying, carefully cut off the tied end of the balloon and let it deflate inside the shell. Pull the balloon out through the hole. Then allow students to paint their models with tempera paints. Provide green and brown (for land), blue (for water), and white (for clouds). When dry, suspend the Earth models from your classroom ceiling to set the mood for the remainder of your Earth Day unit.

What's It All About?

When students have had a chance to reflect on their planet, both up close and faraway, lead a discussion about Earth Day and why it's observed each year. Make a list of what Earth provides for humans: water, food, air, energy, and shelter. Then assist students in listing some threats to the environment, such as pollution, deforestation, overflowing landfills, and acid rain. Divide students into small groups and assign each group an environmental problem to research. Have groups give oral presentations on what they learn. If all the problems leave your students feeling overwhelmed, read some ideas from John Javna's *50 Simple Things Kids Can Do To Save The Earth* (Andrews and McMeel, 1990). Then gear up for some Earth-saving activities!

The Planet Pledge

Create a bulletin board with environmental energy! Duplicate the paper-topper pattern on page 204 for each student. Have each child write one thing she plans to do to help save the Earth on a sheet of writing paper. Let students color the paper toppers and glue them to their writings. Display the papers on a bulletin board with the title "Take The Planet Pledge!"

Letting The Trash Out Of The Bag

Introduce the topic of recycling with this hands-on activity. To prepare, save all your trash at home (without removing recyclable materials) for about three days. Bring your trash to school, and have students weigh it and determine the amount of space the bag of trash takes up in cubic inches. Then have students wear rubber gloves and sort through the trash, removing all items that can be recycled, such as cans, cardboard, plastic containers, glass, newspaper, and other paper. Then have students weigh the trash again and determine its reduced space consumption. Discuss the value of recycling to save space in landfills. Read *Trash!* by Charlotte Wilcox (Carolrhoda Books, Inc.; 1988) for a closer look at what happens to the trash we throw away.

Who Recycles— And How?

How about a garbage-day graphing activity? Duplicate and send home the recycling checklist on page 205 for each student to complete for homework. Then create a class graph on a large sheet of bulletin-board paper to show what your students' families recycle. Cut a supply of index cards in half lengthwise. Have each child take the number of card strips equal to the number of recycling items checked on his paper. Have the children label the strips with their names, then mount them on the graph in the appropriate columns. When the graph is complete, compare the results by asking some questions such as the following: "Which item is most commonly recycled? Which is least? How many more [less] students recycle newspaper than aluminum cans?"

A Conservation Conversation

Recycling is one way to reduce the amount of trash in landfills; conservation is another. Show students how they can conserve materials with this simple demonstration. Place two lunches side by side on a table for students to observe. Pack one lunch in a paper bag with a paper napkin and several items wrapped in plastic wrap or plastic bags. Include a drink in a disposable container. Pack the other lunch in a reusable cloth or thermal bag or lunchbox. Put in a cloth napkin and several items in reusable plastic containers with lids. Include a drink in a thermos or plastic drink bottle.

Lead a discussion with students about these two options for lunch packaging. Ask students to consider the amount of trash that might be generated by your school during one lunch period if everyone used disposable wrappers and containers. What if everyone used plastic containers and cloth napkins instead? Point out that some disposable items (such as paper bags and plastic bags) can be reused a few times. Ask students to write a follow-up paragraph addressed to their parents explaining the demonstration.

We Are Not Alone

Of course, humans are not the only living things who need the Earth and its resources to stay alive. Plants and animals need a healthy planet for their survival, too. And many animals and plants are threatened, endangered, or extinct due to changes in the balance of nature—sometimes caused by humans.

To better explain the concepts of *endangered species* and *extinction,* play this game with your students. Designate one student to be your assistant; then seat all the others in a circle on the carpet. Explain that the seated students represent members of an imaginary species of animal. Your student assistant will portray humankind and their effects on this animal population. Have your assistant walk around the outer perimeter of the circle, tapping each student on the head and repeating, "Going, going, gone," stating one word as he taps each child. Each student who is tapped on the word *gone* gets up and leaves the circle. Stop the game when about one-half of the students are left in the circle. Explain that your imaginary animal species is now *threatened.* Continue the game until one-fourth of the students are left in the circle. Stop and explain that the species is now *endangered.* Let your assistant continue until all students have left the circle. Explain that your imaginary animal species is now *extinct.*

What's Happening In The Rain Forest?

In the forefront of endangered environments is the tropical rain forest. Acquaint your students with this fast-disappearing habitat by sharing *Rain Forest* by Helen Cowcher (Scholastic Inc., 1988). Take a picture walk through the first few pages of the book before reading the text. Ask students to describe what they see on those pages. Then tell students that in this story, something is frightening the animals and ask them to predict what it might be. Read the text aloud and discuss the ending of the story. Tell students that rain forests once covered 20 percent of Earth's land surface. They now cover only 6 or 7 percent. Ask students to write and illustrate continuations of Cowcher's story. Let students share their writings and illustrations. Compare positive and negative scenarios envisioned by the students.

Tropical Products

Many products that we use every day originated in the rain forest. For homework, ask students to fill out the checklist on page 206 to show which rain forest products they can find in their homes. Bring in a few of the more unusual food items, such as *guavas* or *plantains,* to show to students who may be unfamiliar with them. Point out that when people buy rain forest items that can be sustainedly harvested, such as cashews, this gives people living in rain forest regions a reason to preserve the rain forests.

Rain Forest Recipes

After discussing their completed homework assignments, treat students to a snack of Rain Forest Treat. Mix together two cups each of mixed nuts, chocolate chips, dried banana chips, and shredded coconut. While students are snacking, distribute a blank index card to each student. Challenge students to write and illustrate their own recipes using some food items from the rain forest products lists. Compile the recipe cards and add a cover labeled "Rain Forest Recipes" to create a mini cookbook for your classroom.

To Whom It May Concern

Practice letter-writing skills with a planetary purpose! Invite students to write letters to lawmakers, requesting their assistance with a local or global environmental issue of students' choice. Here are the addresses for your congressional representatives:

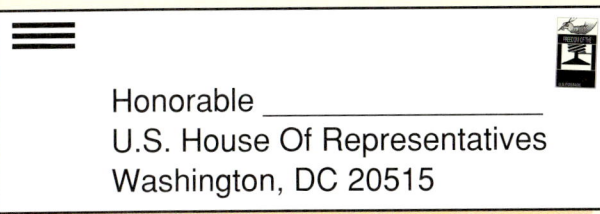

Honorable _____
U.S. House Of Representatives
Washington, DC 20515

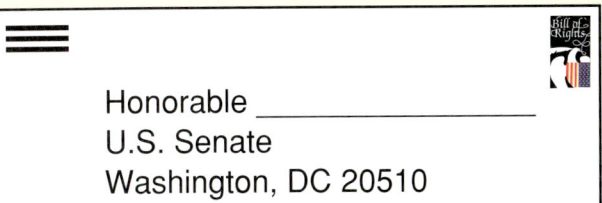

Honorable _____
U.S. Senate
Washington, DC 20510

Conservation Is Catching On!

Brainstorm other ways to conserve natural resources. Challenge students to list ways to conserve water (turn off the faucet while brushing teeth), paper (clean up spills with sponges instead of paper towels), and energy (turn off the lights whenever you leave a room). Have each student choose a conservation tip, write a catchy phrase to convey it to others, and then create a poster featuring her phrase and an illustration. Display the posters in your school library or cafeteria.

Environmental Organizations

Here are just a few organizations you can contact for educational materials and information on preservation of the earth and its animals.

The Nature Conservancy
4245 North Fairfax Dr., Suite 100
Arlington, VA 22203-1606
1-800-628-6860
www.tnc.org
(Adopt An Acre program to preserve an acre of tropical rain forest)

American Forests
Sharing in a Better World
P.O. Box 2000
Washington, DC 20013
1-800-545-TREE (8733)
www.americanforests.org
(Tree-planting program)

Save The Manatee® Club
Adopt-A-Manatee Program
500 North Maitland Avenue
Maitland, FL 32751
1-800-432-JOIN (5646)
www.savethemanatee.org
(Adoption of endangered manatees)

International Wildlife Coalition
Whale Adoption Project
70 East Falmouth Highway
East Falmouth, MA 02536-5954
www.iwc.org
(Adoption of humpback whales)

Paper-Topper Patterns
Use with "The Planet Pledge" on page 201.

Name _____   Recycling

 # The Recycling Routine

Check the items that are regularly recycled at your house.

❑ newspaper

❑ aluminum cans

❑ plastic

❑ glass

❑ tin cans

❑ cardboard

❑ phone books

❑ magazines

❑ clothing (passed to younger children or given away)

❑ yard wastes (made into mulch)

❑ compost

❑ other: _____

_____

_____

Note To The Teacher: Use this reproducible with "Who Recycles – And How?" on page 201.

Name_____   Rain forest

Fruits Of The Rain Forest

Many foods, spices, and other products come from the tropical rain forest. Check the items below that you find in your home.

Foods
___ banana
___ guava
___ lemon
___ lime
___ orange
___ grapefruit
___ passion fruit
___ pineapple
___ plantain
___ Brazil nuts
___ cashews
___ coconut
___ coffee
___ macadamia nuts
___ tapioca
___ tea
___ sesame seeds
___ hearts of palm

Spices
___ pepper
___ cocoa
___ cinnamon
___ cloves
___ turmeric
___ nutmeg
___ cayenne
___ allspice
___ cardamom
___ paprika
___ vanilla

Other
___ camphor oil (insect repellent)
___ coconut oil (foods, lotions, soaps)
___ palm oil (foods)
___ chicle (gum base)

©The Education Center, Inc. • Big Book of Monthly Ideas • TEC1487

Note To Teacher: Use this reproducible with "Tropical Products" on page 202.

FESTIVE FUN FOR THE FIFTH OF MAY

Embark on a journey south of the border for a fiesta of learning about Cinco De Mayo. Olé!

The History Of Cinco De Mayo

Introduce your little *amigos* to our southern neighbor by helping them locate Mexico on a map. Read the book *Mexico* by Karen Jacobsen (Childrens Press®, 1982) to give students a better understanding of our Mexican neighbors. Then share this information about one of Mexico's most important fiesta days, Cinco De Mayo:

—Cinco De Mayo, or the Fifth of May, is a national holiday that commemorates the Battle Of Puebla, which was fought on May 5, 1862.
—During the Battle Of Puebla, Mexican troops defeated the French forces of Napoléon III. The French had planned to take over the country, but Mexican peasants defeated the well-trained French.
—Cinco De Mayo is celebrated in Mexico and in American communities that have large Mexican-American populations.
—Cinco De Mayo events include parades, patriotic speeches, bullfights, barbecues, beauty contests, mock battles, fireworks displays, and mariachi bands.

Locate a copy of the book *Fiesta!: Cinco De Mayo* by June Behrens (Golden Gate, 1978), and read it to your students to give them more information on this holiday.

Comparing Cultures

Build on students' knowledge of Independence Day by comparing it to a Cinco De Mayo celebration. Put one Hula-Hoop® on the floor; then place another Hula-Hoop® over it so that they overlap. Print *"Fourth of July"* and *"Cinco de Mayo"* on separate index cards; then place a card at the top of each Hula-Hoop®. Invite students to write traditions about the respective celebrations on sentence strips. Collect the sentence strips and read each one aloud. As you read the information on a strip, have students decide which holiday the information is describing; then place the sentence strip in the appropriate Hula-Hoop®. If the information describes both celebrations, it should be placed in the area where the circles overlap.

Culminate the lesson by reminding students that people all over the world celebrate holidays to remember momentous historical events in ways that are both similar and different.

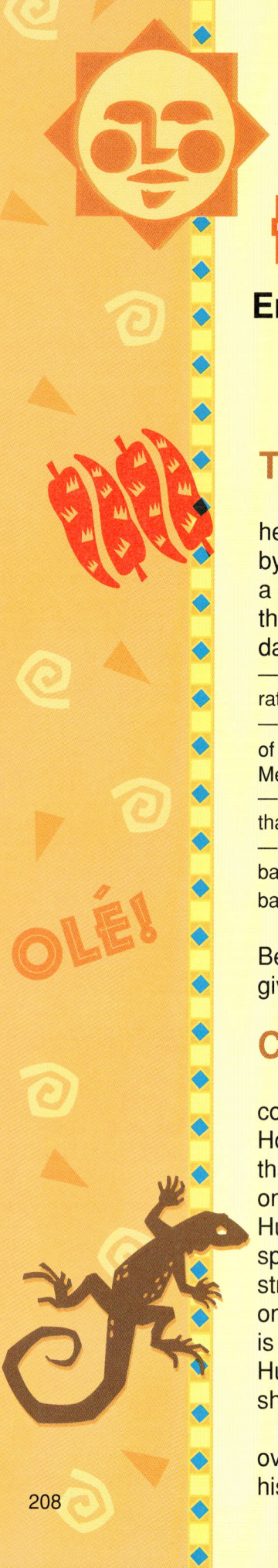

A Fiesta Of Red-Hot Facts

Ignite interest in Mexico with this festive student-made bulletin board. Begin by providing a sheet of black bulletin-board paper, plastic straws, and several small containers of colored liquid tempera paints. Have each student pour a bit of the paint on his paper; then have him use his straw to blow the paint. This creates the effect of sparklers in the night sky. If desired, sprinkle clear glitter on the wet paint for a shimmery result. Staple the black paper to the board to create a background. Then provide each student with a firecracker pattern similar to the one shown. Instruct each student to write a fact about Mexico or Cinco De Mayo on the cutout. Mount the cutouts on the bulletin board. Create a border by attaching a string of chili-pepper lights around the board. Complete the board by adding the title "A Fiesta Of Red-Hot Facts."

Pretty Pottery

Capitalize on students' interest in Mexican art with these pretty pottery projects. Explain that Mexican pottery is an ancient art distinguished by its bright, beautiful colors and detailed designs. If possible, bring in samples of Mexican pottery, or reference books that illustrate colorful pottery.

Then provide each student with a small terra-cotta pot and paint pens (available from your local discount or craft store). Allow each student to use her paint pens to decorate her pot. When the paint is dry, assist each student in planting a small cactus. Display each cactus-filled pot on a sunny shelf.

Speaking Spanish

Read the book *Count Your Way Through Mexico* by Jim Haskins (Carolrhoda Books, Inc.; 1989) to introduce students to Spanish—the official language of Mexico. Then, with students' help, make a chart that has the numbers from one to ten with the Spanish number words printed next to them. Practice the pronunciation of each Spanish word. Then play a game called What's Your Number? Ask each student a question such as "How old are you?" or "How many sisters do you have?" Ask each student to give his response in Spanish.

Numbers in Spanish

1	one	uno
2	two	dos
3	three	tres
4	four	cuatro
5	five	cinco
6	six	seis
7	seven	siete
8	eight	ocho
9	nine	nueve
10	ten	diez

Lotto...Mexican-Style

After students are familiar with the Spanish number words, play a game of lotto with a Mexican flair. Create a gameboard similar to the one shown; then duplicate one for each student. Have each student program each block of the *M* column with a number between one and ten, without repeating a number. Have each student continue in this manner until all the columns on the gameboard are programmed.

Then place ten index cards that have each been programmed with a number between one and ten into a lunch bag. To play, select a card from the bag and say the number word in Spanish. Instruct each student to look for that number in his *M* column. If the student has the number, he may cover that space on his gameboard with a *frijole* (kidney bean). Return the card to the bag and repeat the process for the remaining columns. Continue in this manner until one student has six spaces covered vertically, horizontally, or diagonally. At that time, the student should call out, "Mexico!"

Cinco De Mayo Bells

These jolly jinglers will add flair to your Cinco De Mayo festivities. Explain to students that most Mexican fiestas begin before the crack of dawn with the traditional ringing of bells. To make a jingle-bell bracelet in honor of Cinco De Mayo, provide each student with three 12" x 1/4" lengths of ribbon in the following colors: red, white, and green. Each student will also need three small jingle bells. To make the jingler, have the student thread a different ribbon length through each of her bells. When all the bells have been strung, have each student lay her three ribbons side by side. Instruct the student to tie a knot in the ribbons on each side of the bells, as shown, to keep them from slipping off. Then assist each student in tying the resulting bracelet around her wrist to create instant music.

A Perfect Piñata

Engage your *muchachas* and *muchachos* (girls and boys) in the making of a piñata for a Cinco De Mayo celebration. Blow up a large balloon and provide students with strips of newspaper. After dipping the strips in wheat paste, completely cover the balloon with the strips. After the newspaper has dried overnight, decorate the piñata with pieces of colored tissue paper that have been dipped in glue. When this has dried, cut a small hole in the back of the piñata and insert individually wrapped treats. Attach a string to the top of the piñata and suspend it from the classroom ceiling.

Then give each student a chance to break the piñata. After blindfolding the student, provide her with a stick (such as a wooden dowel) and give her three chances to hit the piñata. When the piñata has been broken and children are enjoying their treats, read aloud *Treasure Nap* by Juanita Havill (Houghton Mifflin Co., 1992) to end this exciting activity on a restful note.

Celebrate Cinco De Mayo

Culminate your study of Cinco de Mayo with a fiesta—complete with music, merrymaking, and munching! Invite parents, relatives, and classmates to attend the celebration.

Festive Flair

On the day of the fiesta, invite students to wear colorful clothing, *sombreros, serapes,* and sandals. Have the boys wear crepe-paper sashes around their waists, and have the girls pin colorful tissue-paper flowers in their hair. Allow students to parade from room to room wearing their jolly jinglers and rousing the other students to attend the fiesta.

Culminate the fun by preparing and serving *tortillas, salsa, guacamole,* and *polvorones.* (See the recipes below.) While students and other guests are enjoying the food, play musical selections from *Papa's Dream*, available from Music For Little People at 1-800-346-4445. End the fiesta by breaking a piñata that students have helped create.

Spicy Salsa
(Serves approximately 15–20)

You'll need:
4 tomatoes, diced
1/2 onion, chopped
1 can mild green chilies, drained
1/2 tsp. garlic powder
1/8 tsp. salt
1/8 tsp. pepper

Mix all ingredients in a small bowl. Add garlic powder, salt, and pepper to taste. Serve with tortilla chips.

Tantalizing Tortillas
(One tortilla will result in 4–6 wedges)

You'll need:
tortillas (available in the dairy case at the supermarket)
griddle or electric skillet
oil
grated cheese

Heat a tortilla on the griddle or hot skillet in a small amount of oil for about 20 seconds; then turn it over and heat the other side. Sprinkle cheese over the top, and then cut it into bite-size wedges. Serve with salsa.

Pleasing Polvorones
(Makes 2–3 dozen cookies)

You'll need:
refrigerated sugar-cookie dough
sugar
cinnamon

Slice and bake the dough as directed. Sprinkle the cookies with sugar and cinnamon while they are warm.

RED-HOT LITERATURE

Hello, Amigos!
by Tricia Brown
(Henry Holt And Co., Inc.; 1992)

Read the story *Hello, Amigos!* to take a look at how birthdays are celebrated south of the border. Frankie Valdez, a Mexican-American boy, is celebrating his birthday with family and friends in rich, traditional style.

After reading the story, brainstorm and list on the board foods mentioned in the book. Use the glossary for help with the translations. Then make a graph to determine which foods students have, and have not, tried. Allow students to mark which foods they have eaten. Discuss the results of the graph and determine which food was the most popular with students. Provide samples of Mexican foods for students to try. Feliz cumpleaños!

Family Pictures/Cuadros De Familia
by Carmen Lomas Garza
(Children's Book Press, 1990)

The story *Family Pictures/Cuadros De Familia* is full of warm illustrations that portray many memorable occasions in the life of the author while growing up in a Hispanic-American home. After reading this story, create a classroom book titled "Our Family Traditions." Provide each student with a sheet of white construction paper. Ask the student to draw a picture of her favorite family celebration or event. Have the student write a story about the event beneath her picture. After students have shared their pictures, bind them together.

My favorite family event is when the whole family decorates the Christmas tree. We string popcorn and cranberries to put on the tree. And we sing carols.

Diego
by Jeanette Winter
(Alfred A. Knopf, Inc.; 1991)

The book *Diego* recounts the life of Diego Rivera, a famous Mexican muralist. After reading the story, motivate students to create Mexican murals. First divide students into groups of four. Provide each group with a length of bulletin-board paper, tempera paints, and paintbrushes. Have each group paint a mural depicting a fiesta or other Mexican scene. If desired, provide students with travel posters or pictures of Mexican scenes to refer to while painting the murals. Display the colorful murals in the hall or cafeteria where all school members may enjoy them.

A COWPOKE ROUNDUP

Howdy, pardner! Saddle up for this rootin'-tootin' roundup of Wild West activities. Yippee-yi-yo—here we go!

BOOT-SCOOTIN' BEGINNING

The *Old West*, or *Wild West*, is a fascinating part of our American heritage. Invite your young wranglers to share what they already know about the Wild West. Use colorful markers to record their responses, graffiti-style, on a large boot-shaped cutout. Then display the resulting poster and a second blank boot-shaped cutout on a classroom wall within your wranglers' reach. As new facts and trivia are learned about the Wild West, ask different students to record the information on the blank boot cutout. When it's time to hit the trail, this pair of boots will be a colorful reminder of how much learning has taken place! Yee-haa!

COWBOY LIFE AND LEGEND

To help students discover what cowboy life was like on the western frontier, share the following facts. Have students compare this view of the American cowboy to the image portrayed on television or in the movies.

- The first cowboys were Mexican *vaqueros*, called *buckaroos* by the Texans.
- Approximately one-half of all cowboys were either African-Americans or from Mexico.
- Cowboys had to be excellent riders, ropers, and animal handlers. Few were sharpshooters. Bullets were too expensive to practice shooting.
- Cowboys carried guns to shoot snakes and turn stampeding cattle.
- A cowboy's most prized possession was his saddle. His most useful tool was a rope.

You'll find plenty more fascinating facts in *Cowboys* from the Fact Or Fiction series by Stewart Ross (Copper Beech Books, 1995). This colorful resource is packed with facts about cowboys.

COWBOY CAMPFIRE

A mock campfire is a must for your Wild-West theme! You'll need a construction-paper-covered oatmeal container, tree branch trimmings (each about 1 inch in diameter and 12 inches long), craft glue or a hot glue gun, red and orange tissue paper, and several smooth rocks. Prop the tree trimmings against the container's rim; then glue them in place. Tear the tissue paper to resemble flames. Glue the flames just inside the rim of the container so that they resemble a campfire. Locate the campfire where students can be seated around it; then surround the campfire with a circle of rocks.

COWPOKE SING-ALONG

On the trail, a rider was always alert to the possibility of a stampede. At night, each cowpoke slept next to a saddled horse. The night guards would sing to the animals in the herd to calm them. These cowboy lullabies are a rich part of our American heritage.

Invite a guitar-playing volunteer to lead a sing-along featuring old cowpoke standards like "Git Along Little Dogies"; "Old Chisholm Trail"; and "Home On The Range." Or play a recording of cowboy songs for your sing-along.

SINGIN' AROUND THE CAMPFIRE

Round up your wranglers and sing this cowpoke song around your classroom campfire!

(sung to the tune of "She'll Be Comin' Round The Mountain")

Oh, a cowpoke sings a riding song. Yee-haa!
Oh, a cowpoke sings a riding song. Yee-haa!
When a cowpoke goes a-ridin',
When a cowpoke goes a-ridin',
Oh, a cowpoke sings a riding song. Yee-haa!

Oh, a dogie sings a roaming song. Moo-oo!
Oh, a dogie sings a roaming song. Moo-oo!
When a dogie goes a-roamin',
When a dogie goes a-roamin',
Oh, a dogie sings a roaming song. Moo-oo!

Oh, a coyote sings a howling song. Ah-ooo!
Oh, a coyote sings a howling song. Ah-ooo!
When a coyote goes a-howlin',
When a coyote goes a-howlin',
Oh, a coyote sings a howling song. Ah-ooo!

Additional verses:
Oh, a pony sings a bucking song. Neigh-ay!
Oh, a rattler sings a sliding song. Hiss-sss!

CIRCLE THE WAGONS

How can a classroom of buckaroos learn to live in peace and harmony? Holding weekly circle meetings is one strategy. Each week round up your youngsters for a class discussion. Topics may range from ways to keep the art center tidy to the significance of friendships. During the first meeting, establish a list of circle rules. List these rules on a piece of chart paper; then carefully burn the edges to give the resulting poster an Old West look. Post the guidelines in a prominent location.

KEEP THIS UNDER YOUR HAT!

Keep wranglers motivated to do their very best work with this idea. Each youngster needs a hat-shaped punch card (see page 222). Explain that one number will be punched from the card for each perfect paper the student completes. Encourage students to give their completed assignments a careful critique before turning them in. When the papers are graded and returned, students sort through them to determine the number of punches they have earned. When a buckaroo's card is completely punched, he redeems it for a free-time privilege or a small prize. Hats off to success!

COMPLIMENT ROUNDUP!

Boost each buckaroo's self-esteem with a student-created display. Cover your bulletin board with background paper; then mount a character cutout (enlarge the pattern on page 222) and the title "Hats Off To You!" Nearby, in a cowboy hat, place several watercolor markers. Invite students to write complimentary phrases about their classmates on the bulletin-board paper. Also invite staff members to write positive comments about your students. Yee-haa!

WRITE 'EM, COWPOKE!

These easy-to-make journals are guaranteed to steer students into writing! To make a journal, fold an 18" x 6" piece of brown construction paper in half. To form the nose, round the bottom corners of the front cover. Cut horns from a 12" x 1" strip of construction paper; then glue the horns along the fold. Attach a construction-paper topknot atop the horns as shown, and glue two construction-paper ears to the back cover. Add facial features using construction-paper scraps, markers, or crayons. To complete the journal, staple several 5 1/2" x 8" sheets of paper between the journal covers.

Each day have students write and/or draw in their journals. Suggest writing topics such as "The Wildest Roundup Ever," "A One-Of-A-Kind Outlaw," "The End Of The Trail," and "Ropin' A Rattler!"

HOWDY, PARDNER!

Corral your buckaroos and boost their spelling scores with this partner activity. At the beginning of each week, have students copy their spelling words onto individual flash cards (card patterns on page 223) and then store the cards in resealable plastic bags. Also assign students spelling partners for the week. Each morning set aside five to ten minutes for your buckaroos to meet with their partners and practice spelling their weekly words. This extra study time helps cowpokes stay in their saddles when the weekly test is given!

THE WILD-WEST GAZETTE

Every buckaroo needs a chance to boast now and then. Here's the opportunity your cowpokes have been waiting for! Ask each student to create a Wild-West name for herself that includes her real name (such as Quick-Draw Kevin or Buffalo Beth). Then invite each buckaroo to write and illustrate an outlandish Wild-West tale about herself—the more far-fetched the better! To display the projects, decorate the front page of a newspaper to show the title "The Wild-West Gazette," the date, and a class byline. Mount your students' projects on the newspaper pages. Laminate the pages for durability; then place the newspaper in your class library for all to read!

READING CORRAL

Round up reading enthusiasm at a reading corral. In a classroom corner, place a mattress covered with a colorful sheet. If desired, border the mattress with a cardboard or tagboard fence. Decorate the top of the mattress with pillows. To limit the number of readers entering the corral, duplicate, cut out, and laminate a desired number of reading badges (see page 223) that must be worn inside the corral. Using a hole puncher, punch two holes near the top of each badge. Thread a length of colorful cord through the holes; then tie the cord ends. Keep the badges in a designated location or distribute them as rewards.

FINGER-LICKIN' GOOD

In the Wild West, the cowboy slang for food was "chuck." Serve each of your hardworking wranglers a serving of chuck—commonly known as trail mix! To make your trail mix, combine equal amounts of Honey Nut Cheerios® cereal, raisins, peanuts, and M&M's® candies. Now that's "ding-dandy" delicious!

COWPOKE PATTERNING

Invite your cowpokes to round up some creativity at this patterning center! Duplicate the patterns on page 224 for students to color and cut out. Place the cutouts, along with a supply of 4" x 18" construction-paper strips, pencils, and markers or crayons, at a center. Using the cutouts, a student creates a pattern by gluing six shapes onto a construction-paper strip. Displayed together, the completed projects make a bronco-bustin' bulletin-board border!

ROOTIN'-TOOTIN' MATH JOURNALS

Corral your cowpokes' problem-solving skills into these appealing student-made journals. To make a journal, have each student tightly crumple a 6" x 9" piece of brown paper bag; then have the student flatten the paper. Repeat this process until the flattened paper feels smooth and has a leatherlike appearance. Fold the rectangle in half and staple a supply of 4" x 5 1/2" blank paper inside. Using crayons or markers, the student "brands" the front cover with her initials. Each day present a problem-solving challenge for your cowpokes to solve in their journals, such as, "Eight wranglers ate three biscuits each. How many dozens of biscuits were eaten?"

STAMPEDE!

Here's a rip-roarin' way to review math facts! To make this partner game, label 30–40 blank cards (card patterns on page 223) with desired math facts. Label four more cards with the word "Stampede!" Store the cards with an answer key in a gift bag at a center.

To play, one partner shakes the bag to shuffle the cards. Then, in turn, each wrangler draws a card and answers the fact. His partner verifies his answer. If the answer is correct, the wrangler who drew the card keeps it. If an incorrect answer is given, the card is returned to the gift bag. If a wrangler draws a "Stampede!" card, he places the card in a discard pile and returns all his math-fact cards to the bag. The student with the most cards at the end of the game wins. Giddyap!

SUNSET SILHOUETTES

It's a gorgeous sight—the wide-open range at sunset. Your cowpokes can create their own colorful images with this picturesque project. To make a sunset, you need colorful chalk, facial tissue, an 8" x 11" piece of white construction paper, and an 8" x 11" piece of manila paper. Align the manila paper atop the white paper and staple the top two corners. At the bottom, tear off a narrow strip of the manila paper. Pressing heavily, draw a chalk line along the torn paper edge; then use a tissue to rub the chalk downward onto the exposed portion of the white paper. When this step is completed, tear off another narrow strip of manila paper and repeat the process, using a different color of chalk and a clean portion of tissue. Continue in this manner until you have used the last strip of manila paper. Remove the staples and any remaining manila paper. Smear the top chalk layer upward to cover any white space at the top of the page. Cut a western silhouette from black paper and glue it on your colorful sunset. Then mount the project on a 9" x 12" sheet of black paper. Wow! It's the Wild West at sundown!

HOWLING GOOD WORK

Is your buckaroos' best work worth howling over? You bet it is! And these cute coyotes are ready to howl! To make his coyote, a student sponge-paints a 9" x 12" sheet of colorful construction paper. When the paint is dry, he traces the coyote pattern (page 225) onto the paper and cuts out the coyote design. Using colored glue, he traces the outline of the coyote and adds other desired details. While the glue is drying, he traces the bandana pattern (page 225) onto wallpaper or gift wrap, and cuts on the resulting outline. Then he glues the bandana to his cute coyote. Showcase a student's coyote and a sample of his best work side by side on a display titled "Howling Good Work!" Ah-ooooo!

A RIP-ROARIN' ROUNDUP!

If you're looking for a unique alternative to a school play that brings parents into the classroom and involves all students, here's the perfect solution. Make plans to host a Rip-Roarin' Roundup! The guests of honor can view the projects and activities your wranglers have rustled up during their study of the Wild West. After a meal of Chuck-Wagon Chili and warm biscuits, gather around the classroom campfire for a cowpoke sing-along and some storytelling fun. It's the perfect chance for your buckaroos to boast about their Wild West experiences! You might even want to prepare a slide or video production for the affair.

CHUCK-WAGON CHILI

This recipe makes approximately 30 servings of mild chili. Warm biscuits or rolls are a nice addition. Or, if your cowpokes aren't fond of chili, consider serving sloppy joes from your classroom chuck-wagon!

Chuck-Wagon Chili

Ingredients:
- 3 lb. ground beef
- 2 medium onions, diced
- 2 cans (26 oz. each) kidney beans
- 2 cans (16 oz. each) stewed tomatoes
- 1 can (46 oz.) V-8® juice
- Optional: chili powder

Directions:
Brown ground beef and onions together. Drain fat and add remaining ingredients. Simmer one hour and serve.

DRESSED FOR SUCCESS

A cowboy's outfit was more than a costume. Each piece of clothing and gear had a purpose. Display pictures or bring in examples of a cowboy's clothing and gear. Have children guess the purpose of each item. (See the list below.) Then discuss the types of clothing and gear that are worn today for protection. Compare these items to a cowboy's outfit.

- **hat**—broad-rimmed for protection from sun and rain
- **bandana**—used as a napkin and towel; protection from sun, dust, and cold
- **chaps**—leggings worn over trousers to protect legs from brush and thorns
- **lariat**—rope (also called a lasso); a cowboy's most useful tool
- **spurs**—used to prod horses
- **saddle**—a cowboy's most prized possession; needed for roping, riding
- **boots**—high-heeled to hold feet in the stirrups
- **leather gloves**—protected the hands from rope burns
- **vest**—for warmth (coats were too bulky)
- **slicker or poncho**—rainwear slipped easily over the head while riding
- **canteen**—carried water on the trail

Invite students and their guests to wear western attire to your classroom roundup. Suggest blue jeans and bandanas. If extra bandanas are needed, cut colorful sheets of tissue paper in half diagonally; then loosely wrap and tie one tissue-paper triangle around each wrangler's neck. Mighty fine!

Patterns

Use with "Reading Corral" on page 218.

Use with "Howdy, Pardner!" on page 217 and "Stampede!" on page 219.

Patterns
Use with "Cowpoke Patterning" on page 218.

Award

Yahoo, Buckaroo!

_____ stayed in the saddle for an outstanding performance!

From: _____
Date: _____

Patterns
Use with "Howling Good Work" on page 220.

IT'S BEEN A GREAT YEAR!

Celebrate individual and class accomplishments with these memory-making activities and awards.

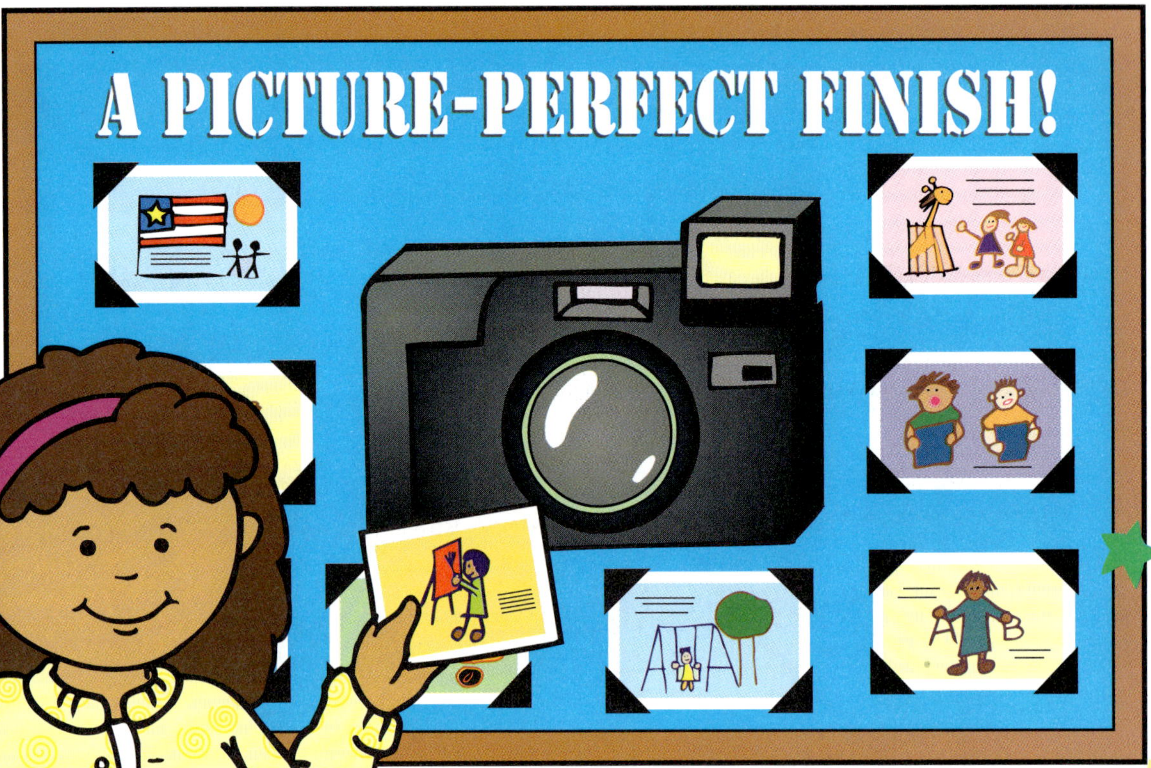

A PICTURE-PERFECT FINISH!

Say good-bye to a successful year with this picture-perfect display. Enlarge the camera pattern on page 233. Color, cut out, and mount the camera on a bulletin board; then have each child create a photo for the display. To make a photo, each child needs a 4" x 6" piece of white construction paper, crayons or markers, and a pen with black ink. On his construction paper, have each child draw and color a favorite memory from the past year. Using the black pen, the child writes a caption for his photo. After students have shared their photos with their classmates, mount the projects on the bulletin board along with the title "A Picture-Perfect Finish!"

LEMONADE-STAND FUND-RAISER

As summer approaches, refresh your math curriculum by having students sell lemonade to raise money for a worthy cause. In advance gather several gallons of lemonade, packages of small cups, several empty pitchers, and coins for making change. Divide students into groups of four or five. Provide each group with poster board, markers, and crayons. Ask each group to design posters for a lemonade stand; then display the posters around the school.

When Lemonade Day arrives, have parent volunteers help you set several tables up around the school (particularly on the playground). Equip each group with pitchers of lemonade, packages of cups, and a small amount of money for making change. At the end of the day, count your profits. Use the money to donate a plant to the school or to purchase needed library materials. Invite students to help select, purchase, and present the item(s). What a capital way to quench youngsters' thirsts for fund-raising fun!

ON THE HUNT FOR MATH

Fit in one final math lesson on the last day of school by leading students on a math scavenger hunt. Divide students into small groups, and provide each group with a supply of rulers marked in inches and a list of mathematical problems to seek out and solve. Below are some questions to get you started. Enlist the assistance of other teachers, school personnel, and parent volunteers to ensure a successful hunting trip.

1. How tall in inches is the water fountain that is closest to our room?
2. How much does it cost to buy _____ in the cafeteria?
3. What is today's outside temperature?
4. How many lunch tables are in the cafeteria? How many chairs?
5. Are there more boys or girls in Mr./Ms. _____ 's class?
6. How many letters are in the last names of all the third-grade teachers combined?
7. What is the perimeter of your desktop in inches?
8. How old is this school building?
9. How many children can sit around one reading table comfortably? What if we had two tables? Five? Ten?
10. Ask one adult and a student who is not in your class to make up a story problem for you.

BE A TRAVEL AGENT

Book your reservations now to encourage creative writing. Set up a writing center that contains travel brochures (check with local travel agents for free literature), U.S. maps, reference books, calculators, paper, pencils, markers and crayons, construction paper, and a computer (if available). Invite each student to choose a summer vacation spot and write a travel itinerary that includes such information as her destination, mode of transportation, number of traveling miles, and some sights that she will see. If desired, have each student draw and cut out a suitcase shape from construction paper and fill it with items that she will carry on her trip. Invite students to share their itineraries aloud; then display the projects on a bulletin board titled "Our Dream Destinations."

WHAT A SUPER SECRETARY!

Show your appreciation for your school secretary by giving her a basket filled with fresh fruits and flattering letters. Make a basket by cutting off the top half of a brown paper grocery bag. Have each student personalize and decorate a portion of the bag; then attach a tagboard handle that is wrapped with decorative curling ribbon. Have each child write a letter to the secretary praising her for her contributions. Ask each child to bring a fresh fruit to school; then invite the secretary to come to your classroom. Place the basket beside her seat. Have each child personally thank the secretary for something nice that she has done; then have the student give her the piece of fruit and the letter that he composed.

A HANDFUL OF MEMORIES

Show off your "hand-some" group by wearing this autographed apron. You will need a plain apron (available at arts-and-crafts stores), fabric paints in various colors, and several small paintbrushes. Lay the apron on a newspaper-covered surface. Using a paintbrush, cover a student's hand with fabric paint. Have the student press her handprint on the apron. Allow the handprint to dry; then, using a bottle of black fabric paint, help each student write her name on top of the handprint she made. Repeat the process until each child has taken a turn. Give this colorful keepsake to your teacher assistant as a reminder of this class.

THE HELLO PAGES

Students can easily keep in touch with each other this summer after creating these individual directories. Distribute to each student a supply of plain or colored half-sheets of paper and two 6" x 9" sheets of construction paper. To make a directory, a child staples the half-sheets of paper between the construction-paper covers, labels the front cover of his directory "The Hello Pages," and decorates the front and back covers. Next the student draws a picture of each classmate on a different page. Beside each picture he writes his classmate's address and phone number. Now this is a book youngsters will love to thumb through!

MADE IN THE SHADE

Create these cool shades before heading out into the summer sun! Provide each student with a copy of the pattern on page 232. Have each student cut out the pattern on the solid lines and then cut out the eyeholes as indicated. Provide each student with a 4" x 15" sheet of tagboard or poster board, two 2-inch squares of colored acetate (or overhead transparency film), markers, glitter, and glue.

To make the sunglasses, a child folds the tagboard in half; then he places the pattern on the fold. He traces and cuts out the pattern. Next he glues an acetate square behind each eyehole to create the lenses. Trim excess acetate as needed. Using markers, glitter, and glue, the child decorates his glasses. A youngster can wear his glasses by tucking the bows of the glasses behind his ears. Have an adult volunteer take a photo of you with each of your cool children individually; then present a photo to each child as a memento of his year in your class.

SUNFLOWER CHILDREN

Add a touch of class to your principal's desk by designing this child-centered sunflower arrangement. Each child will need a wallet-sized photograph of himself that has been cut into a circle. Provide each student with one petal and one leaf pattern on page 234, one 6-inch yellow paper plate, one container of unshelled sunflower seeds, scissors, one wooden tongue depressor, one 9" x 12" sheet of yellow and one 3-inch square of green construction paper, adhesive tape, and glue.

To make a sunflower, a child glues his picture in the center of the plate; then he glues sunflower seeds around the picture in two concentric circles. Let the glue dry. Using the petal pattern, the student traces and cuts out 12 petals from yellow construction paper; then he glues the petals onto the back of the paper plate. Next the child uses adhesive tape to attach a tongue-depressor stem to the flower. The child uses the leaf pattern to trace and cut out a green construction-paper leaf and attaches it to the stem.

Arrange the flowers by sticking all of the stems into a block of Styrofoam® that you have secured in the bottom of a decorative container. Then have your class present the gift to your principal. It's the perfect reminder of how your students have bloomed throughout the year!

PACK UP A PICNIC

Plan a class picnic for an end-of-the-year send-off that your youngsters will always remember. As the last month of school approaches, ask parent volunteers and/or local businesses to assist you in providing food items and beverages, favors, napkins, paper plates and cups, and plastic utensils. Also organize a variety of games and activities to be held on Picnic Day.

Sponsor a bubble-blowing contest. Provide each student with pipe-cleaner wands and the bubble solution indicated below. Students will enjoy trying to blow the biggest, smallest, fastest, slowest, and most long-lasting bubbles. Be sure to provide alternatives for a rainy day—just in case!

Recipe For Bubble Solution
1 cup liquid dishwashing detergent
2 cups warm water
4 tablespoons glycerine (found at your local drugstore)
1 teaspoon sugar

CATERPILLAR CRAWL

Do the Caterpillar Crawl. Separate your class into two teams. Position half of the members of each team at the starting line and the other half at the finish line. Set up obstacles, such as cones or chairs, along each race route. To begin play, the first player on each team runs from the starting line to the finish line—darting around and between obstacles along the way. At the finish line, the next player from each team wraps her arms around the leader's waist and follows along. The two-person caterpillar runs back to the starting line, where a third team member joins the caterpillar. Play continues in the same manner until all team members have been added. If the caterpillar breaks apart during the race, the player who becomes unattached must go back to the starting line where she joined it and rejoin the caterpillar when her turn arrives again. The first caterpillar to cross the finish line with all team members in tow wins the game.

UNPACK THE BASKET

Clue youngsters in to the importance of giving clear directions by playing Unpack The Basket. Divide your class into two teams. For each team fill a basket with an assortment of picnic items, such as a saltshaker, a napkin, a plate, a sandwich bag, a soda can, a tablecloth, utensils, and various food items. Label an index card for each item for each team.

To play the game, the first player for each team holds his team's index cards while the second player sits in front of the team's basket. The first player selects a word card, reads the word silently, and then gives the second player three oral clues that will help her guess the identity of the object. If the second player correctly guesses the name of the object, she removes that object from the basket. Play continues with a new player and the same clue-giver. The first team to remove all of the picnic items from its basket wins the game.

Pattern Use with "Made In The Shade" on page 230.

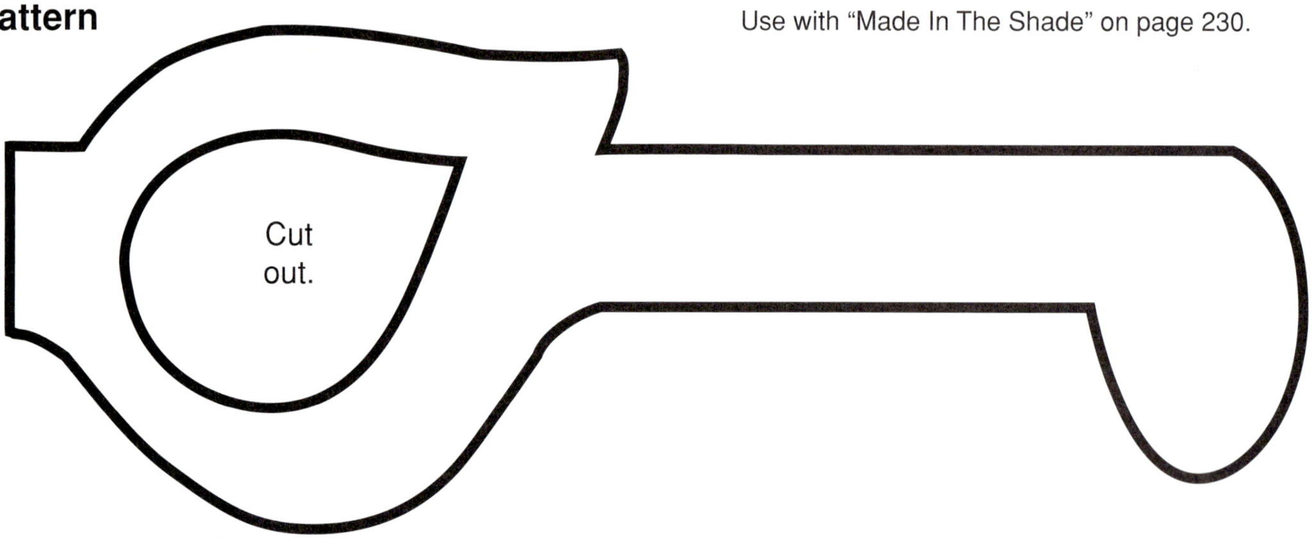

Place on fold.

Cut out.

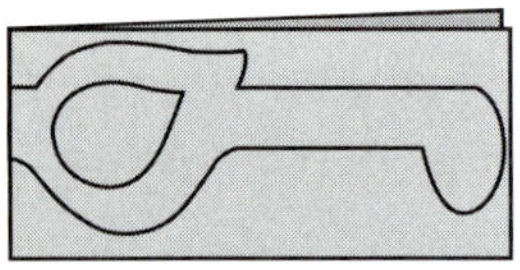

1. Fold tagboard. Trace and cut out pattern.

2. Unfold.

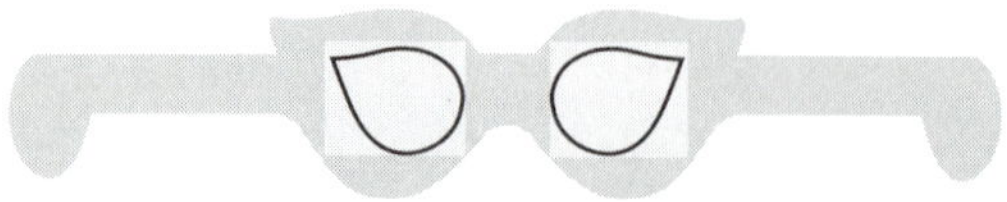

3. Glue on squares.

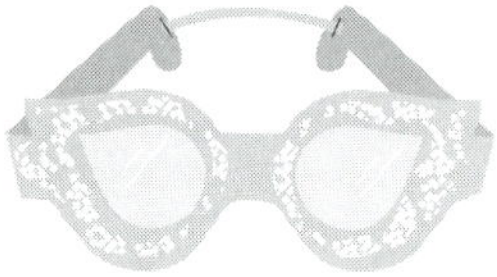

4. Decorate.

Note To The Teacher: Staple elastic, as shown, to each bow to ensure a secure fit.

Pattern

Use with "A Picture-Perfect Finish!" on page 226.

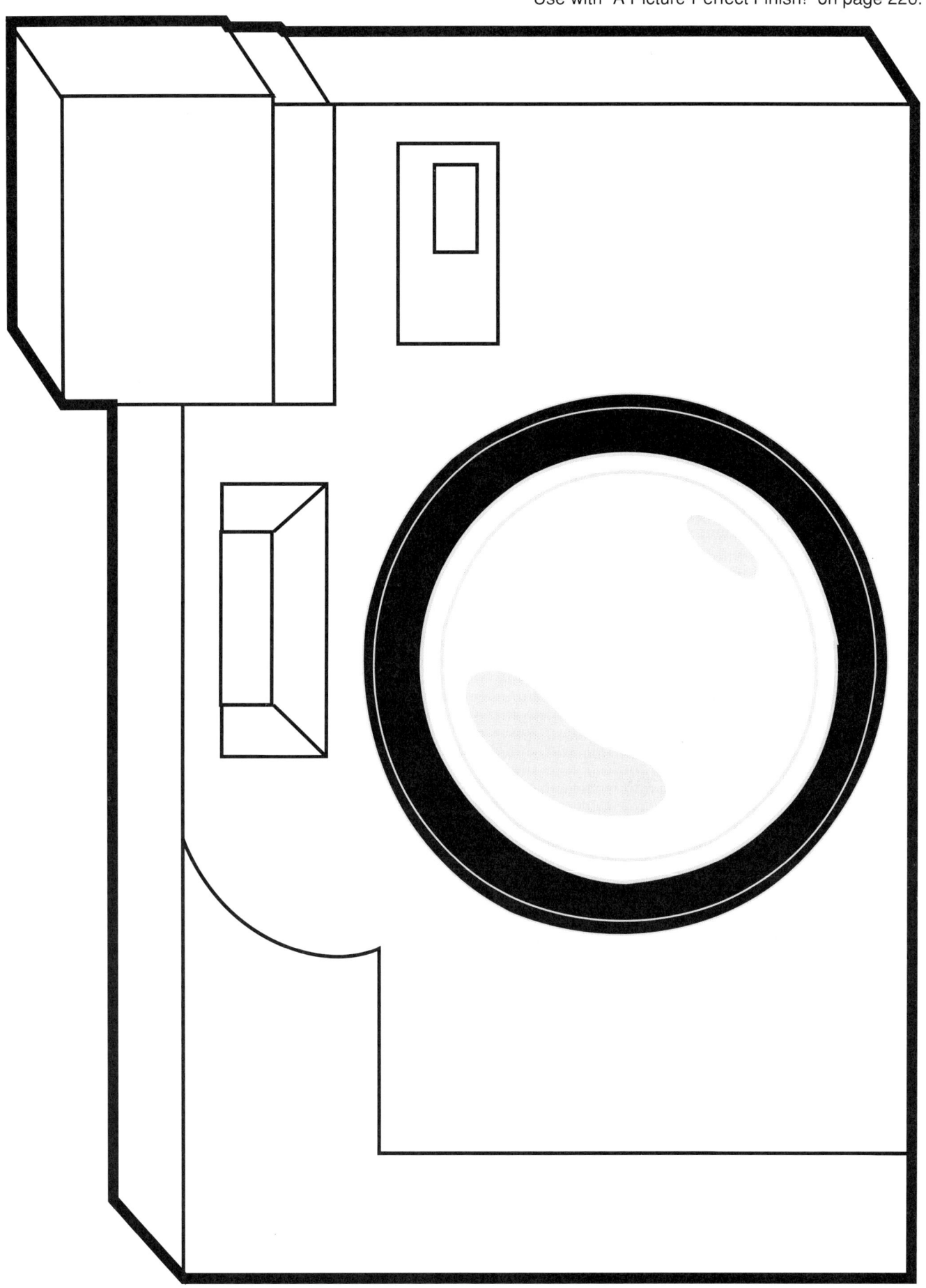

©The Education Center, Inc. • *Big Book of Monthly Ideas* • TEC1487

Patterns

Use with "Sunflower Children" on page 230.

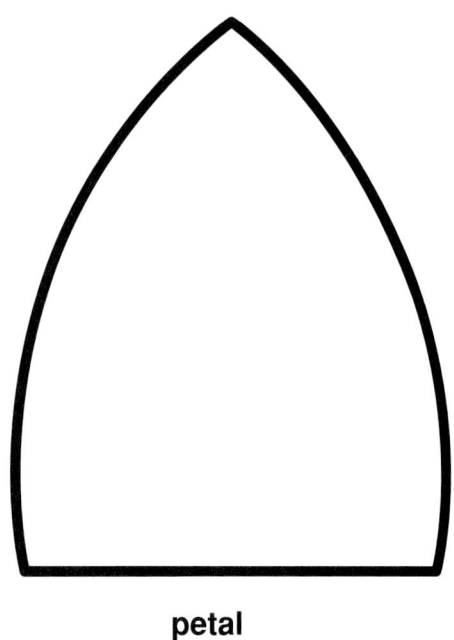

petal

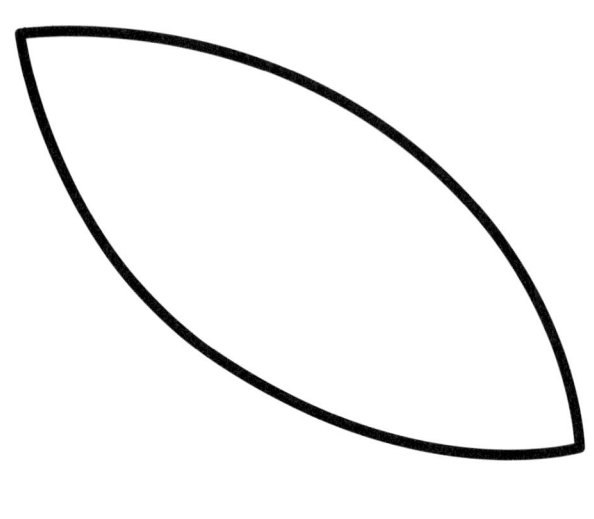

leaf

Award

2... 4... 6... 8...

Who do we appreciate?

_____,

for being a super student

in _____ grade!

Signed: _____

Date: _____

Index

Addition (see Math)
Adjectives (see Parts of Speech)
Adler, David A.
   A Picture Book of Rosa Parks, 136
Africa
   geography, 138
   Swahili, 111
African-Americans
   Black History Month, 134–145
   Bridges, Ruby, 126
   Civil Rights Movement, 121–132
   King, Martin Luther, Jr., 121–132
   Kwanzaa, 109–114
AFRO-BETS® Book of Black Heroes From A to Z
   Wade Hudson and Valerie Wilson Wesley, 134
Alphabet Books
   Eating the Alphabet: Fruits and Vegetables From A to Z, 11
   I Unpacked My Grandmother's Trunk, 46
   making, 46
Amazing Grace
   Mary Hoffman, 138
Analytical Writing
   book reviews, 77
Anderson, Marian
   biography, 135
Animals
   bats, 66
   ducks, 186–192
   endangered, 202
   penguins, 116–120
   spiders, 68
   squirrels, 24–34
Appelt, Kathi
   Watermelon Day, 11
Apples
   arts and crafts, 69
Armstrong, Louis
   biography, 137
Arts and Crafts (see also Bookmaking)
   apron, 229
   baskets, 195
   book jackets, 75
   bookmark, 38, 74
   bracelet—bell, 211
   braiding, 138
   brooms, 100
   candles, 89
   chalk techniques, 220
   Christmas cards, 96
   coat of arms, 61
   coins, 155
   collage, 105
   cornucopia, 97, 111
   door, 17, 35
   door hanging, 98
   dough, 88, 148
   drawing, 17, 123, 137, 200
   ducks, 186
   Earth, 200
   egg tree, 195
   fire helmets, 52
   friendship bracelets, 138
   handprints, 186
   hat, 59
   hearts, 147, 148
   invitations, 35, 45
   kites, 178
   leprechauns, 165
   magnets, 38, 53
   menorah, 88
   mkeka mat, 111
   necklace, 110
   paint techniques, 176, 209
   peace prize, 122
   penguins, 117, 118
   Pilgrim cottage, 83
   pin art, 148
   piñata, 211
   pinwheels, 176
   placemats, 16
   planters, 209
   poinsettia, 104
   posters, 213
   present, 102
   printing, 69, 165, 229
   pumpkins, 67, 68
   scherenschnitte, 99
   scrapbook, 48
   shamrocks, 165
   spiders, 68
   sponge painting, 9
   squirrels, 28
   stationery, 9
   St. Lucia crown, 102
   suitcase, 94
   sunflowers, 230
   sunglasses, 230
   telescope, 59
   treat bag, 69
   Valentine cards, 148
   watermelons, 6
   weaving, 16
   wreath, 31
Australia
   Easter, 194
Authors
   Adler, David A., 136
   Appelt, Kathi, 11
   Behrens, June, 208
   Branley, Franklyn, 30
   Brown, Tricia, 213
   Bunting, Eve, 149
   Chocolate, Deborah M. Newton, 113
   Coles, Robert, 126
   Columbus, Christopher, 59
   Cowcher, Helen, 202
   Czernecki, Stefan, 105
   de Brunhoff, Jean, 98
   de Groat, Diane, 149
   Delton, Judy, 196
   dePaola, Tomie, 96, 98, 99, 100, 104
   Dorros, Arthur, 175
   Earle, Ann, 66
   Egan, Tim, 11
   Ehlert, Lois, 11
   Fox, Mem, 17
   Ga'g, Wanda, 20
   Garza, Carmen Lomas, 213
   George, Jean Craighead, 83
   Geraghty, Paul, 116
   Gibbons, Gail, 82
   Good, Elaine W., 30
   Greenfield, Eloise, 136
   Haskins, Jim, 210
   Havill, Juanita, 211
   Heine, Helme, 17
   Heyward, Du Bose, 193
   Hoffman, Mary, 138
   Hoguet, Susan Ramsay, 46
   Hudson, Wade, 134
   Hunt, Joyce, 66
   Isadora, Rachel, 137
   Jacobsen, Karen, 208
   Javna, John, 201
   Keats, Ezra Jack, 100
   Kessel, Joyce K., 146
   Kroll, Steven, 67, 83, 193
   Lester, Helen, 119
   Levine, Ellen, 124
   list of popular, 81
   Manushkin, Fran, 88
   Marzollo, Jean, 60, 121
   McBratney, Sam, 149
   Metzger, Barbara, 126
   Milhous, Katherine, 195
   Perlman, Janet, 119
   Peters, Lisa Westberg, 188
   Pinkney, Andrea Davis, 113
   Raschka, Chris, 17
   Rhodes, Timothy, 105
   Roop, Peter and Connie, 59
   Ross, Stewart, 214
   Rydberg, Viktor, 102
   Schlank, Carol Hilgartner, 126
   Selsam, Millicent E., 66
   Shelby, Anne, 48
   Smith, Kathie Billingslea, 126
   Stevenson, James, 196
   Thaler, Mike, 37
   Towle, Wendy, 136
   Ward, Cindy, 24
   Waters, Kate, 83
   Wesley, Valerie Wilson, 134
   Wiesner, David, 176
   Wilcox, Charlotte, 201
   Wildsmith, Brian, 29
   Wilhelm, Hans, 193
   Winter, Jeanette, 138, 213
   Yarbrough, Camille, 138
   Yolen, Jane, 61

Babar and Father Christmas
   Jean de Brunhoff, 98
Back-to-School (see also Open House)
   math unit, 20–26
   watermelon theme unit, 6–13
Bats
   bulletin board, 66
   pattern, 71
Behrens, June
   Fiesta! Cinco de Mayo, 208
Ben's Trumpet
   Rachel Isadora, 137
Big Bunny and the Easter Eggs, The
   Steven Kroll, 193
Biggest Pumpkin Ever, The
   Steven Kroll, 67
Biographies
   writing, 36, 59, 124, 134, 213
Birthdays
   King, Martin Luther, Jr., 121
   math, 23
   wish list, 23
Black History Month (see African-Americans)
Bookmaking
   alphabet, 46
   biography, 59
   cookbook, 46, 202
   fairy tales, 119
   family, 113
   historical fiction, 60
   journal, 24, 124, 217, 219
   King, Martin Luther, Jr., 124
   presidential hopefuls, 152
   safety tips, 53
   school, 38
   telephone directory, 21, 229
   wind, 176

Books (see also Reading)
   AFRO-BETS® Book of Black Heroes From A to Z, 134
   Amazing Grace, 138
   Babar and Father Christmas, 98
   Ben's Trumpet, 137
   Big Bunny and the Easter Eggs, The, 193
   Biggest Pumpkin Ever, The, 67
   Bunny Trouble, 193
   Chestnut Cove, 11
   Christmas Tomten, The, 102
   Cinderella Penguin or the Little Glass Flipper, 119
   Cookie's Week, 24
   Cornrows, 138
   Country Bunny and the Little Gold Shoes, The, 193
   Count Your Way Through Mexico, 210
   Cowboys, 214
   Diego, 213
   Early American Christmas, An, 99
   Eating the Alphabet: Fruits and Vegetables From A to Z, 11
   Egg Tree, The, 195
   Encounter, 61
   Fall Is Here! I Love It!, 30
   Family Pictures/Cuadros de Familia, 213
   Feel the Wind, 175
   Fiesta! Cinco de Mayo, 208
   50 Simple Things Kids Can Do to Save the Earth, 201
   First Look at Bats, A, 66
   First Thanksgiving, The, 83
   Follow the Drinking Gourd, 138
   Friends, 17
   Great Big Especially Beautiful Easter Egg, The, 196
   Guess How Much I Love You, 149
   Happy Birthday, Martin Luther King, Jr., 121
   Hello, Amigos!, 213
   Homeplace, 48
   Hurricane, 176
   I, Columbus: My Journal 1492-3, 59
   …If You Lived at the Time of Martin Luther King, 124
   In 1492, 60
   I Unpacked My Grandmother's Trunk, 46
   Latkes and Applesauce, 88
   Legend of Old Befana, The, 100
   Legend of the Poinsettia, The, 104
   Little Drummer Boy, The, 100
   Log of Christopher Columbus—The First Voyage: Spring, Summer and Fall 1492, The, 59
   Martin Luther King, Jr., 126
   Martin Luther King, Jr.: A Biography for Young Children, 126
   Mexico, 208
   Millions of Cats, 20
   My First Kwanzaa Book, 113
   National Children's Book Week, 74–81
   Oh, What a Thanksgiving!, 83
   Pancho's Piñata, 105
   Picture Book of Rosa Parks, A, 136
   Rabbit Finds a Way, 196
   Rain Forest, 202
   Real McCoy, The: The Life of an African-American Inventor, 136
   Rosa Parks, 136
   Roses Are Pink, Your Feet Really Stink, 149
   Sarah Morton's Day, 83
   Seven Candles for Kwanzaa, 113
   Solo, 116
   Squirrels, 29
   Story of Ruby Bridges, The, 126
   Sunshine Makes the Seasons, 30
   Tacky the Penguin, 119
   Teacher From the Black Lagoon, The, 37
   Thanksgiving Day, 82
   Tomie dePaola's Book of Christmas Carols, 96, 98, 99
   Trash!, 201
   Treasure Nap, 211
   Valentine Bears, The, 149
   Valentine's Day, 146
   Watermelon Day, 11
   Water's Way, 188
   Wilfred Gordon McDonald Partridge, 17
   Yo! Yes?, 17
   Zipping, Zapping, Zooming Bats, 66
Boxing Day
   generosity, 96
Branley, Franklyn
   Sunshine Makes the Seasons, 30
Bridges, Ruby
   The Story of Ruby Bridges, 126
Brown, Tricia
   Hello, Amigos!, 213
Bubbles
   recipe for, 231
Bulletin Boards and Displays
   African-Americans, 134
   bats, 66
   border, 218
   campfire, 214
   Christmas, 94, 102, 104
   Cinco de Mayo, 209
   classroom helpers, 7
   Columbus Day, 58, 62
   ducks, 186
   Earth Day, 200, 201
   Easter, 193
   end of year, 226
   fall, 28, 30
   fire safety, 50
   friendship, 14
   kindness, 121
   Kwanzaa, 111, 113
   languages, 147
   penguins, 117, 118
   poinsettias, 104
   presidents, 154
   pumpkins, 67
   reading, 74, 177, 187
   self-esteem, 216, 220
   squirrels, 28
   St. Patrick's Day, 163
   Valentine's Day, 147
   wind, 177
Bunny Trouble
   Hans Wilhelm, 193
Bunting, Eve
   The Valentine Bears, 149

Caldecott Awards and Honors
   Yo! Yes?, 17
Calendar (see Life Skills)
Candy
   jelly beans, 197
Carver, George Washington
   biography, 135
Celebrations (see individual celebrations and holidays, Parties)
Centers
   math, 10, 23, 32, 151, 178, 197, 218
   reading, 218
   various, 118
Chants (see also Poems, Songs)
   "Watermelon Chant, The," 8
   "Who Took the Melon From the Melon Patch?," 7
Character Education
   cooperation, 11, 216
   family, 45–48, 113, 213
   friendship, 14–19, 138, 149
   generosity, 82, 96, 228, 230
   goal setting, 62, 124, 201, 227
   kindness, 82, 121, 201
   Kwanzaa, 109–114
   responsibility, 7, 201
   self-esteem, 119, 122, 123, 135, 138, 216, 220
   various, 123
Chemistry
   oxidation, 156
Chestnut Cove
   Tim Egan, 11
Children's Day
   kites, 178
Chocolate, Deborah M. Newton
   My First Kwanzaa Book, 113
Christmas
   thematic unit, 94–108
Christmas Tomten, The
   Viktor Rydberg, 102
Cinco de Mayo
   thematic unit, 208–213
Cinderella Penguin or the Little Glass Flipper
   Janet Perlman, 119
Classification (see Critical Thinking)
Classroom Management
   cooperation, 216
   grouping students, 116
   helpers, 7
   motivation, 216
Clothing
   problem solving, 24
   Wild West, 221
Coles, Robert
   The Story of Ruby Bridges, 126
Columbus, Christopher
   The Log of Christopher Columbus—The First Voyage: Spring, Summer, and Fall 1492, 59
Columbus Day
   thematic unit, 58–65
Communication—Verbal (see also Drama)
   discussions, 126
   giving directions, 232
   parade, 77
   reports, 134, 152, 201
   show-and-tell, 45
   tour guides, 36
Compare and Contrast (see Critical Thinking)
Consumer Math
   budget, 23
   business, 227
Cookie's Week
   Cindy Ward, 24
Cooking
   bunny cake, 196
   cannolis, 100
   chuck, 218
   Chuck-Wagon Chili, 221
   cookbook, making, 46, 202
   Easter egg cookies, 196
   Friendship Salad, 16, 111
   latkes, 88
   Leprechaun Pie, 166
   Old-Meets-New Fruit Salad, 60
   Pleasing Polvorones, 212
   Pot o' Green Punch, 166
   Rain Forest Treat, 202
   Spicy Salsa, 212
   Squirrel Crispies, 29
   Tantalizing Tortillas, 212
   Watermelon Pops, 11
   Witches' Brew, 70
Cooperation (see Character Education, Cooperative Groups)

Cooperative Groups (see also Games)
    cooking, 196
    environment, 201
    friendship, 15
    grandparents, 47
    math, 219
    spelling, 217
    13 colonies, 152
    writing, 15, 228
Cornrows
    Camille Yarbrough, 138
Correspondence (see Home-School Link)
Country Bunny and the Little Gold Shoes, The
    Du Bose Heyward, 193
Count Your Way Through Mexico
    Jim Haskins, 210
Cowboys
    Stewart Ross, 214
Cowcher, Helen
    Rain Forest, 202
Creative Thinking
    imagining, 152
    inventing, 136
    planning, 11
Creative Writing
    Babar, 98
    Christmas, 99, 102
    Easter, 193
    fairy tales, 119
    friendship, 14, 15
    grandparents, 47
    historical fiction, 60
    poetry, 15, 30
    presidents, 152
    riddles, 163
    school, 37
    story starters, 147
    St. Patrick's Day, 162, 163
    travel, 228
    Valentine's Day, 149
    watermelons, 9
    Wild West, 217
Critical Thinking (see also Experiments, Problem Solving)
    Civil Rights, 136
    classification, 20, 69, 197
    compare and contrast, 11, 82, 96, 99
    environment, 201, 202
    ethics, 61, 126
    fire safety, 53
    peanuts, 135
    planning, 94, 201
    potatoes, 168
    true or false, 8, 66, 146
Czernecki, Stefan
    Pancho's Piñata, 105

Dance (see Physical Fitness)
de Brunhoff, Jean
    Babar and Father Christmas, 98
Deductive Reasoning (see Problem Solving)
de Groat, Diane
    Roses Are Pink, Your Feet Really Stink, 149
Delton, Judy
    Rabbit Finds a Way, 196
dePaola, Tomie
    Early American Christmas, An, 99
    Legend of Old Befana, The, 100
    Legend of the Poinsettia, The, 104
    Tomie dePaola's Book of Christmas Carols, 96, 98, 99
Descriptive Writing
    characters, 76
    people, 154
Dictionary (see Study Skills)

Diego
    Jeanette Winter, 213
Directions (see Geography)
Directions, Following (see Following Directions)
Displays (see Bulletin Boards and Displays)
Division (see Math)
Dorros, Arthur
    Feel the Wind, 175
Drama
    book characters, 77
    choral speaking, 89
    Columbus, Christopher, 59
    fire safety, 53
    friendship, 15
    music, 137
    Thanksgiving, 83
Ducks
    thematic unit, 186–192
Du Sable, Jean Baptiste
    biography, 135

Earle, Ann
    Zipping, Zapping, Zooming Bats, 66
Early American Christmas, An
    Tomie dePaola, 99
Earth Day
    rain forest, 202
    thematic unit, 200–206
Earth Science
    planet's appearance, 200
Easter
    thematic unit, 193–199
Eating the Alphabet: Fruits and Vegetables From A to Z
    Lois Ehlert, 11
Economics (see also Persuasive Writing)
    advertising, 76
    lemonade stand, 227
Editing
    proofreading, 216
    rephrasing, 154
Egan, Tim
    Chestnut Cove, 11
Egg Tree, The
    Katherine Milhous, 195
Ehlert, Lois
    Eating the Alphabet: Fruits and Vegetables From A to Z, 11
Encounter
    Jane Yolen, 61
Endangered Species (see Animals)
End of Year
    thematic unit, 226–234
England
    Boxing Day, 96
    Christmas, 96–97
Environment (see Earth Day)
Estimation
    measurement, 22, 84
    number of objects, 69, 84, 197
Evaporation (see Water)
Experiments
    chemistry, 156
    oxidation, 156
    physics, 168
    potatoes, 167–168
    seasons, 30
    senses, 167
    water, 31, 187–189
    wind, 175
Expository Writing (see Informational Writing)
Fact and Opinion (see Critical Thinking)
Fairy Tales
    Cinderella, 119
Fall Is Here! I Love It!
    Elaine W. Good, 30

Families (see Character Education)
Family Pictures/Cuadros de Familia
    Carmen Lomas Garza, 213
Feel the Wind
    Arthur Dorros, 175
Field Trips
    fire station, 52
Fiesta! Cinco de Mayo
    June Behrens, 208
50 Simple Things Kids Can Do to Save the Earth
    John Javna, 201
Figurative Language
    similes, 149
Fire Prevention Week
    thematic unit, 50–57
First Look at Bats, A
    Millicent E. Selsam and Joyce Hunt, 66
First Thanksgiving, The
    Jean Craighead George, 83
Five Senses
    fall, 30
    potatoes, 167
Following Directions
    Easter, 194
    Halloween, 70
    shapes, 105
Follow the Drinking Gourd
    Jeanette Winter, 138
Football, 32
Forms
    book review, 79
    passport application, 107
    rain forest, 206
    recycling, 205
    volunteers, 43
Fox, Mem
    Wilfred Gordon McDonald Partridge, 17
Fractions (see Math)
France
    Christmas, 98
    Easter, 194
    French language, 98
Friends
    Helme Heine, 17
Friendship (see Character Education)
Fruit (see also Apples, Watermelons)
    cooking, 16, 111
    graphing, 16, 111

Ga'g, Wanda
    Millions of Cats, 20
Games (see also Physical Fitness)
    fire safety, 52, 53
    friendship, 14, 15
    lotto, 210
    math, 21, 32, 89, 164, 178, 227
    memory, 15
    picnic, 232
    piñata, 211
    scavenger hunt, 29, 166, 194
    Spanish, 210
    spelling, 32
    St. Patrick's Day, 166
    word games, 166
Gardening (see Plants)
Garza, Carmen Lomas
    Family Pictures/Cuadros de Familia, 213
Generosity (see Character Education)
Geography
    Africa, 111, 138
    Australia, 194
    Christmas, 94–108
    England, 96–97
    France, 98, 194
    Germany, 99, 194

Greece, 194
Italy, 100–101
Japan, 178
map skills, 58, 70, 122
Mexico, 104–105, 208–213
Norway, 194
Sweden, 102–103
United States, 135, 152
Geometry
    shapes, 105
George, Jean Craighead
    The First Thanksgiving, 83
Geraghty, Paul
    Solo, 116
Germany
    Christmas, 99
    Easter, 194
Gibbons, Gail
    Thanksgiving Day, 82
Goal Setting (see Character Education)
Good, Elaine W.
    Fall Is Here! I Love It!, 30
Grandparents Day
    thematic unit, 45–48
Graphing
    candy, 69, 197
    cereal, 164
    fruit, 16, 111
    grandparents, 45
    recycling, 201
    watermelon facts, 8
Great Big Especially Beautiful Easter Egg, The
    James Stevenson, 196
Greece
    Easter, 194
Greenfield, Eloise
    Rosa Parks, 136
Guess How Much I Love You
    Sam McBratney, 149

Halloween
    thematic unit, 66–72
Handwriting
    contact information, 229
    practice, 154
Hanukkah
    thematic unit, 88–93
Happy Birthday, Martin Luther King, Jr.
    Jean Marzollo, 121
Haskins, Jim
    Count Your Way Through Mexico, 210
Havill, Juanita
    Treasure Nap, 211
Health and Safety (see also Physical Fitness)
    fire safety, 50–57
Heine, Helme
    Friends, 17
Hello, Amigos!
    Tricia Brown, 213
Helpers, Classroom (see Classroom Management)
Heyward, Du Bose
    The Country Bunny and the Little Gold Shoes, 193
History (see also Inventions and Inventors)
    Black History Month, 134–145
    civil rights, 121–132
    coat of arms, 60
    Columbus, Christopher, 58–65
    family, 46, 48
    fire safety, 51, 52
    Presidents' Day, 151–160
    slavery, 138
    Thanksgiving, 82
    Wild West, 214–225
Hoffman, Mary
    Amazing Grace, 138

Hoguet, Susan Ramsay
    I Unpacked My Grandmother's Trunk, 46
Holidays (see individual holidays)
Homeplace
    Anne Shelby, 48
Home-School Link (see also Open House)
    grandparents, 45–48
    love notes, 38
    parents, 125
    volunteers, 37, 47
Hudson, Wade
    AFRO-BETS® Book of Black Heroes From A to Z, 134
Hunt, Joyce
    First Look at Bats, A, 66
Hurricane
    David Wiesner, 176

I, Columbus: My Journal 1492-3
    Peter and Connie Roop, 59
...If You Lived at the Time of Martin Luther King
    Ellen Levine, 124
Incentives (see Reading, Writing)
Independence Day (see also Cinco de Mayo)
    logic, 208
Informational Writing (see also Biographies)
    book reports, 187
    environment, 201
    fire safety, 50
    instructions, 165, 202
    summarizing, 226
In 1492
    Jean Marzollo, 60
Inventions and Inventors
    Carver, George Washington, 135
    McCoy, Elijah, 136
Isadora, Rachel
    Ben's Trumpet, 137
Italy
    Christmas, 100–101
I Unpacked My Grandmother's Trunk
    Susan Ramsay Hoguet, 46

Jack-o'-Lantern (see Pumpkins)
Jacobsen, Karen
    Mexico, 208
Japan
    Children's Day, 178
    kites, 178
Javna, John
    50 Simple Things Kids Can Do to Save the Earth, 201
Jelly Beans (see Candy)
Journals
    King, Martin Luther, Jr., 124
    math, 219
    travel, 194
    week, 24
    Wild West, 217

Keats, Ezra Jack
    The Little Drummer Boy, 100
Kessel, Joyce K.
    Valentine's Day, 146
Kindness (see Character Education)
King, Martin Luther, Jr.
    thematic unit, 121–132
Kites (see Wind)
Kroll, Steven
    Big Bunny and the Easter Eggs, The, 193
    Biggest Pumpkin Ever, The, 67
    Oh, What a Thanksgiving!, 83
Kwanzaa
    thematic unit, 109–114

Language Arts (see Books, Communication–Verbal, Figurative Language, Parts of Speech, Punctuation, Reading, Spelling, Vocabulary, Writing)
Latkes and Applesauce
    Fran Manushkin, 88
Learning Centers (see Centers)
Legend of Old Befana, The
    Tomie dePaola, 100
Legend of the Poinsettia, The
    Tomie dePaola, 104
Lester, Helen
    Tacky the Penguin, 119
Letter Writing
    Christmas, 99
    fall, 28
    lawmakers, 203
Levine, Ellen
    ...If You Lived at the Time of Martin Luther King, 124
Life Skills
    money, 23
    passport, 94
    telephone, 21, 229
    time, 22, 24
Literature (see Books, Reading)
Little Drummer Boy, The
    Ezra Jack Keats, 100
Logic
    Venn diagram, 17, 20, 126
Log of Christopher Columbus—The First Voyage: Spring, Summer and Fall 1492, The
    Christopher Columbus, 59

Management, Classroom (see Classroom Management)
Manipulatives
    acorns, 32
    candies, 69, 197
    cherries, 151
    coins, 155, 164
    watermelon seeds, 10
Manushkin, Fran
    Latkes and Applesauce, 88
Maps (see Geography)
Martin Luther King, Jr.
    Kathie Billingslea Smith, 126
Martin Luther King, Jr.: A Biography for Young Children
    Carol Hilgartner Schlank and Barbara Metzger, 126
Martin Luther King, Jr. Day (see King, Martin Luther, Jr.)
Marzollo, Jean
    Happy Birthday, Martin Luther King, Jr., 121
    In 1492, 60
Math (see also Centers, Critical Thinking, Manipulatives, Time)
    addition, 21, 23, 197
    basics, 10, 32, 48, 89, 110, 178, 219, 227
    consumer, 23, 164, 227
    estimation, 22, 69, 84, 197
    fractions, 197
    geometry, 105
    graphing, 8, 16, 45, 69, 111, 164, 197, 201
    journals, 219
    logic, 17, 20, 21, 126, 208
    measurement, 22, 31, 153, 201
    multiplication, 197
    patterning, 218
    problem solving, 24
    statistics, 84, 155, 164
    subtraction, 151, 197
McBratney, Sam
    Guess How Much I Love You, 149
McCoy, Elijah

biography, 136
Measurement
   nonstandard, 22
   size, 153, 201
   water, 31
Metzger, Barbara
   Martin Luther King, Jr.: A Biography for Young Children, 126
Mexico
   Karen Jacobsen, 208
Mexico
   Christmas, 104–105
   Cinco de Mayo, 208–213
   language, 210
Milhous, Katherine
   The Egg Tree, 195
Millions of Cats
   Wanda Ga'g, 20
Money (see Consumer Math)
Movement (see Physical Fitness)
Multiplication (see Math)
Music (see also Songs)
   Anderson, Marian, 135
   appreciation, 137
   Armstrong, Louis, 137
   bells, 211
   cowboys, 215
   dance, 110
   "Follow the Drinking Gourd," 138
   "I Love the Mountains," 200
My First Kwanzaa Book
   Deborah M. Newton Chocolate, 113

National Children's Book Week
   thematic unit, 74–81
Native Americans
   Christopher Columbus, 61
Newspapers (see Informational Writing)
Nobel Peace Prize
   Martin Luther King, Jr., 122
Norway
   Easter, 194
Nouns (see Parts of Speech)

Oh, What a Thanksgiving!
   Steven Kroll, 83
Old West (see Wild West)
Open House
   unit, 35–44

Pancho's Piñata
   Stefan Czernecki and Timothy Rhodes, 105
Parent Communication (see Home-School Link)
Parks, Rosa
   biography, 136
Parties
   Cinco de Mayo, 212
   end of year, 231
   St. Patrick's Day, 166
   Wild West, 221
Parts of Speech
   adjectives, 6
Patterning
   Wild West, 218
Patterns
   acorn, 33
   airplane, 95
   arrow, 180
   badge, 223
   barrel, 64
   bats, 71
   bookmarks, 78
   bookworm, 78
   boot, 224
   bow, 180

   box/cube, 18, 145
   boy, 41
   cactus, 224
   camera, 233
   clothing, 26
   coat of arms, 65
   coins, 159
   corn, 112
   cornucopia, 97, 114
   cowboy, 222
   coyote, 225
   dog, 54
   dreidel, 93
   duck, 190, 191
   egg, 199
   elf, 103
   feather, 86
   fire helmet, 56
   fire hydrant, 54
   fire truck, 55
   flower, 234
   fruit, 114
   gift tag, 103
   girl, 42
   hat, 63, 180, 222, 224
   horseshoe, 224
   hot-air balloon, 180
   kinara, 112
   kite bow, 180
   leaf, 34, 80
   leprechaun, 170
   map—United States, 140
   map—world, 106
   Mayflower, The, 85
   menorah, 92
   mirror, 172
   passport, 108
   peace-prize awards, 127
   peanuts, 141
   penguin, 120
   pinwheel, 179
   pot, 169
   presidential seal, 158
   rabbit, 199
   rainbow and pot of gold, 172
   sailboat, 180
   shamrock, 173
   shield, 65
   ship, 85
   squirrel, 33
   stationery, 44
   St. Lucia crown, 103
   suitcase, 95
   sunglasses, 232
   turkey, 86
   watermelon, 12
   windmill blades, 180
Peanuts
   George Washington Carver, 135
Penguins
   thematic unit, 116–120
Perlman, Janet
   Cinderella Penguin or the Little Glass Flipper, 119
Personal Writing (see Biographies, Journals)
Persuasive Writing
   book promotion, 75
   civil rights, 126
   environment, 203
   rodeo, 137
Peters, Lisa Westberg
   Water's Way, 188
Physical Fitness
   coordination, 231
   dance, 110
   relay race, 29, 166, 231

Physics
   gravity, 168
Pickett, Bill
   biography, 137
Picnic
   end of year, 231–232
   game, 232
Picture Book of Rosa Parks, A
   David A. Adler, 136
Pinkney, Andrea Davis
   Seven Candles for Kwanzaa, 113
Plants
   bulbs, 31
   potatoes, 167–168
   pumpkins, 67
Poems (see also Chants, Songs)
   friendship, 15
   Hanukkah, 90
   squirrel, 29
   wind, 177
   writing, 15, 30, 149, 177
Potatoes (see Plants)
Presidents' Day (see History)
Prewriting (see also Research Skills)
   brainstorming, 15, 146, 163, 186, 213
Problem Solving
   anger management, 136
   clothing, 24
   fire safety, 52, 53
   friendship, 15
   inventing, 136
   names, 21
   riddles, 102
Properties of Matter
   candles, 89
Public Speaking (see Communication—Verbal)
Pumpkins
   jack-o'-lantern, 67, 68
Punctuation
   correcting, 151

Rabbit Finds a Way
   Judy Delton, 196
Rain (see also Water)
   experiment, 189
   thematic unit, 186–192
Rain Forest
   Helen Cowcher, 202
Rain Forests (see Earth Day)
Raschka, Chris
   Yo! Yes?, 17
Reading
   centers, 218
   comprehension, 91, 137, 142, 143, 144, 154
   genres, 187
   incentives, 9, 74, 75, 77, 177, 187
Reading Centers (see Centers)
Real McCoy, The: The Life of an African-American Inventor
   Wendy Towle, 136
Reasoning (see Problem Solving)
Recipes (see Cooking)
Reproducibles
   Anderson, Marian, 142
   candy, 72
   chemistry, 160
   Christmas, 101
   dictionary, 128
   friendship, 19
   Hanukkah, 91
   math, 13, 19, 164, 197
   Parks, Rosa, 143
   Pickett, Bill, 144
   plants, 174

punctuation, 157
reading, 91
self-esteem, 120
time, 25
Valentine's Day, 146
water cycle, 192
watermelons, 13
writing, 139
Research Skills (see also Informational Writing)
African-American heroes, 134
dictionary, 123
environment, 201
food, 60
penguins, 118
presidents, 152
states, 152
storms, 176
surveys, 164
Responsibility (see Character Education)
Rhodes, Timothy
Pancho's Piñata, 105
Rivera, Diego
biography, 213
Role-Playing (see Drama)
Roop, Peter and Connie
I, Columbus: My Journal 1492–3, 59
Rosa Parks
Eloise Greenfield, 136
Roses Are Pink, Your Feet Really Stink
Diane de Groat, 149
Ross, Stewart
Cowboys, 214
Rydberg, Viktor
The Christmas Tomten, 102

Sarah Morton's Day
Kate Waters, 83
Schlank, Carol Hilgartner
Martin Luther King, Jr.: A Biography for Young Children, 126
Science (see Critical Thinking, Earth Day, Earth Science, Experiments, Five Senses, Physics, Plants, Properties of Matter, Rain, Seasons, Water, Watermelons, Wind)
Seasons
experiment, 30
Self-Esteem (see Character Education)
Selsam, Millicent E.
A First Look at Bats, 66
Sequencing
history, 152
writing, 122
Seven Candles for Kwanzaa
Andrea Davis Pinkney, 113
Shelby, Anne
Homeplace, 48
Smith, Kathie Billingslea
Martin Luther King, Jr., 126
Social Studies (see African-Americans, Character Education, Economics, Geography, History, Informational Writing, Native Americans, Nobel Peace Prize)
Solo
Paul Geraghty, 116
Songs (see also Chants, Poems)
cowboy song, 215
"Follow the Drinking Gourd," 138
"I Love the Mountains," 200
"We Shall Overcome," 124
Sorting (see Critical Thinking)
Spanish
numbers, 210
Spelling
game, 32, 217
Spiders

arts and crafts, 68
Squirrels
Brian Wildsmith, 29
Squirrels
thematic unit, 28–34
States (see Geography)
Statistics
coin toss, 164
St. Patrick's Day, 164
Thanksgiving, 84
Stevenson, James
The Great Big Especially Beautiful Easter Egg, 196
Story of Ruby Bridges, The
Robert Coles, 126
St. Patrick's Day
party—classroom, 166
science, 167–168
thematic unit, 162–174
Study Skills (see also Reading)
dictionary, 123
proofreading, 216
research, 60, 118, 134, 152, 176, 201
Sunshine Makes the Seasons
Franklyn Branley, 30
Sweden
Christmas, 102–103

Tacky the Penguin
Helen Lester, 119
Teacher From the Black Lagoon, The
Mike Thaler, 37
Technical Writing (see Informational Writing)
Thaler, Mike
The Teacher From the Black Lagoon, 37
Thanksgiving
thematic unit, 82–86
Thanksgiving Day
Gail Gibbons, 82
Theater (see Drama)
Thinking (see Critical Thinking)
Time
age, 48
calendar, 24
clocks, 22
timelines, 51, 62
Titles (see Books)
Tomie dePaola's Book of Christmas Carols
Tomie dePaola, 96, 98, 99
Towle, Wendy
The Real McCoy: The Life of an African-American Inventor, 136
Trash!
Charlotte Wilcox, 201
Treasure Nap
Juanita Havill, 211

Valentine Bears, The
Eve Bunting, 149
Valentine's Day
Joyce K. Kessel, 146
Valentine's Day
thematic unit, 146–150
Venn Diagram (see Logic)
Verbal Communication (see Communication—Verbal)
Vocabulary
bulletin board, 84
character education, 123
Hanukkah, 91
Volunteers (see Home-School Link)

Ward, Cindy
Cookie's Week, 24
Water

absorption, 187
condensation, 189
cycle, 188
evaporation, 31, 188
precipitation, 189
Watermelon Day
Kathi Appelt, 11
Watermelons
thematic unit, 6–13
Waters, Kate
Sarah Morton's Day, 83
Water's Way
Lisa Westberg Peters, 188
Wesley, Valerie Wilson
AFRO-BETS® Book of Black Heroes From A to Z, 134
West (see Wild West)
Wiesner, David
Hurricane, 176
Wilcox, Charlotte
Trash!, 201
Wildsmith, Brian
Squirrels, 29
Wild West
thematic unit, 214–225
Wilfred Gordon McDonald Partridge
Mem Fox, 17
Wilhelm, Hans
Bunny Trouble, 193
Wind
thematic unit, 175–184
Winter, Jeanette
Diego, 213
Follow the Drinking Gourd, 138
Worksheets (see Reproducibles)
Writing (see also Bookmaking)
analytical, 77
biography, 36, 59, 124, 134, 213
creative, 9, 14, 37, 47, 60, 98, 99, 102, 119, 149, 152, 162, 163, 193, 217, 228
descriptive, 76, 154
editing, 154, 216
incentives, 77
informational, 50, 165, 187, 201, 202, 226
journals, 24, 124, 194, 217
letters, 28, 99, 203
persuasive, 75, 126, 137, 203
poetry, 15, 30, 149, 177
prewriting, 15, 146, 163, 186, 213
sequencing, 122
story starters, 147
Writing Centers (see Centers)

Yarbrough, Camille
Cornrows, 138
Yolen, Jane
Encounter, 61
Yo! Yes?
Chris Raschka, 17

Zipping, Zapping, Zooming Bats
Ann Earle, 66